artichoke to za'atar

Modern Middle Eastern Food

artichoke to za'atar

GREG MALOUF AND LUCY MALOUF

University of California Press
Berkeley   Los Angeles

In loving memory of our fathers, Kevin Malouf and John Rushbrooke

University of California Press, one of the most distinguished university presses in the United States, enriches lives around the world by advancing scholarship in the humanities, social sciences, and natural sciences. Its activities are supported by the UC Press Foundation and by philanthropic contributions from individuals and institutions. For more information, visit www.ucpress.edu.

University of California Press
Berkeley and Los Angeles, California

Published by arrangement with Hardie Grant Books, 85 High Street, Prahran, Victoria 3181, Australia, www.hardiegrant.com.au

Text design by Gayna Murphy, Greendot Design
Photography by William Meppem
Food styling by Caroline Velik

Library of Congress Cataloging-in-Publication Data

Malouf, Greg.
Artichoke to za'atar : modern Middle Eastern food / Greg and Lucy Malouf.
p.   cm.
Includes bibliographical references and index.
ISBN: 978-0-520-25413-8 (cloth : alk. paper)
1. Cookery, Middle Eastern.   I. Malouf, Lucy.   II. Title.

TX725.M628M34   2008
641.5956—dc22   2007026371
Manufactured in China

17   16   15   14   13   12   11   10   09   08
10   9   8   7   6   5   4   3   2   1

contents

acknowledgments

Artichoke to Za'atar is the result of a lifetime's journey in, through, and around food. It has been fueled by my travels and the people I've met along the way, by the books I have read, and by the countless meals I have cooked and eaten.

My deepest gratitude must go to my family: to my mother, May, and my grand-mothers, Adele and Madeleine. This formidable trio taught me to love cooking and to understand that feeding others was a gift, not a chore. They influenced my childhood years and were the first to nurture my interest in the classic flavors of the Middle East. I also especially thank my sister-in-law Amal Malouf and her mother, Victoria Baroud, for their constant support and advice. Their breadth of knowledge and expertise in the cooking of Lebanon and Syria is unrivaled.

On a personal note, my appreciation goes to Pat McDonald, who was one of the first to encourage my decision to become a chef. I thank too Michelle Garnaut, my partner in Hong Kong during the 1980s, who believed in my passion for the flavors of the Middle East long before they became fashionable. Throughout my career I have been fortunate to work with many extraordinary and inspirational chefs. In particular, I owe a debt to Abla Amad, the undisputed queen of Lebanese home cooking here in Melbourne, who has been a source of inspiration and support over the years, and to Stephanie Alexander, Andrew Blake, and Fred Chalupa.

The first edition of this book was published in 1999, while I was cooking at Melbourne's O'Connell's Hotel. During my years there, the owners, David Blackley, Geoff Burrows, Kent Lovell, and Bill Regan, gave me the freedom to develop my modern Middle Eastern food style within a framework of unwavering support, and I remain eternally grateful to them for that opportunity.

Many of the dishes in *Artichoke to Za'atar* evolved during that time at O'Connell's, and all of them benefited from the input of the talented chefs who passed through my kitchen there. In particular, Kurt Sampson, Harry Hajisava, and Miranda Epstein gave up hours of their time to help refine and test my ideas to turn them into the dishes that I dreamed of.

While the recipes and words that follow remain essentially the same as in the first edition, *Artichoke to Za'atar* now has a gorgeous new look. For this we thank William Meppem for his beautiful photography, Gayna Murphy for her stunning text design, and Caroline Velik for her inspired styling and infinite patience.

Brooke Payne and Simone Watts were tireless workers on the photo shoot and helped ensure that things ran like clockwork. Thanks too to Dean and Geremy Lucas and the entire MoMo team for allowing me time away from the kitchen (yet again!).

Many generous people lent us equipment and beautiful props for the photography, for which we are very grateful. We'd like to thank Manon, Bliink Interiors, Colours of Provence, Mud Australia, and Minimax. And we especially thank Lyn Gardener for opening up her lovely light-filled house to us; it proved to be a stunning location for the photographs.

And finally, our grateful thanks to the A1 Middle Eastern Bakery, Eurofruit, Largo Butchers, and Ocean Made for making sure we were supplied with such outstanding produce. As every chef knows, it is the quality of the produce that is really at the heart of good cooking.

Greg Malouf

introduction

This book is for anyone who is interested in discovering more about the culinary influence of the Middle East and how to use these foods and flavors in their own kitchens at home.

Many people have some understanding of cooking from the Arab world, but it is usually based on their experience of limp pita bread and greasy kebabs from a grubby Lebanese takeaway. In more recent years there has also been a fashion for Moroccan food, with every other trendy bistro serving couscous and chermoula. But any deeper interest in Arab-influenced foods seems to have stopped here, which scarcely does them justice. The cuisines of the region we call the Middle East are as refined and complex as many other great cuisines of the world.

My own interest in food and cooking began in the family home in suburban Melbourne. My culinary instincts are rooted in the flavors and traditions of Lebanon, as cooked by my grandmothers and mother. When my classmates were munching on their lunchtime sandwiches of pork sausage and tomato sauce, I was tucking into a garlic-laden falafel. Using ingredients such as chickpeas, allspice, vine leaves, and rose water has always been as natural to me as breathing.

When I embarked on my cooking career, I followed the traditional route for a young Australian apprentice cook. I studied at trade school here in Melbourne while working in the kitchens of several outstanding local restaurants. The formal part of my training over, I then spent a number of years overseas, cooking in France, Italy, Austria, and Hong Kong, honing my skills, extending my repertoire, and scarcely giving a thought to childhood dishes like stuffed vine leaves and kibbeh nayeh.

Over the last 18 years or so, since heading up my own kitchen, I have been able to synthesize the various influences of my culinary life and to produce the sort of food that I have always wanted to cook: not traditional Lebanese dishes, but rather food which, for me, captures the essence of the Middle East and expresses it in the best Western tradition.

I am all for progress and evolution, in the kitchen as in any other field. Never before has the spread of information and ideas been as easy. As a result, most people know a little about many different cuisines, and are happy to incorporate ideas from Thailand, Mexico, Italy, or Morocco in their own cooking.

There are, of course, those purists and traditionalists who abhor this evolution – and when it comes to the arbitrary mishmashing together of completely incongruous ingredients, I too have been known to shudder. Such a lack of discrimination is, I feel, all about the quest for novelty, with little understanding of or respect for the traditions of the cuisines used. But, surely things are no different than they ever were? There have always been fads and fashions in food. Over the centuries, as new ingredients spread to different regions, they were quickly adopted and used experimentally until they found their own place and level in local culinary traditions. Without this eternal quest for new and different ideas, we would still be munching on lentils and cabbage.

While I believe that good cooking is about understanding how to balance flavors and textures and respecting an ingredient's heritage, I also believe that this understanding does not necessarily have to be instinctual. It comes through experience. With this book I hope to encourage people to learn about and use ingredients which are close to my heart. Some, like rice or apricots, are well known; others, like sumac or cardamom, may be less familiar. Most are relatively easy to track down, although a few will require a visit to a specialist Middle Eastern food store or good delicatessen. I have certainly not provided a comprehensive or definitive list of ingredients, but rather a subjective list of my own favorites, used in recipes which I feel best reflect the spirit of Middle Eastern cooking.

This book is not intended for the superchef – Middle Eastern food is, after all, largely just good home cooking. Many traditional dishes, though, are labor-intensive and time-consuming to prepare. They have evolved over hundreds of years, developed by Middle Eastern women whose days and social life revolved around highly labor-intensive cooking techniques. But these days few people have the time or inclination to spend hours stuffing little exquisite morsels.

Indeed, it seems as if the task of providing food every day for family, partner, or oneself has become something of a chore. I firmly believe that one's daily dinner should not be complicated, time-consuming, and overworked. In the Western world we are blessed with an abundant and staggering array of fresh produce, and this should drive our repertoire. A dish can be transformed by the simplest things – and it is this detail which the following recipes are about. Remember, then, that while some of the dishes might sound exotic and mysterious, they are based on traditions which are, after all, everyday fare in another culture.

In the pages that follow, you will find a range of different dishes. Some, like the pickled pork belly, require a certain amount of planning ahead, even if they are not in themselves difficult and complicated to prepare; others are simple ideas, such as soft-boiled eggs sprinkled with dukkah, or a roast chicken stuffed under the skin with preserved-lemon butter. Often it is simply a matter of looking at things from a different angle to make them exciting.

A word about health: my own past has been littered with angioplasty, bypass operations, and even a heart transplant. Today I simply have to be conscious of my cholesterol intake, but I am firmly against the sort of food fascism which dictates many people's eating habits these days. For a healthy constitution, there must be balance. Don't banish all fats from your diet, but make sure, instead, that you eat "healthier" fats such as olive oil, rather than saturated animal fats. Dairy foods are critical for bone and tooth strength – but make sure you don't eat a full-fat triple-cream cheese every day. You might opt instead for yogurt. The desserts, cakes, and cookies in this book are not intended to be eaten every day. In the Middle East, they are rarely eaten, except on special occasions, and for the most part a meal will finish with fresh fruit.

Finally, a word about the construction of this book, and its coauthor Lucy. I am a professional cook; she is not. On the other hand, she can write, whereas I (in good cheflike tradition) can barely manage a shopping list. Together, then, we make a great working partnership, as we divide the responsibilities on the basis of our talents and inclinations. The text of the book is, for the most part, written by Lucy, and it is she, too, who has been largely responsible for the translation of ingredients from commercial quantities to domestic. The recipes are written by me, but are the results of 40 years of eating, talking, and experimenting with families and friends. The influences of my grandmothers, mother, sister-in-law, and sister-in-law's mother, as well as countless other colleagues and mentors over the years, are all visible in this book.

cooking notes

SPECIAL EQUIPMENT

Very few of us have the perfect kitchen and a complete batterie de cuisine, and yet we manage to cook and feed ourselves and our families very satisfactorily most days of the week. The recipes in this book are intended for the average cook, not superchefs, and for the most part can be made with the normal range of pots, pans, mixing bowls, baking tins, knives, and wooden spoons.

Having said this, there are a few items of equipment that make life much easier, especially when cooking Middle Eastern recipes. At the top of our list of essential items is a mortar and pestle. These are inexpensive and widely available from kitchen stores and Asian markets. They are indispensable when it comes to pounding and grinding nuts, seeds, and spices. We also have a small coffee grinder, used for grinding larger quantities.

Also inexpensive and in constant use is our set of measuring cups and spoons. These are useful for measuring liquids and for ingredients which are measured by volume rather than weight. We have as well a set of electronic scales which conveniently weigh in metric and imperial.

It is a rare kitchen these days which has neither an electric mixer (we have a Kenwood) nor a food processor, and our recipes make use of both of these machines. Several dishes are also made much easier with a deep fryer. However, we do not possess one and improvise quite successfully using a small saucepan or a wok for deep- and semi-deep-frying.

Moving further up the expense scale, there are several recipes in this book for ice cream, and we are of the firm view that an ice-cream maker is essential for making the desired, velvet-smooth, light, and creamy product. The freeze-beat-freeze-beat method will make an acceptable ice cream, but it tends to be hard and dense by comparison with ice cream made in a machine. If you love ice creams and sorbets, then you should do your best to buy, beg, borrow, or steal a machine!

CHEF'S NOTES

It may appear that some recipes are very precise, particularly when it comes to baking and pastry making. Others, however, seem to be more flexible – a sprinkle or drizzle of this or that, a medium onion, a small zucchini, or a large eggplant. This of course means that precision is not as important, and quantities are to be taken as guidelines, rather than hard-and-fast rules. Furthermore, unless stated otherwise:

- a medium onion is 4.5 ounces
- a large potato is 7 ounces
- a medium tomato is 3.5 ounces
- a large bunch of herbs is 1½ cups
- juice of one lemon is ½ cup
- olive oil is listed either as extra-virgin olive oil or as olive oil
- milk is whole milk
- cream is heavy (whipping) cream

- butter is unsalted
- eggs are free-range
- sugar is white granulated sugar
- chocolate is the best-quality dark chocolate you can afford
- salt is sea salt, preferable from Maldon, not the iodized version available in supermarkets
- pepper is freshly ground white pepper, unless black is specified

Note that recipes serve 4 generously, unless otherwise stated.

NOTE ON THE NORTH AMERICAN EDITION

For this edition, dry and liquid measurements have been converted to U.S. units. Such conversions are often approximate, so if your instinct suggests adding a little more or less of an ingredient to a dish, you should feel free to do so. The exceptions are dishes like cake batters and custards, in which the balance of leavening agents, dry ingredients, and liquids may be essential to the success of the dish.

Ingredients are referred to by their common North American names, and substitutions have been made or suggested for some ingredients not readily available in North America.

almonds

Many of our most popular foodstuffs are inedible and even poisonous in their wild state. And yet, as long ago as 3,000 BC, in an extraordinary feat of primitive genetic engineering, our ancestors in the eastern Mediterranean learned how to select sweet, nonpoisonous almonds from the bitter majority, and began the cultivation of one of the world's most important nuts.

The extreme bitterness of wild almonds comes from a chemical called amygdalin, which breaks down to form cyanide (also known as prussic acid). A vestige of this remains today in bitter almonds, mainly grown for their volatile oil, which is used by confectioners to add flavor to marzipan. Their cousins, sweet almonds, are what we buy in the shops – usually in neat little plastic packages – sliced, slivered, or whole.

When the Arabs conquered Persia in the seventh century, the almond was just one of many new foods they discovered. From the Persians they learned to use whole almonds in a variety of sweet and savory dishes. They also learned to grind them to a fine meal for use in cakes and cookies, and to use them to thicken and enrich savory dishes and sweet milk puddings.

As they expanded their empire westward, the Arabs took with them many newly discovered foods, such as the almond tree, to cultivate in their new colonies and to trade with customers in Europe. As well as herbs and spices, vegetables, and many varieties of fruit and nut trees, the Arabs also planted cuttings of the sugar cane they had found in Persia.

The sublime partnering of almonds with sugar remains a key element in European confectionery and patisserie today, especially in Spain and Sicily, where it is a legacy of their two hundred years under Arab rule. Callissons and dragées (sugared almonds), nougat, praline, macaroons, and of course marzipan were all delicious outcomes of this marriage. When the Arabs retreated from Europe in the thirteenth century, the tradition of making sweetmeats, in both Spain and Sicily, was carried on by the skilled Arab servant women of Catholic convents and became something of a closed industry.

The tradition and secrecy are still preserved today. On a recent trip to Andalusia, we visited fancy sweet and pastry shops all around the region, and made a point of sampling as many convent sweets and cakes as we could manage. We can report that there are hundreds of different varieties, some flavored with floral, rose water or orange-blossom water, some scented with spices such as cinnamon or cardamom. Others are enriched with egg yolks or chocolate, and many are mixed with candied citrus peel or chopped pistachio nuts for added texture.

Although almonds are probably best known in sweet dishes, they are also used extensively in the Middle East in a range of savory dishes. Persians and Moroccans like to combine almonds with fruit in a range of tagines and braised dishes, in which they cook down to a buttery softness. In Syria and Lebanon they are fried and used as a crunchy garnish for all kinds of chicken and rice dishes.

SELECTING AND STORING ALMONDS

Almond trees have a lovely scented white blossom, making them an ornamental garden favorite. Soft, young, green almonds are considered a real treat, and Greg recalls with great enthusiasm how he and his brothers would eagerly wait for spring, when the rush would be on to pick them straight from their backyard tree.

It is very hard to find green almonds in the shops, so, unless you can pick them straight from the tree, you will have to make do with the mature version. All supermarkets, whole-food stores, and delicatessens stock almonds – mainly the blanched, prepackaged kind, which are certainly easier and more convenient to use, although you also run a greater risk of ending up with stale or occasionally rancid nuts. Around Christmastime there tends to be an abundance of the whole nuts, still in their shells. For cooking rather than nibbling, though, it is easier to buy shelled almonds, and they have a much sweeter, fresher flavor if you buy them in their papery brown skins and blanch them yourself, as described below.

Probably the best place to buy nuts of any kind, if you want to ensure freshness, is from a Middle Eastern or nut specialist store, where you can be ensured a good, brisk turnover.

Fresh nuts have a high oil content and will turn rancid if not stored correctly. For this reason it is preferable to buy all types of nuts in smallish quantities and eat them within a month of purchase. Nuts should be stored in an airtight container in the refrigerator.

USING ALMONDS

It is not really practical to buy almonds whole in their shells, other than for the fun of cracking them around the Christmas dinner table. For cooking, the unpeeled nuts have a fresher flavor than the ready-blanched variety, and it is very easy to blanch and skin them yourself. Soak the almonds in boiling water for around 3 minutes, then drain them well and pat dry. The skin will then slip off easily, although for more stubborn ones making a small slit with a sharp knife will help. Next, they should be thoroughly dried (either on the windowsill in the sun, or in a low oven for 5–10 minutes) before use or storage.

Blanched almonds can be ground to make a rich almond meal, which is infinitely superior to the ready-ground packaged stuff. One word of caution, though: when grinding any nuts it is best to go slowly in short, quick bursts. Their high oil content means that they quickly mush down to an oily paste, rather than the light, fine crumbs you require.

Recipes for cookies and cakes often call for blanched whole almonds or halved almonds. Savory dishes are more likely to suggest dry-roasting or frying them to bring out a deeper, toastier flavor. Middle Easterners nearly always fry almonds, turning them an appetizing golden brown and adding a heady savory flavor and incomparable crunchiness to any dish. Surprisingly, less oil is absorbed in deep-frying than in shallow-frying. The nuts usually take only a few minutes to color, so always watch them with an eagle eye, and drain them well on kitchen paper once you remove them from the heat.

FRIED-ALMOND RISOTTO

Adding fried nuts and vermicelli threads to rice dishes is popular throughout the Middle East for the crunch and visual interest they add.

~~~~~~

¾ cup sliced almonds

¼ cup olive oil

2 ounces vermicelli nests, crumbled

¼ cup olive oil, additional

1 small onion, quartered

2 cups Vialone Nano or other arborio rice

1 quart chicken stock, simmering

2 tablespoons celery leaves, roughly chopped

7 tablespoons butter, chilled and cut into small cubes

¼ teaspoon allspice

¼ teaspoon cinnamon

⅓ cup parmesan cheese, grated

salt and pepper

FRY THE ALMONDS in ¼ cup of the olive oil until they are golden brown. Remove them with a slotted spoon and drain them on absorbent paper. Return the oil to the heat and add the crumbled vermicelli. Fry until golden brown, then tip into a sieve to drain. Dry the vermicelli on kitchen paper.

Prepare the risotto using the four-stage method on page 256, adding the vermicelli to the onions and proceeding as described. Add the third quantity of stock and, when it is reduced by half, add the almonds, celery leaves, butter, and spices, plus ½ cup of stock. Stir well until the butter is incorporated. Add the cheese and stir again. Cover the pan and take it off the heat for one minute, then check the consistency and adjust seasonings.

Serve immediately as an accompaniment to barbecues and grilled or roasted meats.

ALMOND FRITTERS

These golden puffs of airy choux pastry are rolled in toasted almond flakes before deep-frying and then drizzled with a floral honey syrup. A deep fryer makes the task easy, but you can manage just as successfully with a small saucepan of oil. If you don't have a thermometer, the best way of testing whether the oil is hot enough is to throw in a small cube of bread. If it sizzles slowly to the top, turning golden brown in about 30 seconds, you can proceed.

These fritters are delicious served with the rich and sophisticated Burnt Honey Ice Cream (page 155), or perhaps a nutty Pine-Nut Praline Ice Cream (page 232).

3½ tablespoons butter
3 teaspoons honey
½ cup milk
½ cup water
1 cup plain flour

4 eggs
1 quart vegetable oil for deep-frying
1¼ cups sliced almonds
confectioner's sugar to dust

BRING THE BUTTER, honey, milk, and water to the boil. Add the flour and beat vigorously for 4–5 minutes, until the dough comes cleanly away from the side of the pan and forms a ball. Place the dough in an electric mixer and beat in the eggs one at a time. Cover and refrigerate the mixture until ready to fry.

Heat oil to 320°F (or test with a cube of bread). Shape fritter dough into smallish egg shapes using two dessert spoons. Roll each fritter in almond flakes and then deep-fry, four at a time, until the pastry is golden brown and starting to split.

Dust with confectioner's sugar and serve immediately.

BASBOUSSA

Versions of this semolina cake are found all over the Middle East. It is known as Basboussa in Egypt, while in Lebanese pastry shops it is served in little syrup-drenched lozenge shapes, and known as *namoura* or *harisa louz*. It is generally made with ground almonds, fried golden brown in butter. Sliced almonds are used in this recipe to give added crunch.

¾ cup sliced almonds
1 cup (2 sticks) butter
¾ cup yogurt
¾ cup sugar
1½ cup fine semolina
3 tablespoons Frangelico (optional)
½ teaspoon vanilla essence
1½ teaspoons baking powder

SYRUP
1 cup sugar
⅔ cup water
juice of 1 lemon

IN A SHALLOW PAN, melt the butter and lightly fry the almonds until golden brown. Allow to cool.

Beat the yogurt with the sugar, then add the almond-butter mixture, semolina and Frangelico, vanilla and baking powder.

To make the syrup, bring sugar, water, and lemon juice to the boil and simmer for 5 minutes or until slightly reduced.

Grease an 8-inch square baking pan and line with baking parchment. Pour the cake mixture into the pan and bake in a preheated 350°F oven for around 20 minutes, until the cake is just colored. Then remove it from the oven and, with a sharp knife, mark out small diamond shapes on the surface of the cake. Spoon the syrup over the cake and return it to the oven for a further 5–10 minutes.

Serve with a dollop of Lemon-Curd Fool (page 172).

apricots

Every summer we eagerly anticipate the arrival of the first stone fruits. Apricots, with their blushing rosy cheeks and syrupy perfume, are a visual delight. But, sadly, in temperate climates – even the sunnier ones – they never quite live up to their promise and all too often are a furry, bland disappointment, requiring gentle poaching to bring them to life.

Originating in China, apricots spread along the ancient Silk Road to the Mediterranean, flourishing along the way in orchards throughout Persia and Syria, where they are still plentiful today. Some of the best apricots in the world are said to grow in Isfahan in modern Iran. Certainly they so delighted the ancient Romans when they invaded Persia in the first century AD that they took them back to Italy to plant, and within a few decades the cultivation of apricots had spread throughout western Europe.

The Arabs, who overran Persia in an explosion of religious fervor during the seventh century, were also seduced by the vast orchards of fruits growing in Persia – orchards of not just apricots, but also apples, plums, pears, pomegranates, and quinces. It was in Persia that the Arabs learned to combine fruit with meat in fragrant, spicy stews and rice dishes. They took this new fashion, together with their new religion, back through the Mediterranean and the countries of North Africa, finally ending up in Spain. Of all their subjects, it was the Moroccans, at the extreme west of the Arab empire, who embraced this idea most enthusiastically, as can be seen from their national dish, the tagine, which combines fruit, meat, and spices in a very similar way to a Persian (Iranian) *khoresht*.

In the hot Middle East, it seems only natural that many fruits are also sun-dried and then stored to be enjoyed through the winter months. The best dried apricots are said to be the legendary Hunza apricots from Kashmir, which need only a little plumping up in water and then gentle poaching to release their sublime, tart-sweet, intense flavor. They may look rather unprepossessing with their dull beige color when compared with the bright orange dried apricots we usually see on our supermarket shelves, but looks aren't everything. The color of the latter owes much to their treatment with sulfur dioxide, which is used to avoid spoilage and help preserve the color of the fruit.

Sheets of dried apricot purée, or fruit leather, known as amardine, are also common throughout the Middle East. They can be torn into strips and eaten as a chewy snack or cut into little shapes as a garnish for desserts, cakes, or even rice dishes. Greg's sister-in-law, who grew up in Damascus, boils up Syrian amardine to make a thick, creamy summer pudding, studded with almonds and served with a big blob of whipped cream.

SELECTING AND STORING APRICOTS

Selecting apricots to eat fresh can be tricky. Always choose fruit which is unblemished and gives a little to the touch. Color is not always a good guide, as fruit which is a beautiful pinky-orange and feels ripe to the touch may still taste unpleasantly furry and bland. The scent of the fruit is often a better guide to its flavor. If you plan to poach the fruit or use it in a cooked dish, though, the degree of ripeness is less critical.

Most dried apricots usually have a reliable flavor, and brightness of color is not important, as the most expensive Hunza apricots prove. Dried apricots should be stored in an airtight container in a cool cupboard or pantry, where they will keep for up to a year. In very humid climates they should be kept in the refrigerator.

USING APRICOTS

The intense, syrupy sweetness of apricots is delicious in jams, preserves, and jellies. It is also good in sweet tarts, crumbles, and pies, or poached, puréed, and folded into cream for a bavarois or mousse. To prepare apricots for cooking, simply cut them in half lengthways, without peeling (the skin slips off easily once the cooked fruit has cooled a little). Don't discard the kernels, but add a few of them to the fruit for poaching – they contain minute quantities of prussic acid, which adds a slight bitter-almond flavor to the syrup. Dried apricots may be plumped up by soaking them overnight in water before poaching.

POACHED APRICOTS

Poaching is the best and simplest way to bring out the intense sweet-sour apricot flavor. Cut the fruit in half and poach gently in a sugar syrup flavored with lemon or orange zest until soft. Be careful not to overcook them, and treat them carefully once they are poached, as they will easily lose their shape. Poached apricots are delicious served warm with a big dollop of thick yogurt and Cardamom-Orange Wafers (page 46). Or serve them, still warm, with Pine-Nut Praline Ice Cream (page 232) or spoon them over a sleek, trembling bavarois or custard.

2 pounds ripe apricots
juice and zest of 1 lemon
1 cinnamon stick

1½ cups castor sugar
2½ cups water

CUT THE APRICOTS in half and remove their kernels. If you like, crack about 10 of the kernels to remove the nut inside, and add the kernels to the syrup. Place all the ingredients in a pan and slowly bring to the boil. Then remove from the heat and allow the apricots to cool in their syrup.

APRICOT-CARDAMOM ICE CREAM

Apricots work equally well in an intense sorbet or a creamy ice cream. For this recipe you can use fresh apricots poached in a sherry-laced syrup, or, for a slightly different flavor, use intensely flavored amardine sheets, as described on page 10. This ice cream is also delicious if you omit the cardamom seeds and fold in Pine-Nut Praline (page 231) toward the end of the churning process for a toasty, nutty crunchiness.

~~~~~~

1 cup sherry

1 cup water

16 cardamom pods, seeds only, crushed and sieved

1 packet amardine or fruit leather sheets (1 pound)

¾ cup water

1 cup sugar

2 tablespoons mild-flavored honey

½ vanilla bean, split and scraped

8 egg yolks

2¼ cups cream

1 teaspoon vanilla essence

COMBINE WATER, sherry, and cardamom seeds in a heavy-based pan and slowly bring to the boil. Lower the heat, add the amardine sheets, and simmer gently until it all dissolves to a thickish, smooth consistency. Remove from the heat and allow to cool.

To make a syrup, bring water to the boil with the sugar, honey, and vanilla bean, then lower the heat and simmer gently for 5 minutes.

Meanwhile, to make the ice-cream base, whisk the egg yolks until light and fluffy (about 3 minutes in an electric mixer), then pour on the hot syrup, whisking all the time. Add the cream and the vanilla essence, whisk briefly to incorporate, then turn off the mixer.

Allow to cool completely, then fold the amardine fruit purée into the ice-cream base.

Pour into an ice-cream maker and churn according to the manufacturer's instructions.

SERVES FOUR TO SIX.

APRICOT AND ORANGE-BLOSSOM CREAM

Dessert wines such as Sauternes add another dimension to the flavor of poached apricots, fresh or dried. Of course, if you don't wish to break the bank on a Sauternes, you could choose a Muscat or any one of many delicious New World botrytis-affected dessert wines. Other terrific combinations are Marsala, brandy or orange liqueurs, or even orange-blossom water. This perfumed cream makes a delicious accompaniment to a rich chocolate cake.

10 ounces amardine sheets
¾ cup water
⅓ cup castor sugar
½ cup water

1¾ cups cream
¼ cup Marsala wine
1 teaspoon orange-blossom water

GENTLY COOK THE AMARDINE in ¾ cup water for about 10 minutes, until very soft. Remove from heat and purée in food processor until smooth. Chill.

Next make a caramel with the sugar and ¼ cup of the water. Once the sugar has caramelized, add the remaining cold water to thin the syrup a little and prevent it from setting hard. Allow to cool completely.

Combine the apricot purée with the cream, Marsala, and orange-blossom water and whip into soft peaks. Gently swirl in the caramel and serve straightaway.

artichokes

Maybe it has something to do with the fast pace of the world we live in, but many people consider artichokes to be much too much like hard work. It is true that they are not for those who like to eat on the run, as they require a certain level of commitment to prepare. Indeed, it must have been a brave and determined individual who first attacked the artichoke with a view to eating it. First you have to hack off the spiky outer leaves, and then do battle with the hairy, tickly central choke in order to arrive at the prized heart.

Artichokes are viewed much more favorably in the Middle East and Mediterranean countries, where they grow like the thistles they in fact are. They are particularly popular in Italy, not only for the antipasto platter but also for a variety of Jewish-Italian dishes, such as the famous deep-fried artichokes (known as *carciofi alla Giuda*), stuffed artichokes (*carciofi ripieni*), or artichokes with rice (*riso con carciofi*).

The Jews introduced artichokes to the northern cities of Italy in the sixteenth century, after their communities fled Sicily and the ferocious Spanish Inquisition. Sicilians often claim the artichoke as native to their island, but historians think it more likely that it was introduced by the Arabs during their occupation of the island in the ninth and tenth centuries. Whatever the truth, artichokes were clearly greatly enjoyed by the Arabs, who named them *al-kharsuf*. This is the origin of *carciofi* in Italian, *alcachofa* in Spanish, and of course our English word *artichoke*.

Artichokes became popular in Renaissance Italy and then in France, thanks to Catherine de Medici, who moved there on her marriage to Henry II. Her fondness for them was considered most unseemly by the French court, given the artichoke's reputed aphrodisiac qualities — although this is no doubt the very reason that England's King Henry VIII took to them so eagerly.

Nowadays artichokes grow all around the Mediterranean and the Middle East, where they are cheap and plentiful. Fresh artichokes have a delicate, almost nutty flavor, which lends itself particularly well to Arab styles of cooking. For instance, they are delicious crumbed or battered and deep fried, or braised in olive oil with other vegetables. Artichoke hearts with fava beans, in one of many common cross-cultural anomalies, are a popular Friday-night dish in both Jewish and Arab communities. They are also equally popular stuffed with a delicate meat and nut filling or a robust anchovy crumbing mixture.

A good introduction to this refined vegetable is pickled artichokes preserved in oil, which can be found in any good delicatessen. These are good scattered through salads, to which they add a lovely nutty flavor and a slight acidic bite. They also complement the richness of offal and are particularly good with smoked tongue. Although the shop-bought versions can be good, they don't come close to those prepared at home. All that's required for their preparation, really, is a little courage.

SELECTING AND STORING ARTICHOKES

Artichokes come in all sizes; smaller artichokes are not inferior. Choose firm, crisp-looking vegetables which feel weighty. The stalk should still be attached, and the leaves should be tightly packed together. Artichokes deteriorate quite soon after picking, and as they age, the whole plant starts to droop. As they dry out, they slowly turn brown, and the leaves open up.

Quite a few of our recipes include pickled artichokes. The recipe for preparing them follows, but it may be more convenient for you to buy them. They are readily available, although quality varies. The best are preserved in oil rather than brine, which gives an unpleasant tinny flavor.

USING ARTICHOKES

Larger artichokes need first to be trimmed of their tough outer leaves and the stalks sliced off so they will sit flat on a plate. Smaller artichokes may only need to be carefully washed and the stalks cut. Some people also like to trim neatly across the top leaves; this is best done with sharp kitchen scissors. Once cut, artichokes discolor quickly, so drop each trimmed vegetable into acidulated water straightaway, where they will sit quite happily until you are ready to cook them.

The simplest way to cook artichokes is to boil them in plenty of boiling salted water and lemon juice. Cover them with a plate to keep them under the surface, then cover the pan and cook them for 10–20 minutes, depending on their size. To check if they are cooked, carefully remove an artichoke from the pan and gently pull on a leaf. If it comes away easily, it is ready. The artichokes should then be drained and left upside down until you are ready to eat.

Artichokes cooked in this way are best eaten warm, rather than hot from the pan, and need lots of sauce to accompany them. At its simplest, this can be melted butter, with plenty of salt and pepper and a squeeze of lemon. Delicious variations might be a tangy vinaigrette, a rich hollandaise sauce or mayonnaise, or a light, refreshing Avgolemono sauce (page 173).

Braising artichokes in a niçoise or à la grecque manner is merely a variation of the simple boiling method. The whole artichoke should be prepared as above, but cooked in a pan of water with plenty of olive oil and aromatics (see page 19 for recipe). They can be eaten straightaway or preserved in their poaching liquor for future use. We use artichokes cooked in this way in all sorts of dishes.

Other recipes require only the inner artichoke hearts, but these dishes are only worth preparing if you have large artichokes. Prepare them as above, with a pan of acidulated water close to hand. Trim the stalk and then start snapping off the leaves, rubbing the raw edges of the vegetable with half a lemon as you go. Keep going until you get to the pale, thin, tightly furled leaves inside the artichoke. At this point you can slice off the top part of the artichoke, scoop out the fuzzy choke, and discard these parts. Rub the heart all over with the cut lemon and then drop into your acidulated water.

ARTICHOKE SOUP WITH CHORIZO AND ROASTED PISTACHIO NUTS

This is a version of a Renaissance soup which Greg learned in Mantova, Italy. The Italian version uses cocks' combs instead of sausage, and the soup is garnished with jewel-like pomegranate seeds.

6 large artichokes
juice of 4 lemons mixed with 1 quart
    water
2 medium onions
2 cloves garlic
2 medium leeks
½ cup olive oil
2 quarts chicken stock
3 semidried chorizo sausages, grilled
    and sliced into ½ inch diagonal pieces
2 egg yolks

⅔ cup thickened cream
salt and pepper
juice of 2 lemons

GARNISH
½ teaspoon allspice (freshly milled,
    if possible)
¼ cup extra-virgin olive oil
¾ cup unsalted pistachio nuts,
    dry-roasted and coarsely crushed

TO PREPARE THE ARTICHOKES, remove the outer hard leaves as well as the choke and immediately place the heart into acidulated water.

Slice the onions, garlic, and leeks finely. Heat the olive oil in a heavy-based pot.

Drain the artichokes and very quickly slice into thin (⅛-inch) slices. Sauté them in the hot oil with the onions, garlic, and leeks, then cover and simmer for 5–8 minutes. Do not allow the artichokes to color.

Add the chicken stock. Bring to the boil and gently simmer for half an hour. Taste and season with salt and pepper.

When ready to serve, bring the soup back to the boil and then add the grilled chorizo pieces. Mix the egg yolks with the cream and then add to the soup. Slowly return the soup to just below boiling, stirring constantly. Remove from the heat and adjust seasoning with salt, pepper, and lemon juice.

As you serve, finish each bowl with a sprinkling of crushed nuts and freshly milled allspice, and a drizzle of extra-virgin olive oil.

SERVES EIGHT.

ARTICHOKES COOKED À LA NIÇOISE

Prepare these in the spring, when artichokes are plentiful. There are endless uses for these artichokes, from soups and salads to braised vegetable and meat dishes. Having a jar of them in the pantry will enable you to add that distinctive artichoke flavor and texture to your dishes for many months after their season ends.

20 small artichokes, outer leaves
   trimmed
a small bucket of cold water acidulated
   with the juice of 2 lemons
1 quart water
juice of 4 lemons
2 cups white wine
1 cup olive oil
4 shallots, peeled and quartered

1 teaspoon coarsely ground
   black pepper
1 bay leaf
2 sprigs thyme
1 teaspoon fennel seeds
2 cloves garlic
3 dried chilis
8 strands saffron
1 teaspoon salt

TRIM THE OUTER LEAVES from the artichokes and place them in acidulated water.

Bring to the boil 1 quart of water with the remaining ingredients. Boil the marinade for 20 minutes. Drain the artichokes and place them in the marinade. The liquid should just cover the artichokes; top up with boiling water if necessary. Bring back to the boil and cook at a rolling boil for about 5–10 minutes, or until they are just tender.

Remove from the heat and allow to cool in the marinade. Pack the artichokes into four 1-quart canning jars and cover with the marinade. Seal tightly and sterilize by placing the jars in a pan of cold water, bringing to the boil, and simmering for 10 minutes.

These pickled artichokes will keep unopened for five months. Once opened, they will keep in the refrigerator for up to a month.

ARTICHOKE SALAD WITH BACON AND EGGS

This makes a good starter for four people or a light lunch for two, served with plenty of fresh, crusty bread. It is well worth making the Dukkah for the fragrant, nutty flavor, which blends beautifully with the creamy richness of the runny egg yolks.

8 ounces bacon

1 teaspoon honey

8 ounces artichokes cooked à la niçoise
   (page 19) or good-quality purchased
   artichokes preserved in oil

2 shallots, finely shredded

½ cup whole parsley leaves

⅓ cup cilantro leaves

1 tablespoon Dijon mustard

1½ tablespoons white wine vinegar

½ cup extra-virgin olive oil

salt and pepper

4 eggs

1 tablespoon Dukkah (see page 278)

CUT THE BACON STRIPS into little batons and fry until crisp, then drizzle the honey over the bacon pieces to candy them for a few more minutes. Remove from the heat and strain through a colander or sieve. Cut the artichokes into quarters and place them in a large mixing bowl with the bacon, shallots, parsley, and cilantro leaves.

To make a vinaigrette, put the mustard in a bowl and add a splash of vinegar to loosen. Whisk oil in very slowly so it emulsifies, until half is incorporated. Add another splash of vinegar to loosen again. Continue to add oil, whisking until all of it is incorporated. Taste and adjust seasoning.

Poach the eggs, or boil them for 3–4 minutes (counting from when the water returns to the boil). Peel and halve the eggs.

Dress the artichoke salad with the vinaigrette. Place it on a plate and serve it with the eggs on top. Sprinkle with Dukkah.

BASQUE-STYLE CHICKEN

¾ ounce (about ¾ cup) dried porcini
  mushrooms
4 small-to-medium tomatoes
8 artichokes cooked à la niçoise
  (page 19) or good-quality purchased
  artichokes preserved in oil
1 roasting chicken (about 4 pounds)
salt and pepper
¼ cup olive oil
1 tablespoon honey mixed with
  1 tablespoon water
8 shallots, cut in half

6 small cloves garlic, peeled
¼ cup porcini juice from soaking
1 teaspoon tomato paste
½ cup red wine
1¼ cups chicken stock
8 leaves fresh sage

TO SERVE

7 ounces egg noodles
generous knob of butter
juice of half a lemon
salt and freshly ground black pepper

RINSE THE PORCINI MUSHROOMS briefly to remove any clinging grit or dirt, then soak them in a cup of fresh, cold water for 10 minutes. Reserve the liquid to be added to the stock later. Quarter the tomatoes and gently squeeze out the seeds. If you are using fresh artichokes, remove the outer leaves and chokes and drop the hearts into acidulated water. When you are ready to use them, cut each heart into quarters. If you are using pickled artichokes, cut each artichoke into quarters.

Cut the chicken into 8 pieces, or ask your butcher to do it for you. Remove the skin and season with salt and pepper. In a large ovenproof pan, sauté the chicken pieces in very hot olive oil until they turn golden brown. Toward the end of the frying time, add the honey and then cook for a further few minutes to caramelize, but be careful not to burn. Remove the chicken from the pan.

Lower the heat, add the shallots and garlic, and sauté briefly until they are just softened. Add the artichokes, tomatoes, and mushrooms and sauté for 2 minutes. Mix the porcini juice, tomato paste, and red wine with the chicken stock and pour into the pan. Place the chicken back in the pan, on top of the vegetables, sprinkle the sage leaves on top, and bake in a preheated 425°F oven for 20 minutes. Remove the pan from the oven and move the chicken pieces to a warm plate. Over a high heat, reduce the stock by about a third, and then return the chicken pieces to the pan.

Cook and drain the egg noodles, then sauté them briefly in butter. Add a squeeze of lemon, and add salt and pepper. To serve, put the sauce and vegetables on a plate, then the chicken, and top with the egg noodles twirled into a little mound on top.

beans

In the beginning there were beans – fava beans, that is. These ancient, edible seeds grew abundantly all around Central Asia, the Middle East, and the Mediterranean from the earliest times. In the days before humans learned how to cultivate plants and had to scrabble around in the dirt for sustenance, fava beans were a godsend. They were easily gathered, were packed with stomach-filling starch, protein, and other nutrients, and, most important, could be dried and stored for long periods.

Fava beans were also easy to propagate, and they became one of the first vegetable crops to be cultivated. Like other ancient crops, such as lentils and peas, they belong to the plant group known as legumes, which have large, nutritious seeds contained in an outer pod. Legumes were frequently combined with grains such as wheat, barley, or millet to provide the main sustenance for early civilizations. As well as eating them, the ancient Greeks were said to have used fava beans as election ballot counters. The Romans made them into cakes or porridge, while the Egyptians' passion for them endures today in little rissoles known as *tamia* (elsewhere known as *falafel*) and *ful medames*, a humble peasant stew which has been adopted as the national dish.

Numerous other types of beans have been grown around the world since antiquity – soybeans in China and Japan; haricot, butter, lima, kidney, and endless others in the Americas – but fava beans are the only variety native to the Middle East and Europe. Other beans didn't reach Europe until the fifteenth century, as part of the exciting new range of foodstuffs brought by explorer ships from the New World. As is so often the case, these new beans, which came in a dazzling range of colors, shapes, and sizes, quickly overtook dull old fava beans in popularity. And so tender little pale-green flageolets were taken up by the French, and the Tuscans' fondness for mild-flavored borlotti beans led to their reputation as Italy's "bean eaters." The English preferred yet another sort of New World bean, the fresh "green" bean.

Green beans are simply a variety of bean which has been cultivated for eating whole, rather than for its seeds alone. They also originated in the Americas many thousands of years ago, and are grown today by home gardeners the world over. They come in a range of shapes and sizes, from the thin, elegant French beans to wider, flatter runner beans, or the long Asian snake beans. Green beans often used to be called string beans because of the fibrous string growing down the seam, which had to be pulled off before cooking. Today, though, most beans have been bred to be stringless.

SELECTING AND STORING BEANS

Fresh beans, including fava beans and all varieties of green beans, are seasonal and at their firm, snappy best during the summer.

When choosing any sort of green beans, ensure that they are dry and unblemished, not wet and wrinkled, and, above all, crisp and firm, not limp and bendy. The freshness and age of fresh fava beans are a little harder to determine, as they come hidden within their own fleshy pod. This pod is often misshapen and mottled, and it can be hard to tell the condition of the beans within – but certainly avoid soft and floppy pods. Later in the season, both the pods and the beans are likely to be larger. New-season fava beans, though, are small and tender, and can even be eaten in the pod.

Dried beans, of course, are readily available throughout the year, though it is impossible to know how long your particular choice has been sitting on the shelves. As with all legumes, we recommend you buy from a shop with a swift turnover and a knowledgeable clientele. Middle Eastern stores and health-food shops are usually a good bet.

There are numerous different varieties of dried beans available, but for the most part, Middle Easterners tend to use dried fava beans (which can be large, dark, and unpeeled, or smaller, split, and peeled) and white beans, such as haricots, cannellini, and butter beans. Dried beans last well but should be stored in an airtight container in a cool, dark cupboard.

USING BEANS

Green beans these days rarely need stringing but usually require rinsing and a quick topping and tailing. Cook them in plenty of boiling salted water for 2 minutes or until just tender (personal preference should dictate whether you cook them meltingly soft or still with a slight squeak). If you are eating them straightaway, drain them thoroughly and then dress them immediately in a little butter or olive oil. If they are to be used later, they may be refreshed in cold water.

Fresh fava beans need to be removed from their furry pods before cooking. Unless they are baby-small, they will also need to be peeled, which is easily achieved if you boil them rapidly for 2–3 minutes, then drain them and rinse them under cold water. When they are cool enough to be handled, the tender beans can be easily squeezed out of their leathery skins. They need little further cooking, but just a gentle reheating, perhaps in a little butter or olive oil. From this stage they can also be added to pilafs and risottos, or dressed while warm for salads.

Dried beans and other legumes these days are pretty clean, and it is unusual to find little stones and grit lurking among them, especially those in the plastic packages in supermarkets. If you buy them loose, though, it is probably a good idea to wash them well, as they can be dusty, and to pick them over for alien matter.

Some people are put off cooking dried beans because of the need to rehydrate them before cooking. But although it requires a little forethought, the soaking process really requires zero effort on the cook's part. Long soaking overnight in two to three times their volume of cold water is ideal, as it allows for a slow and thorough rehydration. The long soak is also helpful in leaching out some of the indigestible oligosaccharides which create gas in the gut; for this reason you should always throw away the soaking water. A pinch of baking soda added to the soaking water is said to help loosen the skins. Some large beans with very tough skins (like giant dried fava beans) require even longer soaking (one to two days) in order to squeeze them out of their skins.

The quick-soak method can be handy if you need to soak beans in a hurry (it is all relative, of course, as even the quick soak requires several hours). Rinse and pick over the beans as usual, and then place them in a pan and cover them with twice their volume of cold water. Bring the water to the boil and cook rapidly for 2–3 minutes. Then remove the pan from the heat and allow the beans to soak for at least 4 hours. Drain off the water and then proceed to cook.

After soaking, beans should be covered in plenty of fresh, cold water, which is brought to the boil and then lowered to a simmer. The beans will take from 45 minutes to 2 hours to cook, depending on their size and age. As for all other legumes, do not salt the water until the very end of the cooking time, as salt toughens the skins and slows down the cooking process.

WHITE BEAN SOUP WITH SPICY MERGUEZ SAUSAGES

Dried beans form the basis of all sorts of delicious soups, puréed into a delicious, earthy smoothness. This version is spiced with sweet cinnamon and spicy merguez sausages, and has an underlying nuttiness from the hazelnut oil and the crunchy roasted nut garnish. Serve it with harissa toast: mix a spoonful of harissa paste into the Lebanese Bread dough (page 295) and bake as usual.

⅔ cup white haricot beans, soaked overnight in twice their volume of cold water

1 quart chicken stock

1 cinnamon stick

3 tablespoons olive oil

2½ ounces bacon, diced

1 medium yellow onion, finely chopped

1 clove garlic, finely chopped

1 stick celery, finely chopped

3 ripe tomatoes, skinned, deseeded, and finely chopped

1 teaspoon honey

1 teaspoon thyme leaves

zest of ½ lemon

1 tablespoon hazelnut oil

salt and pepper

1 cup spinach leaves, shredded

6 merguez sausages, grilled and sliced

⅔ cup roasted hazelnuts, peeled and crushed

DRAIN THE HARICOT BEANS and place them in a pan with the chicken stock and cinnamon stick. Bring to the boil, then lower the heat and simmer for 1–2 hours until beans are tender; cooking time will depend on their age and freshness.

In a frying pan, heat the olive oil and sauté the bacon, onion, garlic, and celery for about 4 minutes until they are lightly colored and softened. Add the mix to the beans and stock with the tomatoes, honey, thyme, lemon zest, and hazelnut oil.

To serve, bring the soup to the boil and season generously with salt and pepper to taste. Throw in the shredded spinach leaves, then garnish with slices of the merguez sausage and crushed hazelnuts.

SERVES SIX.

FRESH FAVA BEANS, ARTICHOKES, AND PEAS

Use your own home-pickled artichokes or good-quality shop-bought artichokes in oil. This is a vibrant, summery vegetable braise. Flood the plate with a big spoonful of the vegetables and then top with slices of grilled, barbecued, or roasted meat so that the juices and flavors all mingle.

⅔ cup fresh peas, shelled
1 cup fresh fava beans, shelled
1 cup shallots
artichokes cooked à la niçoise (page 19)
   or good-quality purchased artichokes
   preserved in oil
3½ ounces bacon strips

1 teaspoon honey
1 teaspoon butter
¼ cup extra-virgin olive oil
1 small clove garlic, finely chopped
½ cup whole mint leaves
½ teaspoon sherry vinegar

BLANCH THE PEAS in boiling water for 2 minutes, then drain them and refresh in cold water. Blanch the fava beans for 2 minutes, then drain and refresh in cold water. When cool, peel off the skins. Peel the shallots and place in a pan of cold, lightly salted water. Bring to the boil, then lower the heat and simmer until the shallots are just tender, which will take around 6 minutes.
Cut the artichoke hearts in quarters.

Cut the bacon strips into neat batons and fry until golden. Add the teaspoon of honey, cook a further minute, then remove the bacon pieces from the heat and strain them through a sieve or colander.

In a clean pan, melt the butter and oil together and lightly sauté the garlic. Add the whole shallots and mix well in the oil mixture. Add the fava beans and heat for a further minute or so, moving them gently around in the oil. Finally, add the peas, artichokes, and mint leaves and a splash of sherry vinegar.

Season with salt and pepper and serve.

NIÇOISE-STYLE GREEN BEAN SALAD

One of the best green bean salads around. Use fresh tuna, either seared medium-rare and sliced as described here or cooked through and flaked into the salad. The Dukkah adds a wonderfully nutty fragrance and works beautifully with the creamy eggs and rich tuna.

DRESSING
1 tablespoon Dijon mustard
3 anchovies
1 teaspoon salted capers, rinsed well
juice of 1 lemon
1 tablespoon champagne or
    white wine vinegar
1 clove garlic crushed with
    ½ teaspoon salt
½ cup olive oil

6 eggs
2 medium waxy potatoes

1 large Spanish onion, thinly sliced
2 medium tomatoes, cut into 8 wedges
1 cup green beans
½ cup parsley leaves
⅓ cup Ligurian olives
6 anchovies, cut in half
1¼ pounds fresh tuna
2 tablespoons oil for grilling tuna
pepper

GARNISH
1 tablespoon Dukkah (page 278)

TO MAKE THE DRESSING, put the mustard, anchovies, capers, lemon, vinegar, and garlic paste into a blender and purée to a paste. Gradually add the oil drop by drop until the mixture emulsifies. If the mayonnaise is very thick, thin it with a little water: the consistency should be like thin pouring cream.

Place the eggs in a pot of warm water. Bring to the boil and cook for 4 minutes. Drain and refresh in cold water, then peel and reserve.

Steam the whole, unskinned potatoes for about 15–20 minutes, or until tender but still firm. While they're still hot, carefully peel and cut them into ⅛-inch slices. While the potatoes are steaming, prepare the onion and tomatoes and place them together in large bowl. Top and tail the beans, bring to them to the boil in salted water, and cook them for 2–3 minutes, or until they are tender. Drain and refresh them under cold water.

Cut the tuna into three even steaks. Season well with salt and pepper. Heat the oil in a heavy-based pan until it is almost smoking. Sear the tuna pieces on each side (40 seconds per side for medium-rare) and then remove them from the pan and put them to one side. Cut each steak into six even slices.

While the potatoes and beans are still warm, place them in the mixing bowl with the tomatoes and onion, parsley leaves, olives, and anchovy pieces. Gently mix with half the dressing. Choose a large, shallow dish for serving. Cut the eggs in half, sprinkle them with Dukkah, and arrange them on the salad with the tuna slices.

SERVES SIX.

RABBIT HOTPOT WITH WHITE BEANS AND CHORIZO

This rabbit hotpot is rich and smoky, similar to a French cassoulet. It needs only a big green salad and maybe a bowl of Goat-Cheese Mashed Potatoes (page 54) to make the perfect meal on a cold winter's evening.

½ cup white beans, soaked overnight in 2–3 times their volume of cold water

2 pounds rabbit hind legs cut in half, or rabbit pieces

salt and pepper

¼ cup olive oil

1 tablespoon honey diluted with 1 tablespoon hot water

10 shallots

1⅔ cups small button mushrooms, stalks trimmed flush

6 cloves garlic

½ pound semidried chorizo sausage, cut into ½-inch discs

½ cup white wine

2 large ripe tomatoes (or one 14-ounce can), skinned, seeded, and chopped

12 fresh sage leaves

½ teaspoon juniper berries, lightly cracked

peel of ½ orange

2 cups chicken stock

freshly ground black pepper

½ cup home-made Crumbing Mix (page 291)

6 kalamata olives, stoned and finely chopped

COOK THE BEANS in fresh water until they are just tender, then drain and reserve. Pat the rabbit legs dry and lightly season them with salt and pepper. In a large ovenproof casserole dish, sauté the rabbit pieces in olive oil until they color. Toward the end of cooking time, turn up the heat and pour in the honey glaze. Sauté for a further 30 seconds until the mixture gently caramelizes, turning the rabbit pieces so that they are coated with the glaze. Now add the whole shallots, mushrooms, garlic, and chorizo sausage pieces and sauté for 2 minutes, turning everything in the glaze. Add the white wine and stir to lift all the golden bits stuck to the bottom of the pan. Then add the beans, chopped tomatoes, sage leaves, juniper berries, orange peel, and chicken stock.

Season with fresh black pepper.

Bring to the boil, then cover the surface of the casserole with a circle of waxed paper and cover the dish with a lid. Cook on the middle shelf of a preheated 350°F oven for 30 minutes. Remove from the oven and check that the rabbit is tender and the meat is beginning to fall from the bones. Return to the oven and cook for a further 20 minutes. Preheat the broiler to its highest temperature. Remove the baking paper and sprinkle the surface with a mixture of the Crumbing Mix and the olives.

Grill until golden brown and serve immediately.

WHIPPED BEAN PURÉE WITH TALEGGIO CHEESE

You can use any white beans, such as cannellini, haricot, or even large butter beans. The idea is that the smooth, creamy blandness of the starchy purée makes a terrific base for the strongly flavored, rind-washed Taleggio cheese. You could try all sorts of variations on the Taleggio cheese theme, such as crumbled feta or freshly grated parmesan. A tablespoon of mustard, freshly grated horseradish, or salty tapenade works well too, or, if you feel really extravagant, a liberal splash of truffle oil. Serve a dollop of this purée with grilled poultry or rabbit, or some good meaty sausages.

¾ cup white beans, soaked overnight in
2–3 times their volume of cold water
2 tablespoons olive oil
1 medium onion, finely sliced
1 large clove garlic, roughly chopped
1 tablespoon sherry
3 cups water

1 very small clove garlic, crushed to a
paste with ½ teaspoon salt
2 tablespoons extra-virgin olive oil
juice of ½ lemon
2 ounces Taleggio cheese, cut into
½-inch dice
salt and pepper

STRAIN THE BEANS and rinse them well. In a heavy-based pot, heat the olive oil and then add the onion. Sauté for a few minutes, add the chopped garlic, and stir on a gentle heat for 1 minute. Add the beans, stirring well to coat them with oil, and then add the sherry. Add water and bring to the boil, then lower the heat and simmer uncovered for 30–40 minutes, or until the beans are tender and most of the liquid has evaporated.

Toward the end of the cooking time, raise the heat to boil off any remaining liquid, but watch carefully to avoid burning.

Pour the beans into a sieve and strain any residual liquid, then tip them into a blender and add the garlic paste, extra-virgin olive oil, and lemon juice.

Blend the mixture on high until it is reduced to a smooth purée. To serve, heat the purée through and gently fold in the Taleggio cheese.

Taste and season with salt and pepper.

bulgur

Before tabbouleh took the world by storm, it is doubtful that there were many people outside the Middle East who even knew what bulgur was. Even today, while recognizing it as the little sand-colored flecks in tabbouleh, not many of us have the first idea what else to do with it.

Bulgur is actually cracked wheat. To make it, grains are first boiled and then dried and roughly ground to produce the semiprocessed wheat known as bulgur. This can then be steamed or boiled, moistened with a little butter or oil, and served as an accompaniment to all kinds of stews and braises. Its texture is a little like brown rice, and it has a nutty, earthy flavor.

As Middle Easterners know, bulgur can be almost as versatile as rice. It is a prominent staple, traditionally considered peasant food (city sophisticates would mainly eat rice), and it features in everything from pilafs to stuffings and salads, as well as being a key ingredient in the Lebanese national dish, kibbeh.

Devotees of Lebanese restaurants know all about kibbeh. These are the little torpedo-shaped patties of meat stuffed into a crispy shell of bulgur. The art of kibbeh making is the stuff of legend, and much is made of those special women favoured with "kibbeh fingers." Less well-known outside Lebanon is kibbeh nayeh, which is a sort of Middle Eastern version of steak tartare. This uses the best-quality lamb, pounded or minced to a fine paste with onion, bulgur, and spices and served with a drizzle of fruity olive oil, salad onions, fresh mint, and plenty of pita bread.

There are numerous versions of tabbouleh found all around the Mediterranean. In Turkey, for instance, they make a version called *kisir*, which includes green peppers and cucumber and is sometimes sharpened with pomegranate juice or verjuice (unripened grape juice) instead of lemon juice.

SELECTING, STORING, AND USING BULGUR

Bulgur comes in several different grades and colors. The coarsest grade is usually cooked like rice and used to make pilafs and stuffings. The finest grade is used in salads such as tabbouleh, where it is moistened and allowed to swell in a lemony dressing. In Middle Eastern stores you may also find that bulgur is available bleached or unbleached. However, the color of the bulgur doesn't affect the flavor of the dish, so choose whichever you prefer the look of.

Fine bulgur, which is what you use in tabbouleh, needs only minimal pre-soaking. The grains should be thoroughly rinsed in cold water and then allowed to soak for about 10 minutes to soften slightly. You then need to drain them well: tip them into a tea towel and twist it tightly to extract as much excess water as you can.

For stuffings and pilafs, coarser bulgur is cooked in the same way as rice. As with rice, it is better to measure both water and grain by volume rather than by weight, the ratio being 1.5 parts water to 1 part bulgur.

WATERCRESS TABBOULEH

Tabbouleh suffers much abuse at the heavy hands of deli and bistro cooks the world over. At its best, tabbouleh is a simple salad made at home, using whatever vegetables are best from the garden, and lavish amounts of fresh parsley and mint. In the West people often overdo the bulgur, but tabbouleh is lighter and much more refreshing if less bulgur is used. The individual vegetables and herbs may be prepared a little ahead of time, but should not be assembled with the lemon juice and oil until the very last moment.

½ cup fine bulgur

2 bunches watercress, washed well and leaves picked (should yield 1½ cups leaves)

1 cup mint leaves, finely shredded

1 large purple onion, finely chopped

3 medium tomatoes, diced very small

juice of 2 lemons

½ teaspoon allspice

⅓ teaspoon cinnamon

½ teaspoon each salt and pepper

⅓–½ cup olive oil

SOAK THE BULGUR in 1 cup of water for 10 minutes.

Place the watercress leaves, shredded mint leaves, onion, and tomatoes in a large mixing bowl. Squeeze the cracked wheat dry of as much water as you can (place in a tea towel and twist). Add it to the mixing bowl and then pour on the lemon juice, allspice, cinnamon, and salt and pepper. Add the olive oil and mix well using clean hands. Taste and adjust seasoning if necessary.

SALMON KIBBEH NAYEH WITH A SOFT HERB SALAD

Some people balk at the thought of eating raw meat, which is what kibbeh nayeh is – a kind of Middle Eastern steak tartare, using lamb, bulgur, onion, and spices. However, most of us are familiar with sushi and sashimi, and are happy to eat raw fish, so this version of kibbeh nayeh uses fresh salmon or tuna, both of which work very well. The fish requires less mincing and pounding than the traditional lamb and results in a lighter dish, which is delicious eaten with pita bread, white salad onions, and a big blob of Yogurt Cheese (page 320), or as below, with a fresh herb salad.

10 ounces Atlantic salmon, finely minced and chilled

2 purple shallots, finely chopped

¾ cup fine bulgur, soaked for 8 minutes in ¾ cup water, then squeezed dry

⅓ teaspoon allspice

1 very small serrano chili, deseeded, scraped, and finely chopped

1 teaspoon salt

pepper

1 tablespoon extra-virgin olive oil

2 cups natural yogurt, drained in a cloth for 24–36 hours (page 320)

½ clove garlic crushed with ⅓ teaspoon salt

SOFT HERB SALAD

⅓ cup cilantro leaves

⅓ cup mint leaves

⅓ cup flat parsley leaves

4 artichokes à la niçoise (page 19), or good-quality purchased artichokes preserved in oil

1 small purple onion, finely sliced

juice of ½ lemon

½ cup extra-virgin olive oil

salt and pepper

1 teaspoon sumac

CHILL A STAINLESS STEEL (OR GLASS) BOWL and in it mix the salmon, shallots, bulgur, allspice, chili, salt, and pepper with 1 tablespoon of extra-virgin olive oil. Refrigerate until ready to serve.

When ready to serve, blend Yogurt Cheese with crushed garlic. In another bowl mix cilantro, mint, parsley, and artichoke leaves with onion, lemon, half of the extra-virgin olive oil, and salt and pepper to taste.

Smooth the mixture out on a large plate to form a neat, flat circle. Use a sharp knife to mark the surface with the traditional pattern, if you wish. Drizzle with the remaining extra-virgin olive oil. Place a generous dollop of Yogurt Cheese on top and garnish with the Soft Herb Salad.

PIGEON STUFFED WITH CRACKED-WHEAT PILAF

This pilaf makes a delightfully different accompaniment to all kinds of meat dishes. Nutty, cinnamony, and fruity, it also makes a delicious stuffing for farmed young pigeon. The poaching liquor will keep for a week in the refrigerator. Use it as a base to make soup, or for cooking savory rice dishes.

PILAF

¼ cup currants

2 tablespoons sherry

¾ cup coarse bulgar soaked in 1½ times its volume of cold water for 5 minutes

salt and pepper

½ teaspoon allspice

zest of ½ orange

1 tablespoon butter

⅓ cup toasted pine nuts

¼ cup pistachios, roughly chopped

PIGEON

4 squab pigeons, 10 ounces each (or substitute cornish game hens or quail)

2 large onions

2 cloves garlic

1 stick cinnamon

½ teaspoon cinnamon

¼ teaspoon saffron (15 threads)

1 serrano chili, split

3 pods cardamom, cracked

enough water to cover

¾ teaspoon salt

1 tablespoon honey

¾ cup vegetable oil for frying

salt for dusting

SOAK THE CURRANTS in the sherry for 30 minutes.

Rinse the bulgur well in cold water and then put it in a heavy pot with 1½ times its volume of fresh, cold water. Season lightly with salt and pepper. Bring the bulgur to the boil and then simmer, covered, on low heat for 10 minutes. Drain the currants and add them to the bulgur with the allspice and orange zest. Fork through and then cover again and allow to steam for a further 10 minutes. Add butter and season with salt and pepper. Allow to cool.

Dry-roast the pine nuts over a high heat, shaking the pan continuously until all are an even golden color. Add to the pilaf with the chopped pistachios.

If using as a stuffing, spoon 2–3 tablespoons of the pilaf into each bird (no more, or they'll burst). Secure the skin at the opening with a toothpick.

Cut the onions into quarters and smash the garlic roughly. Place them in a pan with the cinnamon stick and cinnamon powder, saffron, chili, and cardamom pods. Add the birds and pour on enough water to cover. Add salt and bring slowly to the boil. Cover the pan and lower the heat, then simmer gently for 40 minutes to 1 hour. When testing to see if the meat is tender, pierce the leg rather than the breast. At the 30-minute mark, add the honey to the poaching stock and stir well.

When the birds are cooked, remove them from the poaching liquor and allow them to steam dry for 10 minutes. Dust the birds with salt and fry in moderately hot oil (a wok is perfect for this). Do two at a time, turning them around in the oil as they color. Cook for about 4 minutes, by which time they should have turned a glossy, golden mahogany.

Remove birds from the oil and sit them on kitchen paper for a couple of minutes to drain off excess oil.

If serving the pilaf as an accompaniment, spoon a generous amount onto each plate. Cut each bird into quarters and arrange next to the pilaf. Serve with Minted Cabbage Salad (page 185) and a little bowl of Cumin Salt (page 104) for dipping.

cardamom

At our local Indian takeout restaurant, there is always a pretty little brass dish of breath-freshening seeds and spices on the counter for customers to nibble on while waiting for their chicken vindaloo. In addition to the more familiar fennel seeds and whole cloves, tiny black cardamom seeds are almost always included in this mix. They are amazingly potent, and crunching them between the teeth releases a powerful citrusy flavor, with more than a hint of cleansing camphor. It is easy to see why they are chewed throughout India and in Arab countries as a digestive, and to sweeten the breath.

In Western countries cardamom is still considered fairly exotic – a true spice of the Orient. It is, in fact, a member of the ginger family, and while it is native to India, it also grows in other tropical regions, such as Asia, South America, and even the South Pacific. We probably know it best for the refined and exotic flavor it adds to Indian curries, dals, and rice dishes. But cardamoms also feature in Persian cuisine and are an important ingredient in the bolder spice mixes of North Africa and Arabia. They add a curious, slightly camphorous undertone to the complex blend *ras el hanout*, used throughout Morocco. In Yemen cardamoms are added to relishes such as the fiery zhoug and the musty, mysterious *hilbeh*.

Cardamoms also work deliciously well in sweet dishes and hot drinks. All around the Middle East they add a sweet perfume to coffee, while in some African countries they are added to both tea and coffee, usually combined with other spices, such as cloves, cinnamon, and ginger. Cardamoms add an exquisite flavor to creamy milk-based puddings, custards, and even ice cream. They work equally well in spicy biscuits and cakes, or with honey as a marinade for poultry and duck.

SELECTING AND STORING CARDAMOM

There are two main varieties of cardamom: green and a larger, less common black one. The green cardamom is the one you are most likely to encounter. It is readily available from most decent supermarkets, although we tend to purchase it from Middle Eastern or Indian grocers, as there the pods tend to be plumper and fresher. Some suppliers prefer to bleach green cardamoms and sell them as white cardamom, but they lose some of their fragrance and flavor in the process. As with all spices, it is really difficult to know when it was harvested and packed, or how long it has been sitting on the shelves. To ensure freshness it is best to buy cardamom in small quantities and use it fairly quickly.

Cardamom seeds and ground cardamom powder are also available, which might seem more convenient, but the flavor is likely to be inferior to that of pods you crack and grind yourself.

USING CARDAMOM

Cardamom's fragrant seeds are crowded into a pretty, pale green pod, shaped like a miniature football. The pod may be used whole, or split to remove the seeds, which are usually ground into a fine, aromatic powder.

To use whole cardamoms, crack them open (a heavy rolling pin does the trick nicely), and add them to rice pilafs, Moroccan tagines, or sugar syrups with other flavorings, such as cinnamon sticks and whole cloves. You will be doing your diners a favor if you fish these aromatics out before serving the dish: nobody wants to crack their teeth on a clove or end up with a mouthful of overpowering camphor.

Crushed to a fine powder, cardamom seeds are added to a range of spice mixes, particularly in North Africa and the Persian Gulf states, where they are used to flavor savory soups and stews. In the Middle East, ground cardamom seeds are used more commonly to scent cookies and cakes, custards and milky puddings, creams and ice creams. Whack the pods with a rolling pin, or pierce them with the point of a sharp knife, and pry loose the tiny black seeds within. They can then be ground in a small coffee grinder or using a mortar and pestle. The essential oils in the seeds begin to dissipate very quickly once ground, so it is always better to grind them yourself at the last minute. The minute you start to pound away, you will be rewarded by a waft of heady, citrusy perfume, which will fill your kitchen with scents of the Orient.

POUSSIN ROASTED WITH CARDAMOM AND OREGANO

Cook the poussin slowly on a barbecue or grill, taking care not to burn or char, or you will overpower the fragrant spices. For four people you need four poussins, or you could use two smallish chickens (about 2 pounds each).

18 pods cardamom

3 cloves garlic, roughly chopped

1 tablespoon salt

2 tablespoons fresh oregano or
  2 teaspoons dried oregano

⅓ cup olive oil

4 whole poussins (¾–1 pound each), cut
  down the back and splayed open

freshly ground black pepper

USING A MORTAR AND PESTLE, pound the cardamoms to loosen the husks. Remove these and continue to pound the seeds to bruise them and release their flavor. Add the roughly chopped garlic, salt, and chopped oregano leaves. Pound for a few minutes, mixing all the ingredients together well. Then add 3 tablespoons of the olive oil and stir in well. Continue crushing until you have a thick, smooth paste.

Rub three-quarters of the paste over the poussins, ensuring that you get in all the little cracks and crevices. Mix the remaining paste with the remaining olive oil and then pour over the poussins. Cover and marinate the poussins for 4–8 hours, turning occasionally. When ready to cook, preheat a barbecue or grill to high heat. Season the birds with plenty of fresh black pepper. Place them on the barbecue and cook them on high for a few minutes, until the birds are golden all over. Then reduce the heat and cook slowly for a further 10–15 minutes, until they are cooked through. Toward the end of cooking, brush the birds all over with the remaining marinade.

Serve with plenty of lavash (flatbread) and a braise of Fresh Fava Beans, Artichokes, and Peas (page 27). Alternatively, serve with a robust salad, such as a traditional Greek salad, the Spanish Chickpea and Potato Salad (page 63), or even the Coarse Tapenade Salad (page 197).

CARDAMOM-CRUMBED LAMB CUTLETS

2 racks lamb (approx. 4 points per
   person)
5 pods cardamom, seeds only,
   lightly crushed
2 tablespoons Dijon mustard
1 tablespoon mild honey
2 tablespoons sherry

freshly ground black pepper
2 tablespoons freshly grated parmesan
½ cup home-made Crumbing Mix
   (page 291)
2 tablespoons olive oil
salt and freshly ground black pepper

FOR A BETTER PRESENTATION, scrape the lamb rack bones back to the meat and then wipe them clean with kitchen paper.

To make the glaze, put the cardamom seeds, mustard, honey, and sherry in a saucepan with a grind of black pepper. Heat gently until the honey melts. Mix the ingredients together to make a thinnish glaze.

Combine the Crumbing Mix with the olive oil. Add the parmesan to the bread crumbs. Lightly season the lamb racks with salt and pepper. Spread the glaze generously onto the meat side of the lamb racks and then press the Crumbing Mix into the glaze, packing it on generously but neatly. Wrap aluminum foil around the bones to stop them from charring.

Drizzle the olive oil in a heavy oven tray, add the lamb racks, and cook in a preheated 425°F oven for 12 minutes for medium-rare or 15 minutes for medium. Allow to rest in a warm place for a further 10 minutes.

Slice and serve with Goat-Cheese Mashed Potatoes (page 54).

CARDAMOM-HONEY–GLAZED ROAST DUCK

Many new ovens these days have a rotisserie, which tends to be sadly underutilized. This is a great shame, as they are easy to operate and result in superbly flavored, moist meats and poultry. If you are lucky enough to have a rotisserie, then immediately hunt down the instruction manual; it is the ideal way to cook duck, as it allows much of the fat to drip away. Of course, the best thing of all is to place a baking dish of vegetables under the rotating bird, which roast themselves in the delicious duck fat.

GLAZE
2 tablespoons honey
1 teaspoon sherry
3 tablespoons water
4 pods cardamom, seeds only, crushed
   (½ teaspoon seeds)
½ teaspoon black peppercorns, crushed
1 teaspoon orange-blossom water

DUCK
2 ducks (approx. 3½ pounds each)
salt and pepper
2 onions, quartered
2 lemons, quartered (or preserved
   lemon, optional)
1 bay leaf
1 cinnamon stick
a few sprigs rosemary or thyme

WARM THE HONEY gently with the sherry and water to dissolve. Then stir in the cardamom seeds and crushed pepper. As it cools, add the orange-blossom water.

Wash and wipe the ducks and season with salt and pepper. Remove the wings and necks and stuff each cavity with an onion, a lemon, a bay leaf, half a cinnamon stick, and a few sprigs of rosemary or thyme.

Use small skewers or toothpicks to close the cavity. Pierce each duck with the rotisserie skewer and attach it securely, using prongs and extra string. The ducks must be very securely attached to the skewer.

Preheat the oven to 425°F. Fix the skewer to the rotisserie. If you want to roast some vegetables as well, place them in a tray underneath the rotisserie, where they will cook in the duck fat. After 30 minutes lower the heat to 400°F. After another 20 minutes increase the temperature to 425°F and brush the ducks liberally and evenly with the glaze while they are still turning. Close the oven and cook for a further 3–5 minutes until the birds are a glossy mahogany color, but don't allow the glaze to burn.

Remove the ducks from the oven and allow them to rest for 15 minutes, covered with foil. Carve them and serve with roasted vegetables.

CARDAMOM-ORANGE WAFERS

Cardamom's warm, citrusy tones have a special affinity with orange. This combination features in all sorts of sweet dishes, ranging from ice creams to crème caramels and brûlées. It works equally well in moist cakes and crisp, buttery wafers such as these. They will keep for around 3 days in a well-sealed container.

⅓ cup sugar

⅔ cup plain flour

zest of 1 orange, finely grated

¼ teaspoon cardamom seeds,
   finely crushed

2 egg whites

⅓ cup butter, melted

½ teaspoon orange-blossom water

small bowl of milk

MIX TOGETHER the sugar, flour, zest, and cardamom seeds. Add the egg whites and mix to a smooth paste. Melt the butter and allow it to cool a little. Add the butter and the orange-blossom water to the mixture and stir to incorporate. The batter will be quite loose and sloppy.

Preheat the oven to 325°F. Line a baking tray with baking paper and dot with small, well-spaced blobs of the batter. Wet your finger in the milk and carefully flatten and smear the batter out to circles about $1/16$-inch thick. Refrigerate these for 10 minutes before baking in the center of the oven for 5–7 minutes, or until golden brown. Remove the tray from the oven and lift the wafers onto a wire rack with a spatula.

When they are cool, store them in an airtight container.

cheese

When Greg was 19, and a young and foolish apprentice, he spent a magical time in France working in the dessert section of a Michelin-starred restaurant. He is fond of describing how he labored from morning to night baking crisp, buttery pastries, whipping up mounds of cream, and lovingly stirring rich, eggy custards. There is little doubt that he was eager to experience as many tastes and flavors as possible and would have spent as much time licking the spoon as stirring it.

Naturally, the dessert section also included cheeses. This being France, there was an extraordinary variety of cheese on offer. The temptation to try every one was irresistible. Ah, but those were the days! The sad result of all this indulgence was that Greg ended up flat on his back on a hospital gurney awaiting bypass surgery. The next ten years saw more heart surgery, ballooning of the arteries, and finally, at the grand old age of 30, a heart transplant.

Not surprisingly, all this surgery has made him a more cautious if not a wiser man, and he has had no choice but to modify his eating habits. Cheese, with its very high fat content, is definitely off the menu, although, as a treat, we will sometimes make fresh yogurt cheese – labna – at home. This is a Lebanese favorite, and dead easy to make. Being a dairy product, it is certainly not fat-free, but it has about a third of the fat content of other soft cheeses, such as Brie or Camembert, and a quarter that of hard cheeses such as cheddar.

Simple curd cheeses are still popular throughout Eastern Mediterranean and Middle Eastern countries today, and many households still make their own. The problem for those of us living in Australia, North America, or any of the EU countries is that all commercially available milk these days is pasteurized – and pasteurization destroys the milk's natural bacteria. If you want to make fresh curd cheese at home, you have to add your own starter: something like cultured buttermilk works well. Another simple way to make your own fresh cheese is to use live natural yogurt, which already contains its own cultures and in which the fermentation process has already taken place. The technique for making labna is described under Saffron Yogurt Cheese on page 320.

In Arab countries there is nothing like the range of cheeses we have in the West. This is partly because few of them have a strong dairy tradition, and olive oil rather than butter is the main cooking fat. Such cheeses as there are tend to be made from goat's or sheep's milk rather than cow's milk.

However, cheese is widely consumed. Fresh curd cheeses are eaten at breakfast with bread, perhaps livened up with fresh herbs and a dish of olives. Other favorites are the very salty, crumbly feta cheeses, which are also made from goat's or sheep's milk. These are popular throughout Greece and Turkey, and also Bulgaria.

Then there are the hard, almost rubbery cheeses, like haloumi, which are delicious dusted with flour and pan-fried, or baked in an Arab-style calzone. Both Cyprus and Lebanon make excellent haloumi cheese: the Cypriot version is usually flavored with dried mint, the Lebanese one with black cumin seeds.

Also used in cooking are milder-flavored hard cheeses, such as kasseri and kashkaval, which are often mashed together as filling for savory pies, omelets, and other egg dishes. Kefalotiri is closer to an Italian parmesan. It is strongly flavored, and usually small amounts are grated to add flavor to a dish.

A BRIEF HISTORY OF CHEESE MAKING

The transformation of plain old milk into so many different products is quite extraordinary. It seems something of a quantum leap from that startling discovery in Neolithic times that the semisolid curds produced from milk left to sour in the sun could actually taste good, to the very sophisticated technology employed in cheese making today. And yet the basic principles remain unchanged.

At its simplest, the curdling process occurs when the natural lactic-acid bacteria which are already present in milk are allowed to flourish – typically by heating. But there are still more things which can be done to speed up the curdling process. Food historians suggest that pastoral nomads in Central Asia used the stomach bags of animals as a sort of prehistoric Tupperware container. They would have discovered that rennet, an enzyme found in the stomachs of young calves, hastened the curdling of their milk, resulting in much firmer curds.

Once the milk has curdled, the next step in the cheese-making process is to drain off the whey. Today this is usually done in cloths, but in ancient times they used woven baskets. The French *fromage* and Italian *formaggio* derive from the Greek word for basket, *formos*. The Latin word for basket, *caseus*, became the German *Käse*, the Spanish *quesoa*, and the English *cheese*.

Variations in flavor and richness depend on the choice of cow's, goat's, sheep's, or buffalo's milk, whether the animals have been fed on rich spring grass or winter hay, and from which part of the country the milk comes. The production of the whole range of cooked, smoked, aged, blue-vein, and surface-molded cheese follows on from the initial curdling process.

SELECTING AND STORING CHEESE

Buying cheese is, of course, all about personal choice. Do you fancy a sharp piece of cloth-wrapped cheddar to munch on with an apple and a hunk of crusty bread? Perhaps you want to pop a slice of aged goat cheese under the broiler until it is all bubbly brown, or to smear some perfectly ripe Brie onto an oat biscuit. Whatever your fancy, these days there is absolutely no reason why it should not be satisfied, unless, of course, you buy plastic-wrapped, slimy cheeses from the supermarket. Far better to visit a decent delicatessen or specialist cheese shop, where they understand that cheeses are living things which need nurturing.

So many of the cheeses which are unique to the Middle East and Mediterranean are simply not available in the West, although some local producers seem enthusiastic about experimenting with new varieties. All the recipes can be made with readily available cheeses, either imported or locally made equivalents, which can be just as good.

Once home, cheese should be wrapped in a damp tea towel and stored in a cool, damp place – or failing that, in the refrigerator. If you intend to eat it as is, then remove it from the refrigerator at least an hour ahead of time, so it can slowly come up to room temperature.

Different cheeses have different life spans. As a rule, the very hard cheeses, with the lowest moisture content, will last the longest, and soft, fresh cheeses like curd, cottage, and cream cheeses will spoil more quickly. As with so many foodstuffs, it really makes sense to buy in small quantities, and consume fairly quickly.

USING CHEESE

Preparing cheese for immediate eating involves first selecting a perfect, ripe specimen, storing it correctly, and bringing it to room temperature before eating with crusty bread or hard biscuits, perhaps some fresh fruit, a wedge of quince paste, or some dried muscatel grapes and, naturally, a glass of an appropriate wine.

PEASE PUDDING WITH GOAT CHEESE

1 medium brown onion, finely diced

2 tablespoons olive oil

2 cloves garlic, finely chopped

1 cup green split peas, soaked
  overnight

1 bacon or ham bone

1¼ cups water

⅓ whole nutmeg, grated

salt and pepper

3 ounces goat cheese

IN A LARGE SAUCEPAN, sauté the onion in the oil over medium heat until it is
soft and translucent. Add the garlic and sauté for a few more minutes. Add the
drained split peas, the bacon bone, and the water (1¼ cups, or enough to cover
the peas by two finger widths).

Bring to the boil, then lower the heat and simmer gently for 30–40 minutes,
until peas are mushy and water has nearly all evaporated. Remove the bone and
season the mixture with nutmeg, salt, and pepper. When you are ready to serve,
heat the mixture and fold crumbled goat cheese through it. Don't cook further —
the heat from the peas is enough.

This makes a delicious accompaniment to grilled lamb or roasts, pickled or
boiled ham, or meaty sausages.

SERVES SIX.

GRILLED HALOUMI TART WITH A WINTER SALAD

The simplest way of serving this rubbery looking, slightly bland cheese is to grill or fry it. This transforms it into a golden, molten appetizer, which just needs a squeeze of lemon to bring it to life. Cypriot haloumi comes plastic-wrapped in brine and needs to be briefly rinsed and patted dry before use. Cut it widthways into slices about ¼-inch thick and dredge it in flour. Add cayenne or hot paprika to the flour for a spicier result. Fry the cheese slices in a little oil or butter and sprinkle them with thyme and a squeeze of lemon. Cook for a minute on each side and eat immediately. If they are allowed to cool down too much, they go rubbery again. Eat them just like this, hot from the pan, as part of a mezze selection, or arrange them in this tart as a delicious starter or light lunch dish. The pastry may be made and even baked ahead of time and the tart easily assembled when ready to eat. This recipe makes enough pastry to line either four individual tart pans or one 8-inch pan.

PASTRY
½ cup plain flour
1 cup self-raising flour
1 teaspoon salt
6 tablespoons butter, chilled
⅔ cup crème fraîche, chilled

FILLING
12 spears white asparagus (approx.
   2 bunches)
4 ounces portobello mushrooms,
   sliced thinly
several leaves frisée lettuce, torn into
   bite-size pieces
½ cup watercress leaves
1 small Lebanese cucumber, deseeded
   and finely shredded
1 Belgian endive, leaves separated

½ cup lamb's lettuce leaves
2 medium shallots, thinly sliced
1 block (4 ounces) Cypriot haloumi
   cheese
plain flour for dusting
3 tablespoons olive oil
1 teaspoon chopped thyme leaves
juice of ½ lemon
½ cup vinaigrette (see below)
salt and pepper

VINAIGRETTE
5 dates
7 tablespoons water
juice of 1 lemon
⅔ cup extra-virgin olive oil
salt and freshly ground black pepper

PUT THE FLOURS, salt, and chopped butter into the food processor bowl. Then chill the bowl and blade in the freezer for 10–15 minutes. Remove from the freezer and process carefully until crumbs form. Add the crème fraîche and process until just incorporated (don't overwork). Work into a ball with your hands. Wrap in plastic wrap and refrigerate for a minimum of 2 hours. Or, if you like, make the pastry a day ahead.

When you are ready to make the tart, roll out the pastry, place it in a shallow 9-inch tart pan, and allow it to rest a further 2 hours. Then line the pastry with foil, fill it with beans or rice, and blind-bake it in an oven preheated to 350°F for 10–15 minutes, until the pastry has set and is beginning to color.

Remove the beans and foil, lower the heat to 325°F, and bake for a further 10 minutes, until the pastry is golden brown and crisp.

Remove it from the oven and allow it to cool in its pan. Do not refrigerate it, but reserve it until needed in an airtight container (up to a day ahead).

Snap the woody ends off the asparagus spears and peel them up to the top. Drop them into boiling, salted water and cook for 10 mins or until tender. Refresh them in cold water and cut each spear into 3 pieces, on the diagonal.

When you are ready to serve, heat the tart briefly in a preheated 400°F oven for 2 minutes. While it is heating, place the asparagus in a large mixing bowl with the mushrooms, lettuce, watercress leaves, shredded cucumber, endive, lamb's lettuce, and shallots.

Remove the haloumi from its packet, rinse it briefly, and pat it dry. Cut the haloumi widthways into 8 slices. Dust in a little plain flour. Heat the olive oil in a heavy pan. When the oil is almost smoking, add the cheese slices and fry them for 30 seconds on each side, until they are a rich golden brown. At end of frying, sprinkle them with thyme leaves and a squeeze of lemon.

Remove the pan from the heat. Dress the salad with half the vinaigrette (see below), season with salt and pepper, and pile the salad into warm tart shell, laying the haloumi slices on the top. Drizzle the remaining vinaigrette around the plate and serve while the haloumi is still hot.

To make the vinaigrette, bring the water to a boil, add dates, and simmer until they are meltingly soft (around 15 minutes). Remove pan from heat and allow to cool. When cold, remove the date seeds and skins. Chop the dates finely and whisk with the lemon juice and extra-virgin olive oil. Season with salt and black pepper.

GOAT-CHEESE MASHED POTATOES

To make this with a really good consistency, mix ordinary white potatoes, which are light and fluffy, but rather tasteless, with flavorsome waxy potatoes, such as Yukon Gold. To get that lovely, light texture, push the mashed potatoes through a sieve, which is a bit tedious, but worth it for the result.

3 large potatoes (about 1¼ pounds in total)
1 large waxy potato (about 7 ounces)
¼ cup extra-virgin olive oil

7 tablespoons butter
½ cup thickened cream
⅓ cup mild-flavored goat cheese
salt and pepper

PEEL THE POTATOES and cut them into large, equal-sized dice. Place them in a large pan and cover with cold, salted water. Bring to the boil, then lower the heat and simmer gently for 15–20 minutes, or until the potatoes are cooked but not mushy.

As they are cooking, place the olive oil, butter, and cream in another pot. Bring these to the boil and then simmer to reduce by a third. Keep warm. When the potatoes are cooked, drain and put them back into the pan and allow them to dry over the heat for a further 40–50 seconds. Then push them through a sieve and pour over the cream mixture. Beat with a wooden spoon. Adjust the seasoning.

Roughly crumble the goat cheese into the potato and mix it well with the mash. Serve immediately.

BULGARIAN FETA FRITTERS

These golden choux puffs are bound to become a firm favourite. With their crunchy exteriors and soft, melting centers, they are good on their own, as an appetizer with a small tabbouleh salad, or as an accompaniment to barbecued meats. For a change, try drizzling them with maple syrup as you serve them.

~~~~~~

1 medium leek, sliced	2½ cups plain flour
1 clove garlic, sliced	6 whole eggs
1 tablespoon butter	5 ounces feta
1 cup milk	freshly ground nutmeg
1 cup water	salt and pepper
4 ounces (1 stick) butter	1 quart vegetable oil for deep-frying

SAUTÉ THE LEEK AND GARLIC in the butter for 5 minutes or until soft, then purée.

Place the milk, water, and butter in a saucepan and slowly bring them to the boil so that the butter completely melts. As the liquid boils up, quickly add the flour, all at once, and mix well with a wooden spoon to incorporate it into the liquid. Continue cooking over a low heat for about 5 minutes, until the mixture is glossy and comes away from the sides of the pan in a smooth ball.

Transfer the choux pastry to an electric mixer and beat for a few minutes on medium. Add the leek purée and then the eggs, one by one. When all is well mixed, quickly mix in the crumbled feta and season with nutmeg, pepper, and a little salt.

Refrigerate the mixture for 2 hours before deep-frying in small balls, shaped with soupspoons if you like.

Cook at 350°F for a couple of minutes, until the balls are golden brown and starting to split.

MAKES APPROXIMATELY 16 FRITTERS.

BLUE CHEESE AND WALNUT TERRINE

For this rich terrine, use a sharp, creamy blue cheese like Bleu d'Auvergnes, Roquefort, or Foundation Blue. Serve it with walnut bread. Or, for an unusual cheese course, serve it with a little Honey-Roasted Pear and Walnut Salad (page 153).

~~~~~~

8 ounces Roquefort cheese
4 ounces (1 stick) butter
1 tablespoon cognac or brandy
¼ cup cream

pepper
1 cup walnut halves, roasted
 and skins rubbed off

CHILL THE BOWL and blade of your food processor for about 15 minutes. Then add the cheese, butter, and cognac and process to a paste. In a separate bowl, whisk the cream until it is thick but not stiff. Mix a tablespoon of the cream into the cheese paste to loosen, then tip the mixture back into the cream and fold it in well.

Season with pepper. Stir the walnuts into the mixture and set in a mold lined with plastic wrap to chill overnight.

SERVES EIGHT.

chickpeas

What goes around comes around. This is as true in food as it is in fashion: who would have thought that all those healthy hippie dishes of the 1960s would return to favor so soon! In a delicious display of inverse snobbery, it appears that *cucina povera* – the cuisine of the poor – and its cousin, the Slow Food movement, are back in style in trendy restaurants the world over.

The fundamentals of this way of eating are reflected in the well-known "food pyramid" philosophy, which recommends grains and legumes aplenty, an abundance of fruit and vegetables, fish as often as possible, poultry and lean meat in moderation, and cheese and other dairy produce for occasional treats.

Middle Easterners are great exponents of this style of eating, and are probably more inventive in their use of grains and legumes that anyone else in the world. Just look at what they do with the humble chickpea! A staple in Arab cooking, chickpeas are used in countless soups, stews, and stuffings. Roasted and salted, they are sold by street vendors as a snack all around the Middle East. Mashed, they form the basis for what are probably the most famous Middle Eastern dishes of all, hummus bi tahini and falafel. Dried chickpeas can even be ground into a flour for thickening stews and making all kinds of fritters, pancakes, dumplings, and breads.

High in protein, easy to grow, and handy to store through the long winter months, chickpeas are almost the perfect food. They are also one of the most ancient of foods, believed to be native to southwest Asia and having spread to the Middle East, India, and southern Europe by Neolithic times. They were supposedly introduced to North Africa and Spain by the Phoenicians, and were later reintroduced by the Moors, who also established their popularity in Spain. They have remained a staple food in all these countries ever since.

SELECTING AND STORING CHICKPEAS

The variety of chickpea most readily available is the creamy yellow garbanzo. It can be found in all supermarkets, dried and in cans. Canned chickpeas are certainly more convenient, as they are ready to eat. But they have a strong, almost metallic kind of smell and flavor which can be quite off-putting. We would only recommend using them in an emergency.

Dried chickpeas vary enormously in age, size, and quality. However, if you buy chickpeas (and indeed any dried beans) from Middle Eastern or Indian grocers, where there is a swift turnover of stock, you are likely to get a fresher, better-quality product. In some specialist stores you may also be able to find a smaller, darker chickpea, which is believed to be closer to the ancient variety.

Chickpea flour, known as *besan* and *gram*, can also be found in Middle Eastern and Indian stores. Both the flour and dried peas need to be stored in a well-sealed container and kept in a cool, dark cupboard.

USING CHICKPEAS

One of the most common complaints about dried chickpeas is that they take so long to prepare. Well, this is true up to a point, but bear in mind that most of the preparation involves soaking, which, although time-consuming, requires absolutely no effort at all.

Always pick over chickpeas before use, discarding any which are dark and shriveled, and rinse them well in several changes of water. Cover them with twice their volume of cold, fresh water and leave them to soak, at least overnight, and preferably for 24 hours. Many Middle Eastern and Asian cooks add a teaspoon of baking soda to the soaking water, especially in hard-water areas, which is believed to help loosen the skins.

If for some reason you forget to soak your chickpeas the night before, then a quick soak will suffice. Rinse and drain the dried chickpeas and place them in a pan with twice their volume of cold, fresh water. Bring to the boil and cook rapidly for several minutes. Remove them from the heat, and leave them to soak for 4 hours before draining and cooking.

When the chickpeas are ready to cook, drain the soaking liquid and rinse them well. Put them in a pan with fresh water and bring them to the boil. Do not add any salt at this stage, as it toughens the skins and prolongs the cooking time. Turn the heat down low, cover the pan, and allow the chickpeas to simmer. From here, the cooking time varies greatly depending on how fresh the chickpeas are. We have found that some take as little as 40 minutes, while others take up to 3 hours (yes, really!). Toward the end of the cooking time you may salt the water.

If you are using canned chickpeas, drain them and rinse them very well in several changes of cold, fresh water.

MOROCCAN CHICKPEA SOUP WITH SAUTÉED GARLIC PRAWNS

Known as *harira*, this soup is a Moroccan favorite, particularly popular during Ramadan, when it is served after a day of fasting. Harira is traditionally eaten with dates and a wedge of lemon or lime. It is often made with lamb in a hearty meat stock. This is a lighter, vegetarian version, all lemony and peppery. Garnish, if you like, with grilled seafood: delicate fillets of red mullet or garlicky prawns work well.

SOUP
¼ cup olive oil
1 medium brown onion, diced
2 cloves garlic, crushed
½ cup brown lentils
½ cup chickpeas, soaked overnight
2½ quarts chicken or vegetable stock
1 can crushed tomatoes (14 ounces)
¼ teaspoon ground cinnamon
¼ teaspoon ground ginger
1 pinch ground saffron, about 10
    threads, lightly roasted and crushed
salt

½ teaspoon pepper
¼ cup sherry
juice and zest of 1 lemon
1 tablespoon parsley, chopped
1 tablespoon cilantro, chopped
1 tablespoon celery leaves, chopped

GARLIC PRAWNS
¼ teaspoon chili flakes
2 cloves garlic, crushed with
    ½ teaspoon salt
2½ tablespoons olive oil
12 king prawns, tails and heads removed

HEAT THE OLIVE OIL in a large saucepan and gently sweat the onion and garlic until they soften. Add the lentils and soaked chickpeas and 2 quarts of the stock. Simmer for an hour, or until the lentils and chickpeas are soft and beginning to break down. Use a hand-held electric beater on low speed to crush the legumes, but make sure not to turn them into a smooth purée. Add the tomatoes, cinnamon, ginger, and saffron. Adjust the consistency with additional stock. Bring the liquid to the boil, season with salt and pepper, and finish off with the sherry, lemon juice and zest, parsley, cilantro, and celery.

Mix the chili and garlic to a paste and rub it into the prawns. Allow them to sit for half an hour before cooking.

Heat a skillet or wok, add the oil, and, when it is smoking hot, add the prawns. Cook them on a high heat for 2 minutes. Serve on top of the soup.

SERVES SIX.

HUMMUS BI TAHINI

Creamy chickpea dips like hummus are popular around the Middle East. Some simple versions balance the sweet nuttiness of chickpeas with sharp lemon and garlic and a hint of savory cumin. The best-known version, though, is probably Hummus bi Tahini, which incorporates the earthiness of sesame paste (tahini).

~~~~~~

1 cup chickpeas, soaked overnight in
  2 times their volume of cold water
  with a pinch of baking soda
2 cloves garlic, crushed with
  1 teaspoon salt

juice of 2 lemons
¼ cup tahini paste,
  well stirred
salt and pepper

SOAK CHICKPEAS OVERNIGHT in water with baking soda. The next day, rub the chickpeas well with your fingers in the soaking water to loosen the skins as much as possible. Remove the skins as they float to the surface. Place the chickpeas in fresh water and cook them for 40–60 minutes or until they are tender. Strain them, reserving the cooking liquid.

Place the chickpeas in a food processor with the garlic paste, lemon juice, and tahini and 2 tablespoons of the cooking liquid. Process until the mixture is very smooth. Add more liquid if the hummus is too thick. Taste and adjust seasoning if necessary.

As the hummus cools down it thickens up, so adjust with more lemon juice or water, as needed.

OYSTERS IN CHICKPEA BATTER

Around India and the Mediterranean they grind chickpeas into a flour, known as *besan* or *gram*, and use it to make all kinds of sweets and pastries. It also makes a lovely delicate batter, with a slight nutty flavor.

BATTER
2 cups beer
1½ cups besan flour (chickpea flour)
2½ cups self-raising flour
⅓ cup cornstarch
½ teaspoon cumin powder
1 pinch salt
1 pinch baking soda

OYSTERS
24 freshly shucked oysters (keep the shells for serving)
flour for dusting
1 quart vegetable oil for deep-frying

POUR THE BEER into a mixing bowl and whisk in the besan, self-raising flour, and cornstarch. Add the cumin, salt, and baking soda and then allow to sit for half an hour before using.

Heat the oil to 400°F. Test by throwing in a small cube of bread. If it sizzles slowly to the top, turning golden brown in about 60 seconds, then the oil is hot enough.

In batches of six, dust the oysters lightly in plain flour, then dip into the batter and gently lower into oil. Fry for about 45–60 seconds, or until the batter is golden brown.

Serve the oysters immediately, back on their shells, with a lemon wedge and a little salad.

SPANISH CHICKPEA AND POTATO SALAD

This Spanish-inspired salad combines waxy potatoes with sweet, ripe tomatoes, savory onions, and fruity olives in a sweet-sour sherry vinaigrette. Serve it as a light lunch dish with plenty of crusty bread, as an accompaniment to Portuguese Marinated Quail (page 73), or as part of a mezze luncheon.

~~~~~~

2 large waxy potatoes

1 cup cooked chickpeas

1 medium purple onion, finely sliced

2 medium tomatoes, deseeded and
   diced very small

1 cup whole green olives

½ cup parsley leaves

salt and pepper

⅓ cup extra-virgin olive oil

3 tablespoons sherry vinegar

PEEL THE POTATOES and trim off the ends and sides. Cut into neat ½-inch dice, or roughly chickpea size. Steam for 10 minutes, or until they are tender.

Combine the onion, tomatoes, olives, and parsley in a large mixing bowl. When the potatoes are ready, season them with salt and pepper, pour the olive oil and sherry vinegar over them, and stir gently.

Tip the potatoes and dressing into the salad mixture. Toss gently, adjust seasoning, and serve immediately.

SPICY PRAWN AND MUSSEL TAGINE

Chickpeas are a firm favorite in Moroccan cooking, featuring in all sorts of couscous dishes and tagines, such as this spicy seafood version. Accompany with a dollop of Saffron Yogurt Cheese (page 320) or Basil Tzatziki (page 321).

1 pound mussels

1 pound king prawns (whole weight), approx. 2 per person

¼ cup olive oil

2 whole shallots, finely chopped

½ cup chickpeas, soaked overnight and cooked

¾ pound waxy potatoes, cut into 1 cm dice

½ can crushed tomatoes (approx. 1 cup)

2 tablespoons tomato chermoula (page 72)

1 cup stock or water

½ cup chopped parsley leaves

½ cup chopped fresh cilantro leaves and stems

DEBEARD AND SCRUB the mussels thoroughly. Peel the body shells and legs from the prawns, leaving their heads and tails intact.

Heat the oil in a large, heavy-based pan. Add the shallots, chickpeas, potatoes, crushed tomatoes, and tomato chermoula. Then add the stock and stir well. Cover and cook for 8 minutes until the potatoes are just tender. Turn up the heat and add the mussels and the prawns. Cover the pan and cook until mussels open (1–2 minutes), then season with pepper and sprinkle with parsley and cilantro.

Serve immediately with crusty bread and salad.

SERVES FOUR AS AN APPETIZER.

NOTE: Do not add any salt, as the mussel liquor is salty enough.

chilis

When it comes to eating, we humans exhibit a sense of adventure in our willingness to try new and different foods and in our persistence with foods that are initially unpalatable. Think of chilis, black pepper, coffee, even alcohol – some of the most widely consumed foods in the world. On a first encounter, however, they are all either horribly bitter or cruelly pungent, and can irritate or even burn the mouth's delicate lining.

We persist in consuming all these foodstuffs – in huge quantities, too – because of their strange addictive power. With chilis, the thrill is all in the burn. They contain a chemical alkaloid known as capsaicin, which acts as both an irritant (the burn factor) and a stimulant. Capsaicin itself has no taste, but it does increase and intensify other flavors. This ability to enliven a limited range of bland ingredients is what makes chili such an attractive food in impoverished countries around the world. More cunningly, capsaicin stimulates the brain to secrete endorphins, the body's natural opiates, which lift and exhilarate us. Chili is said to be eaten daily by at least a quarter of the world's population.

This popularity has occurred only over the last 500 years, however. Chilis were unknown in Asia, Africa, or indeed Europe until Christopher Columbus landed in the New World in 1492. Chilis are native to Central America: archaeological sites suggest that chilis were consumed in Mexico at least 9,000 years ago and have long been cultivated by the Incas, Mayas, and Aztecs.

With the arrival of the spice-seeking Spanish and Portuguese, it was not long before chilis were being shipped back to Europe and thence to Spanish and Portuguese colonies in Africa, India, and Southeast Asia. In Spain itself, chilis were eagerly received as a new kind of pepper. Over time, they have been gradually cultivated to be larger and sweeter, although their spiciness is still prized in products such as chorizo sausages.

From Spain, chilis spread over the sea to Morocco and the other countries of the Maghreb. People in these hot, desert-hugging regions loved the fiery heat of chili and swiftly incorporated it into local spice mixes, such as the Tunisian tabil, and used it as a condiment in the form of chili pastes and sauces. The best-known of these is harissa, which is served all across North Africa but is particularly popular in Tunisia and Algeria, where it is always served as an accompaniment to couscous.

Moroccans tend to enjoy a gentler bite and usually favor the sweeter heat of paprika. However, they are particularly fond of chermoula, a spicy marinade used for fish and seafood. Inhabitants of the Persian Gulf states also enjoy the boldness of really hot chili. The Yemeni relish zhoug, for instance, is hot enough to bring tears to the eyes.

In an interesting reversal of previous trends, the Spanish introduced chilis to the Arabs, who carried them eastward again along well-established trade routes. Chilis tend to be too brash for Persian and Middle Eastern cooks. They prefer other, more complex and delicate spices, which seduce the palate softly. However, the use of chili is spreading not only throughout Western countries, but also through Middle Eastern countries such as Lebanon and Syria, where it is being increasingly used as a condiment. Dried chili flakes, for example, are nearly always offered for sprinkling on minced lamb pizzas, or pickled chilis may be served as part of a mezze selection.

SELECTING AND STORING CHILIS

All chilis and bell peppers belong to the capsicum family. There are many hundreds of varieties of chili grown around the world, of all different shapes, sizes, and colors and with varying degrees of heat. To the neophyte, chilis are merely hot, very hot, or unbelievably hot, but to the true chili aficionado, each chili has a particular aroma and flavor. Better-known varieties include the jalapeño, commonly used in Mexican cooking; the Jamaican Scotch bonnet, which is popular all around the Caribbean; the habañero, widely used in South America; and the bird's eye or serrano chili, both red and green, which is common throughout Southeast Asia.

Red chilis are merely riper than green chilis, and the color is no real indication of heat. When buying chilis, select only those which are plump and firm, have no black spots on their skin, and are not wrinkled or soft, especially close to the stem. Fresh chilis should be stored in the refrigerator, where they will last for several weeks. Remove any which seem to be getting soft, as they will quickly rot and spoil the rest.

Whole dried chilis have often been roasted to intensify their smoky, nutty quality. They tend to be very spicy and are sometimes simply sizzled in hot oil to add chili flavor without too much bite, and then removed before other ingredients are added.

Ground chili also comes in varying degrees of heat and intensity. The most commonly available types are cayenne pepper (which is what most ground chilis are), and hot or sweet paprika. Cayenne is made from grinding several different types of chilis, and it is pretty hot. It should be added to dishes according to your personal taste. Paprikas will be labeled hot or sweet (mild). They vary in color from bright orange to deep ox-blood red, and come from South America, Spain, and Hungary. The Hungarian variety, widely used in Hungary as a mainstay ingredient, is generally considered to be the best.

As with other spices, dried chilis and ground chili should be purchased in small quantities and stored in a cool, dark cupboard.

USING CHILIS

When preparing chilis, it is best to err on the side of caution. Some people suggest rubbing the cut surface of a chili on the back of your hand to give you an idea of its ferocity. It may cause your skin merely to tingle, or it could actually raise a blister. Of course, this won't tell you what it tastes like, but it will give you some idea of the likely effect on your mouth. You can also test the heat by cutting off a small piece from the center of the chili and cautiously licking it.

It is often recommended that you wear rubber gloves when preparing fresh chilis. At the very least, be careful not to touch the seeds or the whitish inner membranes. Wash your hands afterward very thoroughly, and avoid touching your face, particularly your eyes.

Recipes often suggest removing the seeds and the inner white fibers, as these have the highest concentrations of capsaicin (this is rarely done in Asia or South America, of course, where they really believe in going for the burn). To do this, split the chili lengthways and carefully scrape the seeds and fibers away with the point of a small kitchen knife. You should also use this method to remove the seeds from dried chilis.

"RED HOT CHILI PEPPER" SOUP

This spicy soup was created when the American band was touring Australia in 1992. Use between one and three chilis – or more, of course – depending on your stamina. Squat, thick-skinned peppers are best for this soup, as they are easy to skin.

~~~~~~

3 whole large red bell peppers

2 whole medium onions

2 cloves garlic

1–3 serrano chilis

¼ cup olive oil

4 whole tomatoes, skinned and diced

3 tablespoons sherry

2½ cups vegetable or chicken stock

6 sprigs fresh thyme, tied with string

2 whole bay leaves

salt and pepper

1 teaspoon honey

ROAST THE PEPPERS over a gas flame, or under the broiler, turning them constantly until they are blackened and blistered all over. This takes around 20 minutes. Put them into a bowl, cover with plastic wrap, and allow them to steam and soften for another 10 minutes.

In the meantime, slice the onions finely and chop the garlic and chilis, seeds included. Sauté in the oil over a low to medium heat until they are soft and translucent. Then add the peeled, roughly diced tomatoes and sauté for a further 20 minutes. (To skin, pour boiling water over the tomatoes, pierce the skin, and peel it off.)

Once the peppers are cool, peel off the skins, making sure you remove any blackened bits that will make the soup bitter and unattractive. Remove the seeds too, and then roughly chop the flesh and add it to the tomato-onion mixture.

Add the sherry and stock and cook a further 5 minutes. Season with pepper and salt. Add the bundle of thyme and the bay leaves and simmer for 15 minutes. Remove from the heat and stir in the honey. Taste and adjust seasoning if necessary. Blend the mixture until it is very smooth, which will take about 3 minutes on high speed.

If you are fussy about presentation, tip the soup through a fine sieve, which will also remove any chili seeds. Thin the soup down with a little extra stock or water if required.

Serve it with a blob of goat cheese and a drizzle of extra-virgin olive oil.

SERVES SIX.

RED HARISSA

In Morocco, harissa is simply rehydrated dried chilis mixed with tomato paste and salt. This version is closer to a Tunisian harissa, which is more complex, with spices and garlic.

~~~~~~

1 red bell pepper, roasted and peeled

10 small serrano or other hot chilis

2 cloves garlic

½ teaspoon salt

1 teaspoon cumin seeds

¾ teaspoon coriander seeds

¼ cup olive oil

PREPARE THE RED PEPPER and chop roughly. Deseed the chilis, but leave the white inner fibers intact. Crush garlic with the salt. Roast and crush the cumin and coriander seeds. Place all ingredients in a blender and purée with the olive oil. Taste very cautiously for seasoning (it's hot!) and add more salt if necessary.

Store in a sealed jar, under a thin layer of oil. This will keep for a week in the refrigerator.

MAKES ABOUT ¾ CUP.

HARISSA-POTATO SALAD

A touch of harissa will liven up all sorts of soups and stews, or even a creamy potato salad such as this. If you are unable to make your own, then a good-quality purchased paste will do.

6 medium waxy potatoes
1 tablespoon chopped capers
4 whole spring onions, finely chopped

MAYONNAISE
2 egg yolks

1 clove garlic, crushed with
⅓ cup extra-virgin olive oil
⅓ cup vegetable oil
juice of 1 lemon
1 tablespoon Red Harissa (opposite)
salt and pepper

1 clove garlic, crushed with
  ½ teaspoon salt

STEAM POTATOES until tender, and while they are cooking, make the mayonnaise.

Combine the olive and vegetable oils. Whisk the egg yolks well with the crushed garlic. Very gradually whisk in the oil, drop by drop, making sure each addition is thoroughly incorporated before adding the next drop. Once the mixture has thickened to a stiff paste, thin it with half the lemon juice. Continue to add the oil slowly until all has been incorporated. Taste and adjust the seasonings and add the remaining lemon juice. Then stir in the harissa paste.

Peel the potatoes while they are still warm and cut them into ¾-inch dice. Mix them with the capers, spring onions, and mayonnaise, thinned with a little cream if desired.

Season with salt and pepper.

CHERMOULA

Since Moroccan food became all the rage, Chermoula has featured widely on the menus of trendy restaurants around the world. In its homeland, Chermoula is most often used with fish dishes. Its chili-heat content may be varied to taste. This will keep for a month in the refrigerator; top up with a little oil each time you use it.

3 tablespoons cumin seeds, roasted
   and finely crushed
1 tablespoon coriander seeds, roasted
   and finely crushed
2 tablespoons sweet paprika
1 tablespoon ground ginger
2 cloves garlic, roughly chopped

2–4 whole serrano chilis, deseeded,
   scraped, and roughly chopped
juice of 2 lemons
½ cup olive oil
½ teaspoon pepper
½ teaspoon salt

PUT ALL INGREDIENTS into a food processor and process until garlic and chilis have been ground to a paste. For tomato chermoula, add 1 cup crushed tomatoes.

CHERMOULA-ROASTED KING PRAWNS

12 king prawns (approx. 2 pounds)
1½ tablespoons Chermoula
salt and pepper
¼ cup olive oil

1 medium onion, finely chopped
½ cup parsley leaves, roughly chopped
½ cup cilantro leaves, roughly chopped
juice of 1 lemon

PEEL THE PRAWNS, leaving the head and tail intact. With a sharp knife, split along the back and carefully pull away any intestines. Rub the prawns all over with the Chermoula, season lightly, and allow them to sit for an hour. Heat the oil in a wide, heavy-based pan. Sauté the onion for 2–3 minutes. When it is soft, raise the heat, add the prawns, and sprinkle on the parsley, cilantro, and lemon juice. Turn the prawns in the hot oil for 2 minutes or until cooked. Serve immediately.

SERVES FOUR AS A STARTER.

PORTUGUESE MARINATED QUAIL

This is a Portuguese-inspired, twice-marinated and twice-cooked quail dish. The birds are rubbed with a spicy paste and then cooked in a tangy, hot-sour beer marinade. They are left in this marinade for up to 3 days and require only a quick grilling or frying to turn their skin a delightful golden red.

~~~~~~

4 whole quail
2 cloves garlic crushed with
   1 teaspoon salt
2 teaspoons sweet paprika
1 teaspoon crushed cumin seeds
1 tablespoon olive oil
1 cup beer

1 tablespoon balsamic vinegar
1 tablespoon white wine vinegar
2 long red chilis, cut into thirds
4 small sprigs oregano
⅔ cup olive oil for frying
salt and pepper

TRIM THE QUAIL of necks and wing tips. Split down the backbone with a heavy knife and clean inside. Wash and pat dry.

Pound the garlic with the salt to a smooth, light paste, then pound in the paprika and cumin seeds for a few more minutes so you have a thick, stiff paste. Loosen the paste with 1 tablespoon of the oil and rub thoroughly all over the quail.

In a bowl, mix together the beer and vinegars. Marinate the quail in this mixture overnight in the refrigerator.

Place the quail and marinade into a heavy pot and bring to the boil. Lower the heat, add the chilis and oregano, and cook gently for 12 minutes. Remove the quail and drain it on kitchen paper.

Reduce the marinade by ⅔ until it is thick and syrupy, then pour it over the quail. Cover the quail and marinade with plastic wrap and allow to cool completely. Then refrigerate until you are ready to cook. You can do this up to 3 days ahead of time.

To cook, you can grill the wet quails, straight from the marinade, on a griddle or barbecue or under the broiler. They will need about 1½ to 2 minutes on each side. Or pat them completely dry, dust in paprika flour (1 cup flour to 1 teaspoon sweet paprika), and deep-fry until crispy. This will take about 1 minute in 400°F oil. To shallow-fry, heat about ¾ of an inch of oil in a frying pan and fry, skin side down, for about a minute on each side, or until golden brown. Season lightly and serve.

SERVES FOUR AS A STARTER.

SOUTHERN FRIED CHICKEN WITH EASTERN SPICES

This is a dauntingly long list of ingredients, but they are nearly all spices. Otherwise the dish is pretty simple to make. Serve this spicy fried chicken with wedges of lemon, a creamy Harissa-Potato Salad (page 71), or crisp sautéed potatoes and a big green salad.

~~~~~~

1 corn-fed or free-range frying chicken (or 8 thigh and leg pieces)
6 pods cardamom, roasted and crushed
½ teaspoon black peppercorns, roasted and crushed
½ teaspoon fennel seeds, roasted and crushed
1 teaspoon salt
½ teaspoon sugar
2 teaspoons sweet paprika

1 teaspoon ground coriander seeds
½ teaspoon turmeric
½ teaspoon cayenne pepper
½ teaspoon ground cumin
½ teaspoon ground cinnamon
¼ teaspoon ground allspice
⅔ cup cornstarch
⅓ cup fine cornmeal or very fine semolina
2 whole eggs
¾ cup buttermilk

IF USING A WHOLE CHICKEN, cut it into eight pieces.

Roast and crush the whole spices, salt, and sugar, combine them with the other spices, and then mix with the flours. Whisk the eggs into the buttermilk.

Dip the chicken pieces in the flour, then into the egg mix and then back into the flour again. Shallow-fry them in vegetable oil until each piece is golden brown all over.

Place them on a baking tray and cook in a preheated 400°F oven for 20 minutes. Remove them from the oven and allow them to rest in a warm place for 5 minutes.

Sprinkle with salt and serve.

cinnamon

The smell of sweet cinnamon is as homely and comforting as your granny's kitchen, and conjures up happy memories of freshly baked apple pies, cinnamon buns, and Christmassy mulled wine. We take it so much for granted that it is hard to realize that the history of cinnamon, like that of so many other spices, is dark and violent.

The spice trade is almost as old as civilization itself, and the desire for spices such as cinnamon, pepper, cloves, and nutmeg lured Phoenician, Egyptian, Greek, and Roman ships out into uncharted seas. In the fifteenth and sixteenth centuries, enterprising buccaneers began the search for the Spice Islands in the East, which was the catalyst for great European voyages of adventure, and the colonization of new lands – the discovery, in fact, of a whole New World.

Cinnamon and its rougher cousin, cassia, were two of the earliest spices to have been traded between ancient civilizations. Both were prized in early medicine and religious ceremony long before they were used in cooking. Cinnamon is mentioned in the Old Testament as an essential item in holy ritual, and the Egyptians used it for embalming their pharaohs. The queen of Sheba brought it with her as a precious gift for King Solomon; and the vicious Roman emperor Nero, after murdering his pregnant wife Poppaea, reportedly burned her body upon the city's entire stock of cinnamon in a showy gesture of remorse.

Cinnamon is thought to have entered Europe's culinary repertoire in the last few centuries of Roman rule, but with the collapse of the Roman empire, the supply of spices to the West dried up. Throughout the Dark Ages in Europe, however, Persia still had access to spices from the East via the overland route to China and across the Persian Gulf to India. The Persians' imaginative and elaborate use of many spices and herbs in cooking is legendary. Indeed, the lavish banquets enjoyed by Persian kings so dazzled the invading Arabs that they rapidly adopted many Persian dishes as their own.

During their Golden Age, the Arabs established a far-reaching empire and thriving trading networks from Persia in the east across North Africa and up to Spain in the west. Because of their strategic geographic position, Arab merchants had always played a key role in controlling the spice trade between East and West, and, with the expansion of their empire between the eighth and twelfth centuries, they encouraged a renewed interest in spices all around Europe.

A lingering fondness for cinnamon in many Moroccan and Spanish dishes can be traced back to the Moorish occupation. In northern Europe, though, as cooking techniques evolved, the fondness for mixing sweet spices into one-pot savory dishes declined. Cinnamon became, instead, the spice of choice for baking and sweet dishes, and to this day most English, northern European, Scandinavian, and North American cooks limit its use to fancy baked goods, cakes, and cookies.

However, cinnamon remains an important spice in sweet and savory Arab cooking. It features heavily in Moroccan dishes — in the spice mix ras el hanout, or dusted onto soups, salads, couscous, tagines, and, of course, bisteeya, the legendary pigeon pie. Lebanese, Syrian, Turkish, and Egyptian cuisines use cinnamon in many dishes and as a basic component of a range of different spice mixes.

SELECTING, STORING, AND USING CINNAMON

Cinnamon is harvested from the inner bark of the tropical evergreen tree *Cinnamomum zeylancium*, grown mainly in Sri Lanka but also in Madagascar and the Seychelles. The bark is harvested during the rainy season, when it is pliable. As it dries, it curls into long quills, which are then cut into lengths and sold as the cinnamon sticks we use in casseroles and mulled wine, or ground into the powder we use for spice mixes or apple strudel.

The quills of *Cinnamomum zeylancium* (or "true" cinnamon) are a pale yellowish brown with a mild, sweet flavor. *Cinnamomum cassia* (or cassia) is a darker, reddish brown and has a stronger, spicier flavor. Cassia is rarely seen in Australia or in Europe, but it is the more familiar and popular variety in the United States. Cinnamon quills may be added whole to soups and stews to infuse their flavor into the dish. They should always be removed before serving. The quills can also be ground into a powder, but in most instances it is far simpler to buy cinnamon already ground.

The aroma and taste of both cinnamon sticks and cinnamon powder fade with age. There is really no way of knowing how long the spices in the little plastic packets or glass bottles have been sitting on the supermarket shelves. It is best to buy very small quantities at a time, rather than risk having a jar sit on your spice rack at home for years on end.

LITTLE PIGEON BISTEEYA

This Moroccan specialty is baked for special occasions. However, nearly all Moroccan restaurants serve it, along with the ubiquitous tagines and couscous. It is traditionally made as one large pie, from pigeon spiced with saffron and cinnamon and enriched with eggs. A more prosaic alternative to pigeon is chicken, which is often substituted, but duck legs might be a better choice, with their dark, gamier meat. In Morocco, the whole pie is dusted with cinnamon and confectioner's sugar and can be far too sweet for Western palates. These little pies are only small, as the saffron and scrambled eggs make them extremely rich. Serve them on their own as a starter, or maybe with some lemon-sautéed spinach as a main course.

3 pigeons (roughly 10 ounces each)
salt and pepper
½ cup olive oil
1 medium onion, finely chopped
2 cloves garlic, finely chopped
½ teaspoon ground ginger
8 threads saffron, lightly roasted and crushed
½ teaspoon cinnamon
½ teaspoon ground cumin
1 serrano chili, deseeded and finely chopped

¼ cup sherry
2½ cups chicken stock
3 eggs
⅔ cup parsley leaves, chopped
⅔ cup fresh cilantro leaves and a few stalks, chopped
11 sheets phyllo pastry
⅔ cup (1⅓ sticks) melted butter
¾ cup sliced almonds, fried in vegetable oil and drained
¾ cup confectioner's sugar
2½ tablespoons cinnamon powder

WASH THE PIGEONS and pat them dry with kitchen paper. Remove the legs and breasts and season with salt and pepper.

Heat half the oil in a heavy pan and sauté the pigeon pieces until they are golden brown. Add the onion, garlic, ginger, saffron, cinnamon, cumin, and chili, adding more oil if necessary. Stir so the pigeon is well coated with spices.

Add the sherry and stock, bring to the boil, then lower the heat and simmer for 45–50 minutes, or until the pigeon is tender. When it is cool enough, remove the meat from the pigeon, discarding the skin and bones, and shred it finely.

Reduce the poaching liquid by half and then add the eggs and whisk until they are well combined. Pour this mixture into a small saucepan, season, and scramble over a gentle heat until it is creamy and nearly set. Stir in the parsley and cilantro and check the seasonings. Allow the mixture to cool completely. Stir the meat into the egg mixture, taste for seasoning, and refrigerate until it is ready to use.

To make the pies, work with one sheet of pastry at a time. Lay two sheets on the work surface and brush with melted butter. Fold each one in half, and then cut into six equal squares. Put these to one side (you will need ten of the twelve). Lay the remaining phyllo sheets on the work surface, one by one, and brush them with melted butter. Fold them in half and brush them with butter. Fold them in half again.

Place a generous tablespoon of the meat and egg mixture in the center of each large phyllo square. Place one of the small pastry squares on top of the filling and scatter a teaspoon of fried almonds over the square. Brush around the filling with melted butter and then bring the surrounding pastry sides up and over the filling to form a ball. Turn the pie over and, with the palms of your hands, gently shape it into a raised circular pie. Flatten the top slightly and refrigerate the pie until you are ready to bake.

Place the pies on a greased baking sheet and bake in preheated 350°F oven for 10–15 minutes until they are golden brown.

Sift the confectioner's sugar and cinnamon powder together. Remove the pies and sprinkle them with the cinnamon dust. Brand a diamond pattern on the top of each pie with a heated skewer.

MAKES TEN LITTLE PIES.

RAS EL HANOUT

This is the legendary Moroccan spice mix, which loosely translates as "house blend." Cooks swear by their own particular combination of numerous spices and aromatics, which usually include cinnamon, nutmeg, dried rosebuds, ginger, cloves, and chili (as well as other more exotic ingredients such as Spanish fly!). This is a humbler version which is quite spicy. Use it in soups or lamb tagines, or mix it with a little oil and rub it on poultry as a marinade.

6 pods cardamom, seeds only, roasted and crushed

½ teaspoon black peppercorns, roasted and crushed

½ teaspoon fennel seeds, roasted and crushed

1 teaspoon cinnamon

1 teaspoon ground coriander seeds

1 teaspoon turmeric

1 teaspoon cayenne

2 teaspoons sweet paprika

1 teaspoon ground cumin

1 teaspoon salt

½ teaspoon sugar

½ teaspoon allspice

ROAST and crush whole seeds.

Mix all ingredients together.

Store in an airtight jar and use as needed.

MAKES ABOUT ⅓ CUP.

CINNAMON-CHOCOLATE MOUSSE

This is a heavenly chocolate mousse, made sweetly spicy with the addition of cinnamon. It is airy and fluffy and needs time to set, so it should be made a day in advance and allowed to firm in the refrigerator overnight.

1¼ cups pure cream
4 eggs
⅓ cup mild honey
½ cup castor sugar
14 ounces good-quality dark chocolate
1 teaspoon vanilla essence
3 extra egg whites

1 tablespoon sugar
1 teaspoon cinnamon

TO DUST
1 teaspoon cinnamon
1½ teaspoons confectioner's sugar

BEAT THE CREAM into soft peaks and reserve in the refrigerator.

Place the whole eggs, honey, and sugar in a bowl over a pan of simmering water. Whisk for about 5 minutes until light and fluffy. Pour into the bowl of an electric mixer and whisk on high for 5 further minutes. Meanwhile, melt the chocolate over a pan of hot water and then allow it to cool slightly. Stop the mixer and fold the chocolate and vanilla extract into the egg mixture.

In another bowl, whisk the egg whites until they form very loose, soft peaks. With the mixer running, slowly sprinkle in the sugar and cinnamon. Continue beating for a little longer until the mixture reaches the shiny soft-peak stage.

To assemble the mousse, fold the whipped cream into the chocolate base and then gently fold in the egg whites.

Pour into a serving bowl and refrigerate overnight. When ready to serve, mix together the cinnamon and confectioner's sugar and dust lightly over the mousse.

Serve with fresh berries, caramel, or a dollop of crème fraîche.

CINNAMON-DUSTED SNOW EGGS

Serve these with a creamy Date Custard (page 115), or indeed any custard.

~~~~~~

4 egg whites
1 teaspoon lemon juice
½ cup sugar

TO DUST

1 tablespoon cinnamon
1½ tablespoons confectioner's sugar

THREE-QUARTERS FILL a deep baking pan with water. Place it on the heat and bring the water to a simmer.

Put the egg whites into a mixer bowl with the lemon juice and whisk at high speed until they form soft peaks. Then gradually add the sugar, beating until the mixture is thick and glossy.

Using two kitchen spoons dipped in hot water, scoop up a spoonful of the meringue mixture and form it into an egg shape. Drop it carefully into the simmering water and poach it gently for about 5 minutes, basting continuously with the hot water. Do four meringues at a time. Turn them over and poach for a further 4 minutes. Remove the meringues with a slotted spoon and place them on a clean tea towel draped over a cake rack.

Refrigerate them until you are ready to serve.

Dust the meringues with the cinnamon-sugar mix and float them on the date custard.

Artichoke salad with bacon and eggs **20**

Seven-vegetable couscous with onion jam and green harissa broth **98**

Poussin roasted with cardamom and oregano **43**
(served on fresh fava beans, artichokes, and peas **27**)

Grilled haloumi tart with a winter salad **52**

Squid stuffed with pork and pistachios **236**

Preserved-lemon guacamole with smoked eel and pine-nut wafers **171**

Honey-curd pie with rose-scented figs **224**

coriander and cilantro

The coriander plant leads an exciting dual life as both an herb (cilantro) and a spice, and the need for one will not be satisfied by the other. When it comes to its harmless-looking lacy green leaves, passions start to run high: people either love them or loathe them. The scent and flavor of coriander are curiously hard to define. The name *coriander* comes from the Greek word *koris*, meaning "bug," and it is often said that the plant smells just like a bedbug. It is hard to imagine, though, that there are many people around these days who would recognize the smell of a bedbug if it jumped up and bit them on the nose. One of our very dear friends calls it "stinkweed," which probably sums up the feelings of its detractors pretty succinctly.

Cilantro – the herb – is a vitally important ingredient in cuisines as varied as Mexican, Thai, Vietnamese, Indian, Middle Eastern, and North African. It is at its best very fresh – in salads or garnishes, or ground up, roots and all, into a paste. In cooked dishes it is best thrown in at the very last moment, otherwise it can add a soapy flavor to the entire dish.

In Middle Eastern food, fresh cilantro is one of the most commonly used herbs. People buy it in great armfuls and use it with abandon. Its vivid green leaves are scattered into salads, and generous bunches are used to garnish grilled meat, seafood, and poultry, numerous rice dishes, and all kinds of mezze. Cilantro is also responsible for the surprising bright green color you find in a falafel.

Used on its own, cilantro adds a tantalizing flavor to many dishes, but when combined with other ingredients, such as garlic, lemon juice, and chili, it really comes into its own, adding vibrant, zingy flavors which fairly dance across the taste buds. These can be best appreciated in the marinades and the numerous pastes and relishes which feature all around the Middle East. In Lebanon, for instance, roughly chopped cilantro leaves and stalks are mixed with garlic and lemon juice to make a tangy marinade for grilled poultry and fish or to pour over rice pilafs. Some of the most popular relishes are zhoug – a fiery hot chili-cilantro salsa which originates in Yemen, but is now very popular in Israel as an accompaniment to just about everything – and tabil, a spicy cilantro relish from Tunisia.

Even if you are not partial to fresh cilantro, there is no reason why you should not enjoy the flavor of coriander seeds. These tiny golden balls are often found in pickling mixes, where they create little citrusy explosions in your mouth. More often, they are toasted and ground to a fine powder to be used as a spice. Coriander is commonly combined with ground cumin, and together they form the basis of numerous spice mixes throughout the Orient. Indian spice mixes, for instance, nearly all start with this classic combination, as do the North African mixes chermoula and ras el hanout, and the Egyptian dukkah. In many Arab countries they use a spice blend known as *baharat* (which literally means "spices"). Every household will have its own particular blend of freshly ground spices, but all feature ground coriander and cumin, with the addition in varying quantities of peppercorns, cinnamon, cardamom, nutmeg, cloves, and paprika.

SELECTING AND STORING CILANTRO AND CORIANDER

Sometimes all that you can find on the shelves are those flat vacuum-sealed plastic boxes of weedy little cilantro sprigs. Buy these only as a last resort. It is best to buy big, healthy bunches with the roots still attached. The roots prolong the life of the herb and have a strong concentration of that spicy, citrusy flavor. Some recipes for pastes and relishes actually require the roots to be well pounded and incorporated into the mixture.

As with most fresh herbs, store cilantro in the refrigerator. Place the plants, roots still attached, in a jug of water, covered with a plastic bag to create their own little microclimate. They should last 4–5 days – longer if you change the water regularly.

You can buy little bottles or plastic packets of ground coriander powder. Of course, it is hard to know how long they have been sitting on the shelf, and, once ground up, most spices quickly lose their aroma and flavor. It is far better to buy whole coriander seeds, which are also widely available, and to roast and then grind them yourself when needed. A coffee grinder (thoroughly cleaned first) will make easy work of the task, but it is really quite satisfying to grind them into a powder using a mortar and pestle.

USING CILANTRO AND CORIANDER

Before chopping, you always need to wash fresh cilantro very carefully, as the leaves are often sandy, and the roots harbor mud and dirt. If a recipe requires you to use the roots, then you may even like to scrub them well to make sure you get rid of all the dirt.

When grinding coriander seeds to make a powder, first dry-roast them for a minute or so in a hot, dry pan. This toasting brings out the full flavor of the spice.

BARBECUED SQUID WITH ZHOUG

Zhoug is a hot, peppery relish that comes from Yemen. It is eaten with bread and as a condiment to accompany grilled meats, poultry, and fish. It is often blended with tomatoes to make a spicy sauce.

ZHOUG

4 pods cardamom, husks removed
1 teaspoon black peppercorns
1 teaspoon caraway seeds
4–6 serrano chilis, deseeded and
  scraped
2 cups fresh cilantro leaves and
  stalks
6 cloves garlic
¼ teaspoon salt

1 splash water
1 tablespoon olive oil

8 small squid tubes, tentacles still
  attached if possible (about 3 ounces
  each, whole weight)
⅓ cup olive oil
zest of 1 lemon
1 clove garlic, finely chopped
salt and pepper

TO MAKE THE ZHOUG, crush the cardamom pods, peppercorns, and caraway seeds in a mortar and pestle. Sift to remove bits. Purée the chilis, cilantro, garlic, salt, and water in a blender, then add the spices and mix in well. Cover with the tablespoon of olive oil.

If you are not confident about cleaning and preparing the squid yourself, ask your friendly fishmonger to help you. You need the tentacles, head, and beak to be removed, and the tube split and scraped clean. Keep the tentacles for cooking with the body of the squid.

Score the outside of the squid in a crisscross pattern. Marinate for a minimum of 6 hours in the olive oil, lemon zest, and garlic.

When ready to cook, heat the barbecue (or a very heavy pan). Season the tentacles and squid pieces and place on the hottest part of the barbecue grill, scored side down. After 40 seconds, turn them over. In a moment, they will curl back up into a cylinder shape. Cook for a further minute, then remove from the heat.

To serve, stuff the tentacles back into the squid tubes and serve with lemon wedges and a small blob of Zhoug on the side. (Beware, it is very hot!)

GREEN HARISSA

This is an adaptation of the traditional Harissa, which is made with red peppers and fiery red chilis. To serve as a broth, bring stock or water to the boil, mix in the harissa, check for salt and pepper, and serve as an accompaniment to tagines and couscous (see Seven-Vegetable Couscous with Onion Jam and Green Harissa Broth on page 98).

4 ounces large green chilis, deseeded, scraped, and shredded

1 clove garlic

3½ ounces fresh spinach leaves, stalks removed

2 cups fresh cilantro leaves and stalks

1 teaspoon caraway seeds, roasted and crushed

1 teaspoon coriander seeds, roasted and crushed

1 teaspoon dried mint

1¾ cups vegetable stock or water

¼ cup olive oil

salt and pepper

PLACE ALL INGREDIENTS, except for the oil, salt, and pepper, in a food processor. Process for a minute and then, with the machine still running, slowly add the oil until the mixture is the consistency of pouring cream. Season with salt and pepper.

Transfer to a bowl, cover, and chill.

CILANTRO AND SOFT-BOILED-EGG VINAIGRETTE

Serve this vinaigrette straightaway with Chicken Livers Pressed with Dukkah (page 279), poached brains, white fish, or a cos lettuce and avocado salad.

~~~~~~

2 whole eggs, cooked from the boil
    for 6 minutes
juice of 1 lemon
2 whole shallots, finely chopped
1 clove garlic, finely chopped
¾ cup extra-virgin olive oil

⅓ cup cilantro leaves and stalks,
    finely chopped
1 teaspoon coriander seeds, roasted
    and crushed
salt and pepper

SEPARATE THE EGG YOLKS from the whites. Blend yolks, lemon juice, shallots, and garlic in a food processor and very slowly pour in the oil while the motor is running.

Fold in the chopped egg whites, cilantro leaves and stalks, and coriander seeds. Season with salt and pepper.

MAY'S MARINATED QUAIL

These are a Malouf family favorite, as cooked by Greg's mother, May. They are easy to prepare and bursting with tangy flavors. At home we eat them with a big bowl of risotto or Lebanese Nut Rice (page 164) and a simple mixed-leaf salad.

~~~~~~

8 quail, or 1 large chicken, jointed
2 cups cilantro leaves and stalks, finely
   chopped
4 shallots, finely chopped
2 cloves garlic, finely chopped
zest and juice of 1 lemon

2 serrano chilis (optional),
   finely chopped
1 teaspoon coriander seeds,
   roasted and crushed
¾ cup olive oil
salt and pepper

TRIM THE QUAIL of necks and wing tips. Split down the backbone with a heavy knife and clean inside. Wash and pat dry.

Combine the marinade ingredients and the olive oil in a very large mixing bowl. Place the quail in the marinade and rub it all over, thoroughly working into the cracks and crevices of the birds. Cover and allow to marinade for at least 6 hours, or overnight.

To cook, season the birds with salt and pepper. You can then grill the wet quails straight from the marinade on a griddle or barbecue or under the broiler. Cook for 4 minutes, skin side down, then turn and cook for a further 4 minutes.

SERVES FOUR (TWO QUAILS EACH) AS A MAIN COURSE.

FALAFEL

These spicy patties are a favorite snack all around the Middle East, and from Lebanese takeout shops the world over. Different versions of falafel abound: in Egypt they are made using dried fava beans alone, whereas in Israel, Lebanon, and Syria they are usually made with chickpeas. Others still, like the recipe which follows, use a combination of the two. These home-made falafel are far superior to any you can buy. They are spicy and fragrant, and the fresh cilantro adds a lovely bright green color. It is better to use skinless, split fava beans rather than the whole, unskinned variety.

¾ cup split fava beans, soaked in
   1 quart cold water overnight
½ cup chickpeas, soaked in 1 quart cold
   water overnight
1½ cups fresh cilantro leaves and stalks
1 tablespoon ground coriander
1 tablespoon ground cumin

1 teaspoon baking soda
1 small chili, finely chopped
½ medium onion, finely chopped
1 clove garlic, finely chopped
½ teaspoon salt
3 cups olive oil for frying

DRAIN THE BEANS and chickpeas. Rinse well and dry.

In a food processor, process the beans and chickpeas with a pinch of salt until they are the consistency of coarse, sticky bread crumbs. Add all the other ingredients and process until they combine to form a bright green paste which still has a fine crumb. Don't overprocess – the paste should not be smooth and wet. Refrigerate for half an hour before frying.

Heat the oil to 350°F. It is ready when a cube of bread sizzles slowly to the top and turns a pale golden brown. Shape the falafel into little patties and fry for 6–7 minutes until they are a deep brown. Eat the falafel straightaway, dipped into tahini sauce or stuffed into pita bread, with salad and a squeeze of lemon.

MAKES AROUND THIRTY-SIX PATTIES.

NOTE: You can also use fresh yeast as a raising agent instead of the baking soda. This will give you an even lighter, crisper falafel. Use 1 tablespoon yeast blended with a tablespoon of warm water.

WHOLE ROASTED SNAPPER WITH WALNUT-CILANTRO DRESSING

DRESSING

¾ cup walnuts
1½ cups fresh cilantro leaves and stalks
⅔ cup extra-virgin olive oil
juice of 1 lemon
1 pinch sumac
salt and pepper
1 clove garlic, finely chopped
1 whole shallot, finely chopped

SNAPPER

4 whole baby snapper or black bream
 (approx. ¾ pound each), scaled and
 gutted
salt and pepper
3 tablespoons olive oil
1 cup Tahini Whipped with Yogurt (page
 280)

ROAST THE WALNUTS in a preheated 400°F oven for 5 minutes. Take them out and rub them briskly in a tea towel to remove as much of the papery brown skins as possible. Wash the cilantro and chop roughly. Whisk the oil and lemon lightly together with the salt, pepper, and sumac. Add the shallots and garlic and whisk lightly. Add the cilantro and walnuts and whisk again gently.

With scissors, trim the fins from the fish, and on both sides make three shallow slashes in the flesh. Lightly season the slashes with salt and pepper. Heat 1 tablespoon oil in a heavy-based pan until it is close to smoking. Place two fish at a time in the pan and cook for about a minute on each side, until just colored.

Transfer the fish carefully into a large, deep baking pan brushed with olive oil. Repeat the process with fresh oil for the remaining two fish. Place the baking pan on the top shelf of a preheated 400°F oven. Cook for 10 minutes, or until a pale, milky fluid begins to ooze from the slits.

Remove the snapper from the oven and leave to cool slightly. Carefully peel off the skin from one side, then coat with half of the Tahini Whipped with Yogurt. Spoon on the walnut-cilantro dressing and pack it on evenly and neatly over the entire surface of the fish.

Serve at room temperature with the rest of the tahini sauce and plenty of lemon wedges.

couscous

Until a few years ago, couscous was relatively unknown in Western kitchens. Today it is marketed everywhere as the perfect convenience food, and even the big food manufacturers are hopping on the Morocco-mania bandwagon, with a range of boil-in-the-bag and ready-to-cook versions. It all seems a far cry from Fez and its legendary Seven-Vegetable Couscous (see page 98).

Couscous is not a grain or cereal in its own right, but is made from semolina, which is itself a by-product of flour manufacturing. Traditionally, the tiny pellets are laboriously rolled by hand to the correct size and consistency and then steamed over a bubbling, fragrant stew. The grains absorb all the flavors in the steam and slowly swell to a delectable light fluffiness.

Couscous is the name of the little granules, and also of the entire dish – including the savory stew of meat or vegetables and an aromatic broth. Although we think of couscous as being particularly Moroccan, it is, with slight variations, the national dish of the entire Maghreb region (the North African countries of Morocco, Tunisia, and Algeria). Algerian couscous dishes are fairly robust and spicy, while Tunisians like the fiery heat of lots of chili and often include fish and seafood. Moroccan versions tend to be subtler and more refined; they are often slightly sweeter and can include fresh dates or raisins, nuts, and a touch of honey.

Couscous also appears in other Arab countries, such as Lebanon, where it is known as *maghrebia* ("from the Maghreb"). Here the grains are much larger – almost the size of small peas – and are usually cooked in the broth, rather than steamed, with lamb shanks, or chicken and vegetables. Arab-influenced Sicily also has its own version, typically served with fish stews.

Today couscous is eaten as a daily staple throughout North Africa, but it originated as one of the traditional dishes of the indigenous Berbers. In its homelands it can be served in simple Berber style, with *smen* (the strongly flavored preserved local butter), or it can be a lavish and complex medley of ingredients, eaten as part of an elaborate banquet or feast. Couscous can even be eaten for breakfast: a sweet version is prepared in milk with dried fruit and nuts, honey, and a sprinkle of cinnamon. Traditionally, though, couscous is never served as a main course, but as a fill-up at the end of the meal, to ensure that no one goes home hungry.

Here in the West, we have taken couscous to our hearts and adapted it to our own eating habits. As well as being the perfect partner for exotically spicy tagines, it is the ideal accompaniment to all sorts of braises and stews, as it soaks up all the lovely juices. A handful of couscous thrown into a spicy soup thickens it in a most satisfying way. Couscous is even good just on its own, with a knob of butter, a grinding of salt and pepper, and maybe a dollop of thick yogurt.

SELECTING AND STORING COUSCOUS

The packaged instant versions are anathema to food purists. However, it is virtually impossible to buy any other sort outside Morocco, and even in the Maghreb countries these days, the lure of convenience food is irresistible. Very few Moroccans make their own hand-rolled couscous, except for special occasions. In the West most supermarkets stock several brands of the boxed instant varieties, which are all perfectly acceptable if cooked properly. In our view, the only ones to avoid are the boil-in-the bag, ready-flavored versions, which, in the way of one-minute noodles everywhere, end up tasting suspiciously similar and usually collapse into a soggy mess.

Some good delicatessens, specialist food stores, and Middle Eastern grocers also stock a fully dried, noninstant couscous. This is far more time-consuming to cook, requiring several cycles of steaming, separating, and rubbing with well-oiled hands, but it results in a delicious mound of individually fluffy, light grains.

USING COUSCOUS

When cooked, couscous grains should be fluffy and separate, not soggy and water-laden. Some of the instant versions come with poorly translated and completely inadequate instructions, or instructions in French and Arabic. For the traditional steaming method, see page 96.

For everyday, speedy meals, the instant pour-on-boiling-water variety of couscous is really quite satisfactory, although obviously less tasty, as it doesn't allow the grain to absorb the flavors from the dish cooking below. However, it doesn't require any fancy cooking equipment, like a couscoussier, but only a bowl, a fork, and a saucepan. The thing to remember, though, is that steaming couscous really does improve the flavor and texture of the end result – and is less likely to cause indigestion. Couscous has an amazing capacity to absorb liquid, and if inadequately cooked will continue to swell in your stomach! This problem is avoided in the traditional cooking method, which requires several sessions of steaming.

As a compromise, we suggest the following slightly less quick method. Pour on boiling water, following the instructions on the box. If these are unclear, the rule of thumb is to use twice the volume of water or stock as the volume of couscous. Leave it to stand for at least 10–15 minutes, or until the liquid is completely absorbed. Then dot it with butter or drizzle it with olive oil, cover with plastic wrap, and microwave on medium for around 5 minutes. Alternatively, tip it into an oven-proof dish, add butter or oil, cover it with foil, and leave it in a low oven for around 20 minutes. This second step allows the couscous to steam gently under cover and greatly improves its texture.

If you want to jazz it up a little, then add some aromatics (like a stick of cinnamon, a squeezed-out lemon half, a few sliced dried mushrooms, some raisins, or even finely diced apricots) before the second heat-through. When you are ready to serve, fluff it up with a fork, season, and serve. Or sprinkle on finely chopped parsley and mint, or some lightly toasted almonds.

BUTTERED COUSCOUS – TRADITIONAL METHOD

⅓ cup couscous   salt and pepper
cold water to moisten   aromatics (see below)
a few teaspoons olive oil   ½ teaspoon butter

SPRINKLE THE COUSCOUS in a shallow dish, add ¼ cup of cold water, and let it sit for 10 minutes. This helps start the softening and swelling process. Then rake it through with your fingers. Add a teaspoon of olive oil, and lightly salt and pepper.

Line a steamer or couscoussier with a damp cloth. Sit it on top of boiling water, flavored with aromatics if desired – such as a cinnamon stick, half an onion, lemon peel, and a few sprigs of thyme. Tip the couscous into the top section, steam for 15 minutes, and then pour it onto a shallow pan. Fork it through lightly and allow it to cool for about 5 minutes. Sprinkle it with 1 tablespoon cold water and pour a teaspoon of oil onto your hands. Rub the couscous between the palms of your hands to break down the clumps into individual grains. This will take about 5 minutes. Put the couscous back into the cloth and steam it again for about 20 minutes.

Pour out and fork the butter through thoroughly.

MAKES ONE SERVING.

CRAB AND COUSCOUS SALAD

¼ cup extra-virgin olive oil

juice of 1 lemon

3 shallots, finely sliced

1 clove garlic, crushed with
 ½ teaspoon salt

½ pound fresh crab meat

1½ cup cooked couscous (quick-cook
 method, see page 95)

½ large avocado, cut into ½-inch dice

1 large tomato, deseeded and finely
 diced

¾ cup cilantro leaves, roughly chopped

½ cup watercress leaves

1 serrano chili, deseeded, scraped, and
 finely shredded

1 teaspoon sumac

WHISK TOGETHER the extra-virgin olive oil and lemon juice with the shallots and garlic paste to make a dressing. Combine all the remaining ingredients, except for the sumac, in a bowl. Add two-thirds of the dressing to the salad and mix well.

To serve, pile the salad into a high mound in the center of the plate. Drizzle the remaining dressing around, sprinkle with sumac, and serve with plenty of pita bread.

SEVEN-VEGETABLE COUSCOUS WITH
ONION JAM AND GREEN HARISSA BROTH

Serve with Green Harissa broth (page 87) in a separate jug for each person to help themselves. A bowl of rose-water-flavored yogurt cheese (page 320) or Basil Tzatziki (page 321) on the side, although distinctly un-Moroccan, is also delicious.

~~~~~~

ONION JAM

¼ cup (½ stick) butter

5 medium purple onions, finely sliced

1 cup dry sherry

1 cup tawny port

⅓ cup currants, soaked in an additional ¼ cup dry sherry

salt and pepper

1¼ cups couscous

2 medium carrots, scraped and cut into wedges on the angle

1 small butternut squash, peeled and cut into ¾-inch dice

2 small turnips, peeled and cut into wedges

2 small parsnips, scraped and cut into batons

1 small eggplant, cut into wedges

1 medium zucchini, cut into wedges on the angle

½ cup chickpeas, soaked overnight and cooked until just tender

4 small waxy potatoes, boiled until tender, peeled, and halved

1 tablespoon sweet paprika

½ tablespoon powdered ginger

½ tablespoon dried chilis, crushed

½ tablespoon ground cumin

½ tablespoon ground coriander seeds

½ tablespoon ground pepper

4 cardamom pods, seeds only, crushed

1 clove garlic, crushed with ½ teaspoon salt

juice of 1 lemon

½ cup olive oil

2 cups vegetable stock

salt and pepper

2 teaspoons rosewater

MAKE THE ONION JAM ahead of time. In a heavy-based pan, melt the butter and slowly sweat the onions until they are soft and translucent (about 5 minutes). Add the sherry and port and continue to cook for a further 45 minutes over a very low heat, stirring from time to time to ensure the jam doesn't stick to the bottom of the pan. Add the soaked currants and the soaking liquor and cook for a further 10 minutes, or until the onions have become very sticky and almost caramelized. Season with salt and pepper.

If you have a couscoussier, stew the vegetables in the bottom section and steam the couscous on top. Otherwise, proceed as follows.

Prepare couscous with aromatics according to the base method (see page 96). During the second steaming, begin to prepare the vegetables. Preheat the oven to 400°F.

In a mixing bowl, combine all the spices with the garlic, lemon juice, and half the olive oil.

Heat the remaining oil in a large ovenproof casserole and sauté the carrots, squash, turnips, parsnips, and eggplant for around 5 minutes, or until all are lightly colored.

Add the spice mixture and stir to coat the vegetables for a further 2 minutes. Add the stock and cook for 5 minutes.

Add the zucchini, chickpeas, and potatoes. Mix them in well, then place the casserole in the oven and bake for 20–30 minutes, or until the vegetables are tender. Remove from the oven, check for seasoning, and sprinkle the rose water over the top.

To serve, pile the couscous high on a large serving platter and stack the vegetables on top. Serve immediately with the Onion Jam, the harissa broth, and the yogurt cheese.

NORTH AFRICAN COUSCOUS SOUP

Similar to a traditional Moroccan *harira*, this soup is chock-full of nutty chickpeas and meaty lamb, and thick with couscous. Top with handfuls of fresh mint and parsley and serve it with pita bread and a big dollop of creamy, soothing yogurt for a filling winter lunch.

¼ cup olive oil

½ pound lamb, leg steak, cut into
   small chunks

1 medium onion, finely chopped

2 cloves garlic, crushed with
   1 teaspoon salt

1 tablespoon coriander seeds, roasted
   and ground

1 tablespoon cumin seeds, roasted
   and ground

1 teaspoon allspice

1 teaspoon ground chili

1 teaspoon sweet paprika

1 can crushed tomatoes (14 ounces)

1 green chili, deseeded, scraped, and
   finely shredded

1 teaspoon honey

½ cup chickpeas, soaked overnight

3½ cups chicken stock

2 cups water

salt and pepper

¼ cup couscous

1 tablespoon fresh parsley, finely
   chopped

1 tablespoon fresh mint, finely chopped

juice of 1 lemon

HEAT THE OLIVE OIL and sauté the lamb pieces. Remove them with a slotted spoon and drain on kitchen paper. Add the onion and cook over a gentle heat until soft. Then add the garlic, coriander, cumin, allspice, ground chili, and paprika, and mix well with the onion. Cook for a further 2 minutes and then return the lamb to the pan. Next add the tomatoes, chili, and honey.

Stir well before adding the chickpeas, water, and stock. Cover and simmer on low heat for 45–60 minutes, or until the chickpeas are tender.

When you are ready to serve, taste and adjust seasoning. Add the couscous to the pot, cover, and allow it to sit for 5 minutes.

Serve garnished with the parsley, mint, and lemon juice, a dollop of thick yogurt (optional), and plenty of warm pita bread.

SERVES SIX.

cumin

Cumin seeds pack a powerful punch. Their earthy, savory aroma reminds us immediately of Indian curries, but crunching them between the teeth releases a strong, spicy, almost aniseedy flavor, more reminiscent of caraway.

Cumin is indeed a member of the same family of umbellifers as caraway (and carrot and parsley), but whereas caraway is used in northern European cuisines as a flavoring for rye breads and smoked cheeses, cumin has its roots firmly in the East. The plant is believed to be native to Egypt but has been cultivated around the eastern Mediterranean, Arabia, and India for many thousands of years, and it is one of the most ancient spices used in cooking.

Cumin was certainly grown in Egypt during the time of the pharaohs, where it was used in the embalming process, as well as to flavor many savory dishes, and it remains a favorite spice there today. The ancient Greeks and Romans probably imported cumin from Egypt and also used it widely. While they enjoyed eating it, the ancient Greeks also considered cumin a symbol of meanness — a miserly person was said to be a "cumin splitter." In ancient Rome, cumin was often used interchangeably with pepper.

The Romans were probably responsible for the eventual spread of cumin westward, and by medieval times it was popular both in European kitchens and in early medicines as an antispasmodic and as a cure for flatulence! Interestingly, the faith in cumin's carminative qualities persists in the Middle East today, where a pinch of ground cumin is often added to beans while cooking.

Although cumin has rather fallen from favor in European cooking, it remains indispensable in the cuisines of North Africa, the Middle East, and, of course, India. Its savory, spicy flavor is added to all sorts of meat and poultry dishes, rice dishes, soups, and stews. The seeds are typically dry-roasted before being ground to a fine powder, which further intensifies their pungency.

In Morocco, cumin is an essential ingredient in chermoula, the hot and spicy seasoning paste used in many fish dishes. Cumin is also rubbed onto grilled lamb and used to season minced lamb for making kifta kebabs (brochettes). Throughout North Africa, a popular street food is hard-boiled eggs dunked in little dishes of cumin salt. The Egyptian spice mix dukkah, served with bread and olive oil, is also fragrant with roasted cumin. Middle Easterners use cumin and ground coriander seeds as the basis for many spice mixes. Cumin is often sprinkled onto onions and used to garnish rice and lentil dishes, or mixed with garlic and rubbed as a paste onto grilled meats.

SELECTING AND STORING CUMIN

There are three different kinds of cumin seeds: amber, white, and black. The amber seed is the only one commonly available in supermarkets. This is also the variety most widely used in Middle Eastern and Asian cooking. White and black cumin seeds are usually only to be found in Asian or Middle Eastern stores. Black cumin is considered superior to the others, as it is rarer and has a milder, refined flavor, with smaller seeds. Naturally enough, it is also more expensive. Black cumin seeds are used on flat breads, especially in Turkey, Cyprus, and Lebanon. In Lebanon, they are also added to the brine in which haloumi cheese is stored.

Don't confuse black cumin seeds with nigella seeds, which are quite different. Nigella seeds are also tiny and black, and they have a strong peppery flavor. They are most commonly used in Indian cooking, especially in pickles and in spice mixes, and sprinkled over Indian flat breads.

Cumin seeds are available as whole seeds and as a ready-ground powder. Unlike many other spices, ready-ground cumin retains its potency pretty well – although as it ages you will have to increase the amount you use. For a full-on blast of flavor, though, it is better to use whole seeds, roasted first and then ground with a mortar and pestle or in a clean grinder. As for all spices, buy cumin in small quantities and store it in a tightly sealed container in a dark, cool cupboard.

USING CUMIN

Cumin is potent, so it should be used sparingly. Recipes often suggest what looks like a ridiculously small amount of cumin, but a little really does go a long way. If you are unfamiliar with cumin, a good starting point is between one-eighth and one-quarter of a teaspoon of ground cumin, or half a teaspoon of the whole seeds for every four servings.

Dry-roasting cumin seeds reduces their faint bitterness and brings out their nutty, savory taste. To dry-roast cumin seeds, put them in a heavy frying pan on a medium heat and toss them over the heat for few moments until they have darkened and begun to release their aroma. Tip them into a mortar and grind them up by hand, or pour larger amounts into a clean coffee grinder.

BATTERED SCALLOPS WITH CUMIN SALT

Savory cumin salt is also good for dipping hard-boiled eggs into, or to accompany little grilled quail or pigeons. Serve these scallops with a wedge of lemon, or with a dollop of mayonnaise flavored with preserved lemon and a small mixed-leaf salad.

2 tablespoons cumin seeds
2 tablespoons salt
1¾ cups Chickpea Batter (page 62)

24 fresh scallops, cleaned, rinsed,
 and dried
1¼ cups vegetable oil for deep-frying
plain flour for dusting

TO MAKE THE CUMIN SALT, roast the cumin seeds until they are lightly colored, and then pound them to a fine powder using a mortar and pestle. Sieve to remove bits of husk. Crush the salt to a fine powder and combine with the cumin powder. Heat gently in a pan to release the flavor, and then allow to cool and store in an airtight container.

Make the Chickpea Batter and allow it to stand for half an hour. Meanwhile, clean the scallops, wash them briefly, and pat them dry. Heat the oil to 375°F (test with a blob of batter – it should sizzle to the top and turn golden brown in about 30 seconds). Dust the scallops with plain flour, dip them into the batter, and deep-fry, six at a time, for 45 seconds to 1 minute.

Drain the scallops well on absorbent paper. Sprinkle them with cumin salt and serve straightaway with wedges of lemon.

CUMIN ROUILLE

Use to accompany Prawns Wrapped in Almond Kataifi (page 219) and Grilled-Seafood Bouillabaise (page 274).

~~~~~~

1¼ pounds potatoes

1¼ cups water or Crab Stock (page 274)

5 cloves garlic

10 saffron threads, briefly roasted
  and ground

2 serrano chilis, deseeded and
  roughly chopped

2 red bell peppers, roasted, skinned,
  and diced

1 tablespoon cumin seeds, roasted,
  ground, and sieved

juice of ½ lemon

1 cup olive oil

salt and pepper

COOK THE POTATOES in water or stock with the garlic, saffron, and chilis until the potatoes are soft and the water has nearly evaporated. Tip the mix into a blender with the diced peppers, cumin powder, and half the lemon juice and blend to a purée. While the motor is running, slowly dribble in the oil until all is incorporated, then add the remaining lemon juice.

Season with salt and pepper. Taste and adjust seasoning, adding extra lemon juice if necessary. The consistency should be that of a thin honey, not a stiff mayonnaise.

RED MULLET FRIED IN CUMIN FLOUR

Delicate little red mullet are adored around the Mediterranean and Middle East. Deep-fried whole, as here, they make a spectacular but simple dish. You must use whole, spanking fresh fish. Ideally you should clean them yourself, as they are fragile and fishmongers tend to be heavy-handed, often crushing the flesh and impairing the flavor. It is really not hard (see below), but if you are unsure, then ask your fishmonger to be as gentle as possible. A deep fryer with a basket is useful for this dish, as you need the fish to maintain their shape for a spectacular presentation.

8 red mullet (about ¼ pound each)
salt
2 cups plain flour
2 tablespoons cumin seeds, roasted,
  ground, and sieved

1 teaspoon ground ginger
½ teaspoon pepper
3 cups vegetable oil for deep frying

TO CLEAN THE RED MULLET, leave the fins and tail attached for presentation, but scale using your thumb, running it against the scales from the tail to the head; they are delicate and come away very easily.

Using a sharp knife, slice carefully along the underbelly. Hold the sides open and pull the insides away. Insert your finger into the reddish-colored gills and pull them out, too. Rinse the insides of the fish under running water, paying special attention to rubbing away the dark blood line against the backbone. Pat dry.

Season the fish inside and out with salt. Heat the oil to 375°F. Season the flour with the cumin, ginger, and pepper, and dust the fish all over with seasoned flour.

If you are using a deep fryer with a basket, then splay open the fish just under its chin/gills, so it sits up on its own. Place it like this in the basket – you should be able to do two or three at a time. Lower the basket gently into the oil and cook for 3–4 minutes, or until the fish are golden brown and the flesh is firm to the touch. They should "set" into their new shape in the hot oil.

Lift the basket out of the oil and place the fish on kitchen paper to drain.

Serve them with lots of lemon wedges and preserved-lemon mayonnaise.

PICKLED PORK BELLY ROASTED WITH CUMIN SEEDS

Pickled pork belly may be difficult to find in North American markets, although you could try ordering it from a European specialty butcher. Failing that, try substituting raw pork belly or spare ribs, omitting the soaking in milk. Ask your butcher to remove the skin and ribs if you are unconfident about doing this yourself. Start preparing this recipe at least 2 days before you want to eat it: the meat needs to be soaked in milk to tenderize it and remove some of the salt, and then marinated in a cumin-spiced oil before cooking. Cooked quickly over a high heat, pork belly strips resemble spare ribs. When cooked long and slowly, the meat becomes meltingly tender and softly sticky. Either way, serve with a hearty accompaniment, like creamy mashed potatoes or the spicy Harissa-Potato Salad (page 71). This dish is also good with a tangy braised cabbage dish or sauerkraut.

5 pounds pickled pork belly, ribs and skin removed, soaked overnight in milk

2 cloves garlic, crushed with
½ teaspoon salt

MARINADE

1 tablespoon cumin seeds, roasted and lightly crushed

zest of 1 lemon

1 teaspoon black peppercorns, lightly crushed

1 teaspoon allspice berries, lightly crushed

1 tablespoon fresh ginger, grated

⅔ cup olive oil

REMOVE THE PORK belly from the milk, wash, and pat dry. Cut the belly in half widthways, then cut each half into ¾-inch strips. Rub the garlic paste all over the pork strips.

Mix all the marinade ingredients together and add to the pork. Turn the pork so it is well coated. Cover and refrigerate for 6–24 hours, turning occasionally.

The belly strips can be either seared in a hot pan to color and then baked in a 400°F oven for 15 minutes, or placed on a rack and slow roasted in a 350°F oven for 1 hour, until they are meltingly tender. They are also good barbecued over a hot flame for 15 minutes, until golden crispy brown.

SERVES EIGHT TO TEN.

dates

At first glance, dates are not immediately appealing. For many people, they are those hideously sweet, dried things that turn up in bar cookies and steamed puddings. For some reason, dried dates are also a traditional Christmas gift, packed tightly into long oval boxes which are brightly decorated with palm trees, camels, and mysterious foreign writing.

All it took for us to fall under the spell of this ancient fruit was a visit to the Middle East. Here were names and places familiar since primary school: Nazareth, Bethlehem, Jerusalem – and Jericho, the oldest continuously inhabited city in the world, described in the Old Testament as "the city of palm trees." Under the hot desert sun, our guide pointed out a small oasis of date palms swaying gracefully in perfect, picture-postcard fashion. Clustered among the fronds were fresh dates, as big as amber-hued eggs. We could smell their sweetness in the air, and they were soft as warm toffee in our mouths.

It wasn't hard to imagine these most ancient of trees growing in the very same spot ten thousand years ago. As our guide explained, the date palm has been revered for its usefulness since Neolithic times. Although a tree takes up to six years to fruit, once mature it will yield up to 200 pounds of fruit annually, for an average of sixty years. Furthermore, the tree itself provides shade and building materials, while its fronds can be woven into mats and baskets.

Dates have been a staple food in desert lands for many thousands of years. Their high sugar content meant that they became the mainstay of the nomadic Bedouin's austere diet, and the prophet Muhammad was said to have survived entirely on dates and water during his self-imposed fast. Dates still have a special significance for Muslims during Ramadan – the day's fast is often broken with a bowl of dates and a glass of water, or they are served whole with a wedge of lime as a garnish for the traditional *harira* soup.

Today there are hundreds of varieties of date palm, which are grown in the Maghreb lands of North Africa through the Persian Gulf states, Israel, and Iraq to Pakistan, India, and California.

In the West, most of the fresh dates we enjoy probably come from California or Israel. Although they can never match the buttery, brown-sugar flavor of a sun-warmed date fresh from the tree, these are still quite delicious.

It is thought that dates first reached England in the thirteenth century. As with so many of the new foods brought across the seas by returning crusaders and merchants, they were very expensive, and they were used mainly for sweet puddings and desserts. Even today, English recipes for dates revolve around the bakery – recipes for date slices and loaves, scones, cakes, and sticky puddings abound.

In the Middle East, however, cooks are not so restrained. Moroccan and Persian recipes frequently partner dates with lamb or pigeon. Rice and grain dishes are often garnished with chopped dates and a sprinkling of nuts. Dates are also used extensively in sweet dishes: they are preserved in syrup, cooked into a jam, and chopped and stuffed into shortbread cookies. Some of the most exquisite sweetmeats are made by stuffing dates with an almond, a pistachio nut, or a knob of rose-scented almond paste.

SELECTING AND STORING DATES

In North Africa and the Middle East, there is a seemingly infinite variety of dates to choose from, and their selection is a serious business. A purchase from the souks involves much sampling and deliberation, together with long explanations of the differences between the numerous varieties on offer. Elsewhere, we have to be thankful for what we can get, in most cases the *deglet noor*, which are a light golden color. The other dates readily available are the luxurious medjool dates, which are darker, plumper, and larger. When selecting dates, choose those which are unblemished and have a rich and fairly uniform color. Although the wrinkliness of the skin varies, as a general rule, the drier and older the dates are, the more wrinkled the skin is. Because of their high sugar content, dates keep remarkably well. They do not need to be refrigerated and will keep for several weeks.

USING DATES

Really, the only thing you have to remember when preparing dates is to remove the narrow pit inside. Simply slit them along one side, and the pit will easily come away from the sticky flesh.

DATE-LEMON CHUTNEY

This tangy, spicy chutney is absolutely delicious with all kinds of grilled meats, especially poultry. It also works well with rich, creamy offal – serve it, for instance, with crumbed sweetbreads or golden brain fritters. Alternatively, use it as a last-minute glaze when barbecuing. Mix a spoonful with a little olive oil and simply brush it over the meat or chicken for the last turn on the flames. A spoonful of chutney added to a vinaigrette adds a lovely citrus-sweet dimension to a dressing for salads with bitter greens (see Grilled Haloumi Tart with a Winter Salad on page 52). If you can't wait the required time for the chutney to mature, then make a simpler version by slowly cooking fresh dates until they collapse to a thick sludge. The reduction is then puréed and beaten with extra-virgin olive oil and lemon juice to make the vinaigrette.

6 medium lemons, zest and flesh finely chopped

2 tablespoons salt

4 cloves garlic, finely minced

½ cup extra lemon juice

½ cup cider vinegar

1 tablespoon fresh ginger, finely grated

1 teaspoon cardamom seeds, finely ground

1 teaspoon coriander seeds, finely ground

½ teaspoon chili flakes

1¼ cups brown sugar

1⅓ cups fresh dates, stoned and chopped small

MIX THE CHOPPED LEMON, lemon zest, and juice with the salt and leave overnight. The next day, place the lemon mixture in a heavy pan with all other ingredients except the sugar and dates. Bring slowly to the boil and simmer for 5 minutes. Then add the sugar and dates and simmer gently for 45 minutes to 1 hour, until thick and well reduced. Stir from time to time so the mixture doesn't stick and burn. Pour into sterilized jars and store for at least 6 weeks before eating.

PIGEON TAGINE WITH DATES AND GINGER

In the Middle East pigeons are bought live from the souks and grilled over a hot barbecue. Elsewhere we have to make do with the less flavorsome farmed variety, usually sold as squab, which are tender baby birds weighing ½ to ¾ pound. Their rich, dark meat is delicious in this spicy sauce. The combination of pigeon and dates is a Persian and Moroccan favorite, although traditional recipes, which use large amounts of fruit, can be too sweet for Western palates. In this version, the sauce is spiced with pungent saffron and ginger, which help cut the sweetness and richness of the dish. It needs only a simple pilaf or couscous accompaniment.

PIGEON STOCK
4 carcasses and trimmings
1 tablespoon olive oil
1 carrot, roughly chopped
1 celery stick, roughly chopped
1 onion, roughly chopped
1 clove garlic, roughly bashed
1 bay leaf
a few sprigs thyme
12 tablespoons sherry
1½ quarts cold water

TAGINE
4 squab pigeons, breasts and
    legs removed

½ teaspoon salt
2¼ cups water or pigeon stock
7 tablespoons butter
1 tablespoon olive oil
2 medium onions, finely chopped
2 cloves garlic, finely chopped
1 tablespoon fresh black pepper
¼ teaspoon powdered saffron
    (or 10 strands, roasted and crushed
    to a powder)
2 teaspoons cinnamon
1 teaspoon ginger
1⅓ fresh dates, pits removed,
    chopped
⅓ cup parsley leaves

PREPARE THE PIGEONS by cutting off heads, necks, and claws, trimming the wings, and then neatly slicing away the breasts, thighs, and drumsticks from each bird. Season each piece with salt. If you don't feel confident about preparing the pigeons yourself, ask your butcher to prepare them for you and to give you the carcasses so you can make a stock.

To make the stock, briefly sauté the carcasses to add color, then add the vegetables, bay leaf, and thyme and sauté a few more minutes. Add the sherry and scrape any bits from the bottom of the pan. Pour the water over the top and bring to the boil. Skim off any surface fat, then lower the heat and simmer for an hour, skimming off any additional fat from time to time.

To make the tagine, melt the butter and oil and fry the onions and garlic over medium heat until softened. Add the pepper, saffron, cinnamon, and ginger and stir well. Season the pigeon pieces with salt and sauté in the spicy mixture for about 2 minutes, until they are well coated. Add the stock and bring to the boil. Lower the heat, cover, and simmer for 15 minutes. Then add the chopped dates and stir in well. Cover again and simmer for a further 20–30 minutes, or until pigeon pieces are nice and tender.

Sprinkle over the parsley leaves, taste, and adjust the seasoning if necessary.

Serve with plain buttered couscous or a simple rice pilaf.

DATE BRÛLÉE WITH KAHLUA

This is a thick, luxurious, and totally seductive dessert, combining creamy coffee and buttery, toffeeish dates. Use the confit as a base for petits pots, brûlées, soufflés, and custards. Serve with Cardamom-Orange Wafers (page 46) or Sesame-Honey Wafers (page 280).

CUSTARD	DATE CONFIT
5¼ cups pure cream	⅔ cup sugar
10 egg yolks	½ cup water
⅓ cup sugar	1⅔ cups fresh whole dates
1 vanilla bean, split and scraped	½ cup Kahlua
1 cinnamon stick	½ cup sugar for dusting

TO MAKE THE CUSTARD, bring the cream to a rolling boil, then pour it onto the egg yolks, sugar, split vanilla bean, and cinnamon stick, whisking well to incorporate. Pour the mix back into the pan and cook gently for about 15–20 minutes, stirring constantly with a wooden spoon, until the custard thickens. It should be as thick as honey and just beginning to catch on the bottom of the pot.

Pour the mixture into a stainless steel (or glass) bowl and set on ice or in a sink of very cold water for 5–10 minutes. This is important, as it stops the custard from cooking further. Remove from the ice and allow it to continue cooling naturally.

To make the confit, heat the sugar with the water until it is completely dissolved. Add the whole dates and Kahlua and cover the surface with a circle of waxed paper to keep the dates submerged and stop a skin from forming during cooking. Gently cook for 15–20 minutes. Remove from the heat and allow to cool. When cold, remove pits and skins from the dates and chop them finely. Put a heaped teaspoon of the confit at the bottom of ten small ramekin dishes (3-inch diameter) and spoon in enough custard to fill to just below the rim. Chill until ready to serve.

Set your broiler pan to its highest possible level and heat for at least 5 minutes. Remove the custards from the refrigerator and lightly dust with sugar. Grill for a few moments until they are brown and bubbling. Remove and refrigerate for 5 more minutes. Dust with a little more sugar and broil again. Naturally, if you have a domestic blowtorch, this works even better. Serve straightaway.

MAKES TEN SMALL BRÛLÉES.

DATE CUSTARD

Custard might seem a little bit too much like nursery food, but this creamy, caramel-like version is rather adult, and perfect served chilled with Cinnamon-Dusted Snow Eggs (page 82), or as an accompaniment to Sticky Ginger Cake (page 146).

The date confit is made in a similar way to that described in the previous recipe, but with orange and lemon juice for a lighter, tangier flavor. Either of these date confits can be folded through whipped cream to make a simple date romanoff, which would also be delicious served with the Sticky Ginger Cake, or with an orange cake.

CUSTARD
1 cup milk
½ cup cream
4 egg yolks
⅓ sugar

DATE CONFIT
½ cup water
½ cup sugar
1⅓ cups fresh dates
⅔ cup fresh orange juice
juice of 1 lemon

FOR THE CUSTARD, bring the milk and cream to the boil. In a mixing bowl, whisk the egg yolks with the sugar, and then add the boiling milk and cream mix. Whisk well and tip back into the saucepan. Cook gently for about 10 minutes, until the custard thickens. You should be able to draw a horizontal line through the custard on the back of a spoon, without it all running together. Allow the custard to cool a little.

To make the confit, bring the water to the boil with the sugar until the sugar is completely dissolved. Add the dates and the orange and lemon juice and cover the surface with a circle of waxed paper to keep the dates submerged and stop a skin from forming during cooking. Bring back to the boil and then lower the heat and simmer for 15–20 minutes, until the dates are meltingly soft. Remove the pan from the heat and allow to cool. When cold, remove the pits and skins, chop the dates finely, and return them to the syrup.

To serve, mix the confit with the custard, pour into a large glass serving bowl, and decorate with a few pieces of confit.

eggplant

For many Anglo-Saxon cooks, the eggplant is something of a mystery. Its shiny, sensual curves are pleasing to the eye, and its deep purply black hue hints of an opulence within, but many of us still don't really know what to do with it. Maybe make a moussaka? Or that famous Middle Eastern eggplant dip which seems to crop up everywhere these days? Possibly, if we feel a little more adventurous, we might even toy with the idea of stuffing it with a savory rice filling.

This tentativeness is not surprising, really, given that the eggplant has come into our kitchens relatively recently. As with so many other good things which have come our way, eggplant was introduced to Europe by the Arabs. Eggplant was just one of many foodstuffs which they learned about on conquering Persia in the seventh century. From there, they spread the secrets of its cultivation and cooking to all the countries in their new empire, reaching through North Africa and up into Spain, and to the island of Sicily in the Mediterranean. However, it was not until the exodus of the Jews from Sicily in the fifteenth century that the eggplant reached northern Italy, and it didn't arrive in France until the eighteenth century.

The eggplant is surely the most adaptable vegetable on earth, as it lends itself to many diverse cooking styles and regional flavors. It can be fried, grilled, steamed, roasted, and braised. Or mashed, stuffed, pickled, or made into relish. It is equally delicious hot, warm, or cold. The only way it cannot be eaten is raw.

When cooked, the eggplant has a unique, subtle flavor and a silky texture, which allow it to showcase many other, stronger flavors and ingredients without losing its own distinct identity. Blended with sesame paste, it becomes a creamy, smoky purée; with tomatoes, onions, and garlic, a robust braise. Add a touch of sugar, vinegar, and a sprinkle of currants and it becomes a Sicilian-Arabic classic. With yogurt and mint it turns Turkish; with minced meat, rice, and pine nuts, Persian; and spiced with cayenne and saffron, a Moroccan tagine.

Some people are afraid of eggplant because of its reputation as an oil guzzler. When fried, the spongy flesh does absorb extraordinary amounts of oil, but once it cools down, much of the oil seeps out again. Salting before cooking can help to reduce the amount of oil absorbed, as can dipping in seasoned flour before frying. The one thing which is critical, though, is to use really good-quality olive oil, as it becomes an integral part of the flavor of the dish. If you use cheap and nasty oil, it will make the whole dish taste cheap and nasty.

SELECTING AND STORING EGGPLANTS

The variety of eggplants available these days is ever-increasing. We are probably most familiar with the large, oval, purply black variety. But this is just one member of the large eggplant family. These days we can also buy slim, trim little Japanese eggplants in most supermarkets, while better greengrocers will also offer plump little egg-shaped Lebanese eggplants or eggplants which are a delicate white-streaked mauve, the palest green, or even a pure white.

Arab folklore has it that when choosing an eggplant, you should look for an oval-shaped belly button and leaves which reach down a quarter of the whole vegetable – these ones, so the theory goes, have fewer seeds and are less bitter.

Whichever variety or size you wish to use, always choose plump, firm eggplants with a taut, glossy skin. Any which are wrinkled, scarred, or feel flabby should be rejected immediately. As with all vegetables and fruit with a high water content, choose eggplants which feel weighty for their size, as this indicates freshness. They should be stored in the refrigerator and used within a couple of days.

USING EGGPLANTS

If you are frying eggplant, remove the stalk and prickly leaves and slice the eggplant lengthways for an attractive presentation (about ¼-inch thick). Eggplants do not need to be peeled: the skin not only adds an attractive color, but also helps hold them together and maintain their shape.

You may wish to salt them to reduce the amount of oil they absorb in cooking. Place eggplant slices or cubes in a colander, sprinkling them with plenty of salt as you go. Put a plate over them to weigh them down, and leave them to drain for about an hour. Rinse them well and carefully pat them dry before frying. Bear in mind, though, that few eggplants we get these days warrant this degorging procedure just to rid them of bitterness.

Another good trick for limiting the amount of oil absorbed is to deep-fry slices of eggplant before further cooking. It sounds bizarre, but it does have the effect of sealing them and minimizing further oil absorption. Another method is to dip the slices in seasoned flour and shallow-fry them first. If you really want to be virtuous, you can, of course, always steam them or sprinkle them with a little water and microwave them instead of frying them. They do lose some of their rich luxuriance, but if they are to be used in a highly flavored dish, like a moussaka, for instance, then it doesn't really matter.

Plump little Lebanese eggplants are ideal for stuffing and pickling whole. Medium-sized ones are perfect for stuffing and oven baking. Large eggplants are best sliced and fried, layered for gratin dishes, or cubed and used in braises or omelets. To grill, brush the slices with olive oil, and grill on a griddle or barbecue, or under a broiler until soft. Depending on the thickness of your slices, this will take about 4 minutes on each side.

Larger eggplants are also good for making creamy dips. Soften the flesh by roasting the eggplant over a flame until the whole thing is blackened and collapses. The pulp can then be mixed with other flavorings, such as lemon juice, garlic, or tahini paste.

BABA GHANOUSH

This superb dip is found throughout the Middle East, Turkey, and even Greece, and there are as many recipes as there are people making it! Local variations abound, with the addition of yogurt, mint, and cumin on top of the basic oil, lemon, garlic, and tahini. It is really all about personal preference and a balance of flavors. The earthy tahini, sharp lemon, or pungent garlic should not dominate, but all should meld into one rich, creamy, smoky whole, which is infinitely greater than the sum of its parts. One thing which we are adamant about, though, is that the eggplants simply must be roasted over a direct flame. It is the direct heat contact (which could also come from roasting in the white-hot ashes of a bonfire) which chars and blackens the skin and results in that exciting, mysterious smokiness. If you have a gas stove, then cook them directly on the top burners. A similar effect can be obtained on the coals of a barbecue. If you have an electric stove, then you will have to roast them in the oven, but it just won't be the same. Serve as a dip with plenty of pita bread or as a deliciously different accompaniment to grilled or roast lamb.

~~~~~~

4 medium eggplants
1 large clove garlic, crushed with
    ½ teaspoon salt
juice of 3 lemons

3 tablespoons tahini
1⅔ cups natural yogurt
salt and pepper

PRICK THE EGGPLANTS all over with a fork and then sit them directly on the naked flame of your stove burners. Set the flame to low-medium heat and cook for at least 10 minutes, constantly turning each until the whole eggplant is blackened and blistered and has collapsed in on itself. Remove them from the flame and place them on a small cake rack in a sealed container or plastic bag (so juices can drain off). Allow the eggplants to cool for about 10 minutes.

If you prefer a milder smoky flavor, then you can char the eggplants on the flame for 5 minutes and then finish off the roasting in a preheated 350°F oven for about 10 minutes.

When the eggplants are cool, gently peel away the skin from the flesh with a small, sharp knife. Allow the skin to peel away naturally, and do not scrape the flesh directly off the skin, as it will have a burnt flavor. For this reason too, be careful not to allow any pieces of the skin itself into the mix. Set pulp in a colander and allow to sit for 5–10 minutes to drain further.

When you are ready to assemble the dish, mix the garlic with the yogurt, then mix into the eggplant pulp with the lemon juice and tahini.

Season with salt and pepper and mix to combine: the dip should be coarse, not smooth. Don't be afraid to taste and to adjust seasonings, as it should taste sharp. Serve with a big splash of extra-virgin olive oil.

SMOKY EGGPLANT SALAD

The currants and pine nuts give this salad a distinctly Moorish feel.

1 tablespoon currants
3½ tablespoons sherry
3 medium eggplants, charred
3 tablespoons olive oil
2 tablespoons pine nuts
1 medium purple onion, diced
2 medium Roma tomatoes, deseeded
    and cut into ½-inch dice

1 clove garlic, crushed with
    ½ teaspoon salt
juice of 1 lemon
½ teaspoon sumac
1 tablespoon whole oregano leaves
2 tablespoons whole parsley leaves
⅓ extra-virgin olive oil
salt and pepper

SOAK THE CURRANTS in the sherry for 10 minutes. Char the eggplants as described on the previous pages. Once they are cool, carefully peel away all the blackened skin, cut them into rough ½-inch dice, and place them in a large mixing bowl.

Heat the olive oil to medium heat and then fry the pine nuts for 3 minutes or so, moving them constantly to stop them from burning. Remove and drain them on kitchen paper. Then sauté the onion until it is soft and translucent. Add it to the chopped eggplant. Mix the garlic paste and lemon juice and add to the eggplant. Sprinkle the sumac onto the eggplant, then add the extra-virgin olive oil and combine gently. Allow to rest for 5 minutes.

Strain the currants and add them with the remaining ingredients to the salad. Mix gently, taking care not to break up the eggplant.

Taste and adjust seasoning.

EGGPLANT TONNATO

This makes a great accompaniment to fried or grilled fish, such as sardines, red mullet, or whiting fillets. Serve as a light starter with a handful of dressed watercress leaves or as a main-course accompaniment to grilled or fried sardines.

3 medium eggplants
salt
⅓ cup baby capers, finely chopped
1 clove garlic, finely chopped
½ cup olive oil

TUNA MAYONNAISE
6 ounces canned tuna in oil

2 egg yolks
4 anchovies
1 tablespoon mustard
juice of 1 lemon
⅔ cup olive oil mixed with ⅔ cup
    vegetable oil
1 tablespoon white wine vinegar
salt and pepper

CUT THE EGGPLANTS WIDTHWAYS into ¾-inch-thick slices and lightly salt. Leave for about an hour, and then rinse well and pat dry. Mix the capers with the garlic. Heat the olive oil in a heavy-based pan and fry the eggplants until they are lightly colored on both sides. Sprinkle them with the caper mixture, pressing it well into the eggplants. Turn the eggplants and cook them for a few more minutes, and then remove and drain them on kitchen paper. Cover them with a tea towel and place a heavy baking dish (1 to 2 pounds in weight) on top. Leave for about half an hour (this embeds the capers firmly into the eggplant and squeezes out some of the oil).

To make the mayonnaise, drain the tuna of its oil and place it in a food processor with the egg yolks, anchovies, mustard, and lemon juice. Process to a smooth, fine purée. Dribble the oil in drop by drop until it is emulsified, then loosen it with half the vinegar. Slowly add the rest of the oil and, when it has all been incorporated, add the remaining vinegar. Taste and adjust seasonings.

To serve, lay out eggplant slices in an overlapping ring and place a spoonful of mayonnaise and a lemon wedge on each slice.

SERVES SIX.

PICKLED EGGPLANTS WITH WALNUTS AND CHILIS

One of our favorite places to visit in Lebanon is Zahle, the Malouf family's hometown. Zahle lies between Beirut and Damascus, in central Lebanon. It is surrounded by mountains and is a popular summer resort. In winter, though, the town is often snowbound. People here are big on self-sufficiency and home preserving: in the fruitful summer months they bottle, pickle, and preserve in preparation for the cold, dark winters. It was in Zahle that we first tasted these eggplants pickled with walnuts and chilis. The recipe comes from Greg's sister-in-law Amal Malouf.

2 pounds baby Lebanese eggplants
  (no more than 2 inches long)
½ cup salt
1¼ cups walnut halves

2 tablespoons oregano leaves
4 cloves garlic, thinly sliced
2–3 serrano chilis, split
1 quart olive oil

WASH AND DRY THE EGGPLANTS and cook them in boiling water for 5 minutes. Refresh them under cold water and drain. Split each eggplant in half lengthways to within ½ inch of the stem. Open them up and rub salt into each side, then lay them in a colander, weigh down, and allow to drain for 24–48 hours.

Chop the walnuts into quarters. Into each eggplant stuff a few oregano leaves, garlic slivers, and walnuts. Pack the eggplants tightly in a sterilized jar and turn it upside down for an hour in a colander; this will allow more liquid to drain away.

Invert, fill the jar with oil, and drop in the chilis. Seal and leave for at least three weeks. Unopened, the pickles will keep up to a year.

Once opened, keep refrigerated and eat within six weeks.

QUAIL BAKED IN AN EGGPLANT

~~~~~~

4 jumbo quail (6–7 ounces each)
4 small eggplants, about 5 inches long
salt
¼ cup olive oil

salt and pepper
⅓ cup Cardamom Honey Glaze
   (page 45)
4 sprigs thyme

TRIM THE QUAIL by removing the neck flaps and wing tips.

Cut the eggplants in half lengthways, leaving ½ inch intact close to the stalk (do not remove stalk). Sprinkle the insides generously with salt and leave in a colander for half an hour. Rinse them thoroughly, and then sprinkle them with a little olive oil. Roast them in a preheated 350°F oven for 15 minutes. Remove them from the oven and allow them to cool, sealed in a plastic container.

In a heavy pan, heat the olive oil and sauté the quail for a few minutes until they are golden brown. Season them with salt and pepper. Pour the Cardamom Honey Glaze into the pan and turn the quail around to ensure they are well coated. Remove them from the heat and allow them to cool.

To assemble, place a sprig of thyme on one half of the opened-up eggplant, and then insert the quail's bottom right into the center of the eggplant and tie the drumstick legs together around the eggplant's stem. Cook in a preheated 400°F oven for 10 minutes. Remove and allow to rest for 2 minutes. Reheat the glaze and drizzle it over and around the quail.

Serve with watercress leaves for a very attractive starter for four.

BARBECUED SALMON AND EGGPLANT TERRINE

This mosaic terrine is exquisitely pretty and a delicious light, summery starter. When layering the ingredients, remember that the effect is meant to be a random mosaic, rather than neatly symmetrical. If possible, try to get salmon from the head end of the fish, which is thicker.

4½ pounds salmon fillet (approx.
    12 inches long), skin removed
1 clove garlic, crushed with
    ½ teaspoon salt
pepper
3 tablespoons olive oil
4 red bell peppers, roasted and peeled
7 ounces feta cheese, crumbled

4 large leeks, steamed whole
12 Pickled Eggplants with Walnuts and
    Chilis (page 124)
2 teaspoons coriander seeds, toasted,
    ground, and sieved
⅓ cup cilantro leaves, roughly chopped
⅓ cup parsley, roughly chopped

GENEROUSLY LINE A 12-INCH TERRINE MOLD (Le Creuset is ideal) with 4 layers of plastic wrap (you need enough to wrap up and over the terrine). Cut the salmon lengthways into 3 even-sized strips, rub them all over with the garlic paste, and season them with pepper. Heat the oil in a large frying pan until it is smoking hot. Sear the salmon pieces, one at a time, just coloring each side (no more than 20 seconds on each side). Remove them and place them on a wire rack to cool.

Cut the skinned peppers in half and trim to a neat shape. Lay half of them on the bottom of the terrine mold, skinned side down, trimming to fit if necessary. Sprinkle with a little crumbled feta, then lay a piece of salmon down the center, with a leek on one side and 4 pickled eggplants down the other. Sprinkle with half the ground coriander, cilantro, and parsley leaves, and a little feta cheese. For the next layer, place a leek down either side and a strip of salmon and a line of 4 eggplants down the middle. Sprinkle with the remaining spices and herbs and a little feta, as before. For the top layer, lay a leek down the center, the remaining piece of salmon down one side, and the last 4 eggplants down the other side. Sprinkle with the last few bits of feta and cover with the remaining red peppers. Bring the plastic wrap over the top and seal.

Cut out a piece of styrofoam, or a few thick pieces of cardboard just smaller than the mold, and place them so they fit inside the terrine, directly on top of the peppers. Weigh the terrine down with a 5-pound weight and refrigerate it overnight. When you are ready to serve, unwrap the terrine and cut it into ¾-inch slices. Serve it with a drizzle of olive oil, freshly made aïoli, and hot, fresh, crusty bread.

MAKES TEN TO TWELVE PORTIONS.

figs

There can be few greater pleasures in life than a fig. Not a dreary, brown, medicine-sweet disc of pressed dried fig, full of tiny little teeth-sticking seeds, but a perfectly ripe fresh fig, split to reveal its inner red secrets and glistening with a dew as sweet as honeysuckle.

The fig is regarded by many as a quintessentially Mediterranean fruit, but is believed to have originated in Asia Minor. Archeological remains suggest that fig trees were first found in Persia, Syria, and Turkey, and then spread west along ancient trade routes to Greece and Italy and eastward to India and China.

Figs – both fresh and dried – were an important part of the diet of the early peoples of the Middle East and eastern Mediterranean. The very high sugar content of dried figs has made them an ideal source of concentrated energy in lean times, and a syrup of figs was used in many countries as an early sweetener.

Figs have long been celebrated for the simple and exquisite pleasure they provide. Baskets of figs have been found in Egyptian tombs, where they were left to accompany pharaohs on their journey to the afterlife. They were a favorite fruit of the ancient Greeks, who considered them a gift from the gods and fed them to their Olympic athletes. They were popular in the Roman empire, where they were grafted and cultivated with great success: figs are portrayed on the walls at Pompeii, and the Roman gourmet Apicius, writer of the first known recipe book, is said to have fed the best imported Syrian figs to his pigs to sweeten their flesh!

Figs and fig trees feature in the myths and legends of many civilizations, from Ancient Egypt, Greece, and Rome to India, East Asia, and even North Africa. The fig is also firmly entrenched in Christian symbolism. It is the first tree mentioned in the Bible, and its leaves were used by Adam and Eve to hide their nakedness. Fig leaves have been used as a symbolic device by artists ever since, to disguise nudity in their art.

SELECTING AND STORING FIGS

In warm climates, many people are lucky enough to have a hardy old fig tree in the backyard and, come late summer, may gorge to their hearts' content. In fact, the battle is on to get the fruit before the birds do and before the fruit becomes overripe. Most figs available commercially are black (or purple), green, or white, but they are not sold by variety. The green ones are usually the first to reach our markets, followed by the larger, deep purple figs with their luscious deep crimson flesh. Fig trees often crop twice, and true fig fanciers will often hold out for the smaller late-summer fruits, with their intense, honeyed perfume.

Whichever variety of figs is available, it is important to select fruits which are unbruised and unblemished. This is probably more important for figs than just about any other fruit. One of the reasons for their high cost is that they are delicate and highly perishable. Furthermore, once ripe, they ferment rapidly. Figs need to be handled with a little tenderness, as they are so fragile. Reject any which are bruised or sticky and weeping – they are almost certainly overripe and may even have started fermenting.

If possible, eat figs on the day of purchase, and certainly keep them refrigerated until you need them. Remove them from the refrigerator ahead of time, though, as chilling them dulls some of their flavor.

As in ancient times, the best dried figs are still imported from Turkey – the best being the legendary Smyrna figs. Turkish figs are large, plump white figs which are dried in the sun. Over time, the sugar in them rises to the surface and gives them a characteristic white surface bloom. Dried figs may be bought loose or packed in little cardboard cartons (pressed figs), but the very best come strung on raffia loops like a chunky modern necklace.

USING FIGS

As with so many of the best things in life, a perfect fig really requires little tricking out. Many are thin-skinned and don't require peeling, but if you like a fancy presentation you can cut a cross in the skin, over the top of the fruit, and peel the skin away from the flesh in petals.

Dried, salty hams, such as prosciutto, are natural allies of the fig, as are many cheeses. Soft, creamy cheeses, such as a fresh goat or soft blue cheese, are delicious with fresh figs, whereas hard, sharp cheeses, like a good cheddar, are particularly good with the big dried Turkish figs.

Fresh figs make a perfect and easy dessert. Split them by cutting through the flesh to the base (but leave it intact) and eat them exactly as they are. If they are slightly less than perfect, then you might like to sprinkle them with a few drops of rose water and a drizzle of honey. Or shake over Cinnamon Dust (page 81) and caramelize them under a very hot grill (or with a blowtorch) and serve with thick yogurt or mascarpone.

FIGS WRAPPED IN PROSCIUTTO AND KATAIFI

Partnering sweet fresh figs with creamy mascarpone and salty ham is a classic and delicious combination. Here they are briefly baked in a kataifi nest, which provides an extra crunch. The combination of hot, juicy figs, salty ham, and cold, melting mascarpone makes a stunning, luscious starter.

12 small black figs

12 slices prosciutto

½ package kataifi pastry

½ cup (1 stick) butter, melted

1¼ cups mascarpone

freshly ground black pepper

WRAP THE BASE OF EACH FIG with a slice of prosciutto. With a small, sharp knife, make a small cross over the top of each fig and gently squeeze the base of the fig, so it opens out like a little flower.

Carefully divide the kataifi into 12 long sections and brush liberally with the melted butter. Wrap one section around each fig, leaving just the pointed top of the fig protruding. Bake the figs on the top shelf of a preheated 400°F oven for 8 minutes, or until the pastry is golden brown.

Remove from the oven.

Serve with a blob of the fresh mascarpone stuffed into the top of each fig and a grinding of fresh black pepper.

SERVES SIX (TWO EACH) AS A STARTER.

FRESH FIGS POACHED IN GINGER SYRUP

Fresh figs are barely poached with pieces of candied ginger and sweet spices in a light syrup. When fresh figs are out of season, you could also use good-quality dried figs, simmered in the syrup until soft and plump. Serve with thick Greek-style yogurt and a drizzle of honey.

¾ cup sugar

1¾ cups water

peel of 1 lemon

4 cardamom pods, cracked

1 cinnamon stick

1 dried lime, cracked (optional)

⅓ cup candied ginger

12 fresh figs (or good-quality
   Turkish figs, dried)

PLACE THE SUGAR in a pan with the water, lemon, 4 cardamom pods, cinnamon, lime, and ginger. Bring to the boil, ensuring the sugar dissolves completely. Lower the heat and simmer for 5 minutes, then remove the pan from the heat.

Peel the figs and place them in the syrup. Return the pan to a low heat and bring it slowly back to the boil. As soon as the syrup reaches the boil, remove the pan and allow the figs to cool down in the pan – no further poaching is required. (If you are using dried figs, simmer gently for 5 minutes, or until they are soft).

Serve warm.

TOFFEED FIG TART

A simple phyllo-layered pastry base cooked crispy golden and drenched in syrup. Serve with a jug of delicate Ginger Cream (page 147), or, if you prefer, a blob of crème fraîche.

~~~~~~

10 sheets phyllo pastry
7 ounces (1¾ sticks) butter, melted
½ cup sugar
½ cup water
a splash of rose water (optional)

12 fresh figs
2 tablespoons sugar
1 extra tablespoon butter
¾ cup hazelnuts, toasted, peeled, and roughly crushed

LAYER THE SHEETS of phyllo pastry on the work surface, brushing each one with melted butter. Use a ramekin dish or cookie cutter, about 3 inches in diameter, and cut out 4 circles from the stack of pastry.

Place the pastry circles on a baking tray lined with baking parchment and bake in a preheated 350°F oven for 10–12 minutes. Remove the tray from the oven and, while still hot, drizzle a little sugar syrup over each pastry circle.

To make the syrup, place the sugar and water in a small pan and bring to the boil, making sure the sugar is completely dissolved. Lower the heat and simmer for 5 minutes, then add a splash of rose water if desired.

Sprinkle the sugar into a frying pan and add the tablespoon of butter. Heat until the butter dissolves and the sugar caramelizes. Cut each fig in half and place them cut side down in the caramel. Stir them gently in the caramel for a few moments, then remove them from the pan.

To assemble, lay a circle of pastry on each plate and stack the figs, pointing outward, in two layers of three halves. Sprinkle with hazelnuts and serve immediately with Ginger Cream.

garlic.

Since the earliest days of civilization, garlic has been the culinary symbol par excellence of social snobbery and prejudice. Reviled by the aristocracy, garlic was always the poor person's food flavoring and medicine. The Egyptian pyramid builders and the Greek and Roman soldiers all ate garlic with their daily bread for strength and courage. It has traditionally been the common person's cold and flu remedy and an antiseptic for healing wounds and skin conditions; contemporary research suggests that it helps prevent blood clots and even some cancers. To this day in the Middle East, many people still string garlic over their front door to ward off evil spirits, and of course we all know it to be an essential weapon against vampires!

Even up until the last few decades, garlic has been firmly linked in the Anglo-Saxon mind with all that is "foreign." This prejudice centers on garlic's strong smell and the way it lingers on the breath. Generally, though, garlic has enjoyed a surprising reversal of fortune of late. Nowadays people tend to be considered miserably unsophisticated if they claim not to like it.

If you are not keen on garlic, you might think that Middle Eastern food is not for you, as garlic and its companion allium, the onion, are the fundamental savory starting points for nearly every dish from Barcelona to Baghdad and Cannes to Cairo. The trick, though, is subtlety and a delicate hand. Everybody's garlic threshold is different; and besides, garlic shouldn't overpower every other flavor in a dish, but should add an earthy depth and complexity.

Garlic is frequently combined with olive oil in a range of dressings, marinades, sauces, and soups. At its most basic, this can be a simple emulsion, sharpened with a squeeze of lemon juice; at its most unctuous, the legendary aïoli, a rich, garlicky mayonnaise much loved in the South of France. In Lebanon and Syria they make toum, a sublime garlic sauce as light and fluffy as whipped cream. In Greece they pound garlic and oil with bread to make skordalia. In Spain they add tomatoes, peppers, and onion to make the zesty summer soup gazpacho. The Moorish version uses almonds instead and is at once creamy and refreshing. The Turks pound walnuts with garlic and oil to make the delicious sauce known as *tarator*, while the Lebanese usually make their own version of *tarator* using pine nuts.

SELECTING AND STORING GARLIC

Garlic is available all year round but is sweeter and more delicate in the spring. New-season garlic boasts plump, tightly packed heads of white, juicy cloves with soft, moist skins. By winter, the cloves are noticeably looser and harder, with dry, brittle, papery skins that can even become woody. Older garlic can often begin to germinate and develop a green shoot in its center. This has a bitter, unpleasant flavor and should be pinched out and discarded.

Choose heads of garlic which are firm and weighty. Always check for bruising and blemishes, and avoid any heads that have shrunken, withered cloves or are obviously moldy on the outside. Store garlic in a cool, dry place rather than the refrigerator, where it is more likely to go moldy. It will start to sprout if kept too long, so use within a week or so of purchase.

USING GARLIC

To roast individual cloves or a whole head of garlic, they do not need to be peeled entirely. Simply tidy them up and remove the extra layers of papery skin. Individual cloves can be tucked in next to a roast, or you can oven-bake the whole head; some people like to wrap it in foil. When we roast a leg of lamb or a whole chicken at home, we always stuff a handful of garlic cloves alongside, or among the accompanying roasted vegetables. The garlic cloves emerge from the oven all shriveled, but when you pierce the skin you discover that the insides have transformed into a delicate, mellow, buttery paste, which is just divine mushed in with the gravy and smeared over a mouthful of meat or potato. One word of warning, though: only add the garlic to the roasting pan once the initial blast of heat has been turned down. After the mellow, creamy stage, they quickly start to caramelize, becoming sticky and brown. Beyond that they turn to blackened cinders.

If a dish calls for whole cloves of garlic, the best way to peel them is to slice off the base of the clove and carefully peel the skin away with a small, sharp knife. Otherwise, crush the clove firmly with the flat side of a broad, heavy knife, as close to the handle as you can get, for maximum pressure. The skin should then peel away easily.

Many recipes call for finely chopped or minced garlic. The simplest way to achieve this is to crush the peeled garlic and a little coarse salt to a smooth paste using a mortar and pestle. It only takes a moment, as the gritty salt quickly breaks the garlic down to a silky-smooth paste. An added benefit is this paste dissolves away into the food, rather than hanging around as fierce little lumps. Chopping with a sharp kitchen knife is fine, of course, but your fingers and chopping board always end up smelling of garlic.

The flavor and strength of garlic depends partly on its age, but also on whether it is eaten raw or cooked. It is at its most fiery when eaten raw, but both its flavor and its texture soften and mellow on cooking. Dried-up old-season garlic can often be far too astringent to be enjoyable. One way of improving the flavor somewhat is to blanch it in boiling water for 30 seconds before use.

ANDALUSIAN WHITE SOUP

There are many garlic soups to be found all around the Mediterranean. Some are simple bread soups; other, more sophisticated versions use a flavorful stock instead of water; and others still enrich it with egg yolks. Some soups are served hot, others warm or even chilled. One hot day in Seville we ate a delicious version, thickened in true Moorish style with almond meal, sharpened with vinegar, and served with a sprinkling of currants.

7 ounces day-old good-quality white
   bread, crusts removed
⅔ cup milk
1¼ cups blanched almonds
3–4 cloves garlic, crushed with
   ½ teaspoon salt

½ cup olive oil
2–3 cups iced water
3 tablespoons sherry vinegar
salt and pepper
2 tablespoons currants, soaked in
   2 tablespoons sherry

SOAK THE BREAD in the milk for a few minutes, and then squeeze it dry. Place the almonds in a food processor and process to a coarse meal. Then add the bread and garlic paste and blend to a smooth paste. With the motor running, slowly pour in the olive oil, drop by drop, as if making a mayonnaise. When all the oil is incorporated, add the iced water until the soup is the consistency of pouring cream. Add the vinegar and season with salt and pepper if needed.

Keep the soup chilled until you are ready to serve. You can make it a day ahead if it suits.

Serve at room temperature on a hot summer's day, sprinkled with the sherry-plumped currants.

SERVES FOUR TO SIX.

TOUM

This fiercely garlicky sauce is not for the fainthearted, but if you enjoy garlic, you will love this Lebanese/Syrian sauce, which is traditionally served with chicken. Use it to brush on grilled chicken, seafood, and meats at the end of barbecuing, or to accompany roasts or cold meats. Or thin it down with water to make a garlicky salad dressing. But be warned, don't plan any business meetings afterward.

1 whole head of garlic,
   cloves peeled
1 teaspoon salt

juice of 1 lemon
¾ cup sunflower oil
2 tablespoons water

PEEL AND ROUGHLY CHOP the garlic cloves, then place them in a blender with the salt and lemon juice. Blend for about 2 minutes, until smooth, scraping down the sides occasionally. Next, very slowly start to add the oil, as if you were making a mayonnaise, and blend on high until it is emulsified. Continue to dribble in slowly, until all the oil is absorbed. Finally, add the water. The whole process will take about 5 minutes, and you end up with a light, fluffy, garlicky sauce. This will keep in the refrigerator for about a week.

If the sauce separates, you can save it by doing the following. Clean out the blender jar. Put in 2 egg yolks and blend, then very slowly pour in half the mixture. When it begins to emulsify and thicken, add a teaspoon of cold water to loosen it. Then gradually add the rest of the mix. You end up with a mayonnaise rather than a sauce, but it is still delicious.

MAKES APPROXIMATELY 1¾ CUPS.

GARLIC YORKSHIRE PUDDING

A touch of garlic makes a surprisingly different Yorkshire pudding batter. For an even bigger surprise, drizzle the rest of the head of garlic with a drop of honey, wrap it in foil, and bake it in the oven until it is soft (15 minutes at 350°F). Allow it to cool a little, then carefully peel each clove. Drop a soft, buttery clove into each pudding before baking them in the oven. These Yorkies are terrific with Deviled Lamb Loin (page 166) or any roasted joint of beef or lamb.

¾ cup plain flour
1 egg
½ cup milk

2 cloves garlic, crushed with
½ teaspoon salt
vegetable oil or pan drippings

SIFT THE FLOUR into a bowl, make a well in the center and break in the egg. Beat the egg into the flour until it combines to a smooth, lump-free paste. Then add the garlic paste and mix in well. Gradually add the milk, incorporating each amount thoroughly before adding more. When all is mixed in, chill the batter for at least half an hour until you are ready to cook.

Preheat the oven to 425°F. When it has come to this temperature, pour a teaspoon of oil into each of six muffin tins and heat them in the oven for 10 minutes or until the oil is sizzling. Pour in the chilled mixture and bake for 15 minutes.

MAKES SIX SMALL PUDDINGS OR ONE LARGE PUDDING.

PARSNIP SKORDALIA

Skordalia is a traditional Greek garlic sauce, often made with mashed potatoes, stale white bread, or even almonds. This version uses parsnip for a sweeter, mellower taste. Serve it as an accompaniment to any barbecued or grilled dishes.

2 pounds parsnips
2 cups milk
2 cloves garlic, crushed with
   ½ teaspoon salt

juice of 1 lemon
¾ cup fresh bread crumbs
½ cup olive oil
salt and pepper

PEEL AND CORE the parsnips and cut them into even-sized pieces. Cook them in the milk until they are very soft. Purée them in a food processor with the garlic paste, lemon juice, and bread crumbs. Add the oil, in a very slow dribble, until all is incorporated. Adjust the seasoning and allow to cool.

ginger

Times and fashions change in the kitchen as surely as they do everywhere else. These days, if you ask a shop assistant which aisle the ginger is in, they will almost certainly direct you to the fresh produce section, where fresh root ginger is to be found cuddling up next to the garlic. This gnarled, knobbly root certainly seems to have ousted the dried, powdered spice in the popularity stakes in recent years. Those little bottles of sandy ginger powder, most commonly used in puddings, cakes, and cookies, have been pushed firmly to the back of the kitchen cupboard.

It seems that speedy, stir-fried dishes from China and Southeast Asia are better suited to our fast-paced lifestyles. Fresh root ginger combined with garlic and chili forms the unmistakable fragrant and spicy basis for numerous dishes from this region. In traditional Chinese medicine, ginger is also still used as a tonic, particularly for digestive disorders and for the female reproductive system. Ginger is eaten to boost the immune system and used for its general antibacterial properties; in fact, ginger has always been widely used in many civilizations for its medicinal qualities as well as the clean, invigorating flavor it adds to food.

Botanically, ginger, like turmeric and galangal, is a rhizome – the tuberous root of an attractive flowering plant which probably originated in India or tropical Asia. It has been consumed in the Far East for many thousands of years and was one of the first spices to be introduced to the Mediterranean, probably by the sea-loving Phoenicians. It was certainly known in the ancient civilizations of Egypt, Persia, and Greece and was particularly loved in Rome, where it was used as lavishly as black pepper.

In medieval Europe, powdered ginger was one of the most popular spices. It was used in baking, to make all kinds of cookies, cakes, and desserts, and was a popular flavoring in many savory dishes too, often used very liberally to mask the smell and taste of bad meat. With the gradual evolution away from one-pot cooking, the distinction between sweet and savory dishes became more marked, and the use of ginger, like cinnamon, shifted to sweet dishes. This tradition remains in northern European and North American cooking today, in a wide repertoire of ginger cookies, ginger cakes and puddings, gingerbreads, and even ginger wines and cordials.

Dried ground ginger, rather than the fresh root, is used in Middle Eastern cookery and even more so in North African cookery. The Arabs transported ginger all around their empire from the eighth century onward, introducing it to North Africa, where it became a key spice in savory dishes and where it remains one of the primary ingredients in spice mixes such as the Moroccan ras el hanout, which is used in all sorts of soups and tagines. As a result of the Arab enthusiasm for spices, the Spanish too learned to love and value them. From the sixteenth century, both the Spanish and the Portuguese introduced ginger to their colonies in the West Indies, West Africa, and South America, where it is an important flavoring in local dishes.

The Arabs were also responsible for introducing Europeans to crystallized ginger. Once they invaded and conquered Persia, they discovered sugar cane and, more important, the techniques for extracting and refining sugar. Preserved and candied ginger became a real delicacy — although perhaps its success was due less to its sweet flavor than to its reputation as an aphrodisiac.

SELECTING, STORING, AND USING GINGER

When choosing ginger, try to buy the freshest, youngest-looking rhizomes. As ginger ages, it becomes woody and dry, and its flavor becomes hotter and more peppery. Certainly avoid ginger which is shriveled and wizened. Store fresh ginger in the vegetable drawer of the refrigerator, where it will last for a couple of weeks.

To prepare fresh ginger, slice off a knob or section of the ginger and carefully peel it with a sharp paring knife. Cut it into thin slices across the grain. These can be used as they are, or sliced into batons and very finely diced. To grate ginger, use the shredding side of a grater, and then dice it more finely by hand. Large quantities of ginger can be puréed to a paste in a food processor.

Ground ginger is available in little plastic packets or glass jars from all supermarkets. Store it in a tightly sealed container in a dark, cool cupboard.

RABBIT TERRINE WITH GINGER

1½ pounds rabbit meat, minced
½ pound pork belly, minced
½ pound chicken livers, minced
1 egg
½ cup milk
½ tablespoon ginger powder
½ teaspoon cinnamon powder
½ teaspoon ground chili
½ teaspoon ground coriander

4 shallots, finely chopped
1 clove garlic, finely chopped
⅓ cup fresh ginger, grated
⅓ cup olive oil
1 tablespoon salt
½ teaspoon pepper
¾ cup unsalted, shelled pistachio nuts
11 ounces sliced bacon

PLACE THE MINCED RABBIT, pork belly, and chicken livers into a large mixing bowl with the egg, milk, and spices. Stir well.

Sauté the shallots, garlic, and ginger in the olive oil for 2 minutes, until they have softened. Allow to cool for a few minutes and add to the meat mixture and mix in well. To taste for seasonings, take a walnut-sized lump and fry on both sides until it is cooked. Taste and adjust salt, pepper, or spices if need be. Divide the mixture into three batches and purée them in a food processor until they are smooth. Stir in the pistachio nuts.

Line a 12-inch terrine mold with waxed paper and then line the inside with strips of bacon, reserving enough to cover the top. Tip in the meat mixture and pack it in carefully. Cover with the remaining slices of bacon, tucking any ends down the sides. Cover with foil, place in a deep baking pan half-filled with water, and bake in the center of a preheated 350°F oven for 1½ hours. Remove the terrine from the oven and weigh it down while it is still warm (a few heavy bottles or cans will do the job quite well).

Leave it to cool overnight or for at least 8 hours. Turn it out, remove the waxed paper, and slice thickly to serve.

This terrine is good with crusty bread, pickled gherkins, and plenty of hot mustard; or serve it with a lively salad such as Fattouche (page 289), Smoky Eggplant Salad (page 122), or Minted Cabbage Salad (page 185).

MAKES TEN TO TWELVE PORTIONS.

STICKY GINGER CAKE

This cake uses both fresh grated ginger and dried ginger powder. It is deliciously moist, and mouth-tinglingly hot and gingery. Serve warm as a snack or turn it into a dessert with a generous dollop of crème fraîche, Ginger Cream (opposite), or even Burnt Honey Ice Cream (page 155).

⅔ cup molasses or golden syrup
1½ cups sour cream
½ cup soft brown sugar
2 eggs
4 teaspoons fresh grated ginger
1 teaspoon grated lemon zest
10 ounces (2¼ sticks) butter

1⅓ cups plain flour
1⅓ cups self-raising flour
1 teaspoon baking powder
½ teaspoon salt
1 teaspoon ginger powder
2 tablespoons unsalted, shelled
   pistachios

WHISK TOGETHER the molasses, sour cream, brown sugar, eggs, grated ginger, and lemon zest. Melt the butter and whisk it into the mixture. Twice sift the flours, baking powder, salt, and ginger powder. Fold into the warm batter, whisking gently if necessary to break down any residual lumps of flour. The batter will be fairly runny.

Tip it into a well-greased 8-inch springform tin and bake in the center of a preheated 350°F oven for 35–45 minutes, or until a skewer comes out clean.

Soak the pistachios in boiling water for 2 minutes, then use a very sharp knife to peel away the skins. Pat dry and chop them finely.

Sprinkle the pistachios over the cake and serve with a dollop of Ginger Cream.

Minted split-pea soup **184**

Hot mussel salad with feta and fennel **186**

Spring vegetable paella **259**

Watermelon salad with cherry-vanilla ice cream **314**

Chicken livers pressed with dukkah 279

Salmon grilled with sumac and fennel crumbs **291**

Garfish grilled with thyme, lime, and sumac **297**

Whole roasted snapper with walnut-cilantro dressing **91**

GINGER CREAM

Serve this alongside the Sticky Ginger Cake (opposite) or all kinds of steamed puddings. It is also good with Fresh Figs Poached in Ginger Syrup (page 132).

〜〜〜〜〜〜〜〜〜〜〜〜〜〜〜〜〜〜〜〜〜〜〜〜〜〜〜〜〜〜〜〜

1 knob fresh ginger

⅔ cup pure cream

½ teaspoon ginger powder

3 tablespoons palm sugar or soft brown sugar

2 egg yolks, whisked to combine

GRATE THE FRESH GINGER on the shredder side of a grater and chop more finely with a knife (don't use the fine side, as it will just clog up the grater).

Scald the cream with both the fresh and ground gingers and the palm sugar.

Pour the cream onto the egg yolks and whisk well. Return the cream to the saucepan and heat it gently until the cream thickens slightly, which might take up to 10 minutes. Tip it into a bowl and allow it to cool.

Whip the cream when you are ready to serve it.

GINGER SHORTBREADS

Rice flour gives a slightly sandy texture. You could use cornstarch instead for a softer, more melting cookie.

~~~~~~

⅔ cup butter
½ cup confectioner's sugar
1 egg yolk
1½ cups plain flour

¾ cup rice flour
2 generous tablespoons finely
    chopped crystallized ginger

CHILL THE BOWL and blade of your food processor for 10 minutes in the freezer. Then cream the butter and confectioner's sugar. Add the egg yolk and mix in well. Sift in the two flours and then add the chopped ginger. Process carefully until the mixture just comes together. Tip the mixture onto a floured work surface and divide it into two. Roll each half into a log shape (approx. $1^{1}/_{2}$-inch diameter), wrap in plastic wrap, and refrigerate them for at least 2 hours. Slice into $^{1}/_{4}$-inch rounds and bake in a preheated 300°F oven for 6–8 minutes. The cookies should color only very slightly.

Store them in an airtight container.

MAKES 35–40 COOKIES.

honey

While the possession of a sweet tooth is far from being solely a twenty-first-century phenomenon, it has never before been as easy to satisfy. These days confectionery is no longer confined to candy stores. In fact, it seems that wherever we go we are faced with sweet temptations – at gas stations and video stores, supermarket checkouts and newsstands. It is easy to forget that these simple pleasures, which we take so much for granted, have only been readily available since the commercial cultivation of sugar cane and sugar beet during the last few hundred years.

The secret of extracting and concentrating the juice from sugar cane was known in India as early as 3,000 BC, but it didn't reach Europe until the Arabs took it to Spain in the eighth century. However, it was not until Spanish colonists took sugar cane to the West Indies in the fifteenth century that the sugar-refining industry really began in earnest.

Before refined sugar, people's taste for sweetness was satisfied by the concentrated natural sugars found in ripe and sun-dried fruits, and most of all by honey. Honey was one of the very first sweeteners known to our ancestors – prehistoric cave paintings in Spain depict a stone-age man carefully stealing honey from a nest of bees. By 2,500 BC, the Egyptians had learned to avoid some of the danger involved in collecting honey from wild bees by taming them with smoke and forcing them to build their honeycombs in tall, cylindrical hives.

To ancient civilizations honey was a kind of miracle, a food given to us by the gods, rich in energy and delicious to taste. It was used for sweetening and flavoring foods, for making primitive fruit preserves, and for coating all kinds of flowers, nuts, and fruit to make sweetmeats. It must also be said that another of honey's key attractions was its propensity to ferment quickly when mixed with water – especially in hot climates – turning it into mead, one of the very first intoxicating drinks.

In the West, honey is no longer a key ingredient in most kitchens, as it is unable to compete with cheap white sugars in either cost or availability. For most of us, honey is merely a delicious spread to be enjoyed with lashings of butter on good hot toast. In the Middle East, however, honey is still an important basic ingredient in cooking and confectionery making. A spoonful of honey is often added to syrups for pouring over nut-stuffed pastries. Then there are all sorts of honey cookies and puffs, like the Greek *loukoumathes*, honey pies, and even honey-cheese cakes. Honey works well in nutty-earthy sweets, like nougat or halvah, and marries perfectly with several sweet spices, such as cinnamon, ginger, and cloves. All around the Mediterranean, gingerbreads and spice cakes are still made with honey. Honey's affinity with lemon is also well known, not just in throat-soothing winter drinks, but in syrups and marinades for roasts and grills. Honey even adds a warming, sweet base note to all kinds of savory tagines and meat casseroles.

SELECTING AND STORING HONEY

One of the very best things about a weekend in the country is the opportunity it provides for visiting country markets. There always seems to be at least one stall boasting endless varieties of local honeys, and we find it almost impossible to go home without buying at least one jar. As a result, we have a cupboard full of different honeys, ranging from a mild-flavored, cheap supermarket variety to several different intensely fragrant single-flower honeys.

Every honey is different. The flavor, strength, and smell of each one is determined by the flowers visited by the bees, as their fragrance is retained in the honey. The cheap commercial brands always taste pretty much the same because they are blended from lots of different honeys. As a result, they are consistent, reliable, and a little dull, lacking the complexity and subtlety of the finest single-flower honeys. Honeys from small producers tend to be costlier. As with the finest boutique olive oils or wines, the flavor of these honeys is dependent on the local climate, terrain, fauna, and flora that the bees visit.

Delicious single-flower honeys come from a wide range of plants. Some are strongly floral, like orange blossom and apple flower, or more aromatic, like lavender and clover. Some have strong herbal qualities, like rosemary, fennel, and thyme.

Honey should not be kept in the refrigerator but should always be stored in a cool cupboard, well away from light. All honeys start off fairly runny and clear, though some are darker and stronger smelling. Over time, and more quickly if exposed to light, they slowly crystallize, becoming thicker and cloudier, until they eventually set solid. (Don't confuse them with creamed honeys, though, which are whipped to a creamy, opaque consistency.) This is an inevitable process which affects neither the flavor nor the quality of the honey and is easy to reverse by submerging the entire jar in a pan of very hot water. Leave it for half an hour or so, until the honey becomes runny again.

USING HONEY

Everyone knows that honey is delicious on hot, buttered toast or drizzled over a bowl of thick, creamy yogurt with the lightest dusting of cinnamon. If you want to use it in cooked dishes, though, use it with discretion: honey is not simply interchangeable with sugar, and some very strongly flavored honeys are not suited for cooking at all. Furthermore, heat destroys the more complex and distinctive flavors of the most interesting single-flower honeys, so in many cooked dishes it is better to use a milder-flavored supermarket brand.

HONEY-ROASTED PEAR AND WALNUT SALAD

Top this salad with slices of grilled haloumi to make a delicious starter. It is a lovely, light accompaniment to all sorts of earthy vegetable dishes and risottos.

~~~~~~

3 ripe pears

2½ tablespoons mild-flavored honey

3 cardamom pods, seeds only

1 tablespoon orange-blossom water

3 teaspoons sherry

2 tablespoons butter

½ cup extra-virgin olive oil

¾ cup walnuts

2 packets Cypriot haloumi cheese
    (8 ounces each), sliced ⅛-inch thick

1 cup plain flour for dusting

¼ cup olive oil

juice of 2 lemons

1 teaspoon fresh thyme leaves, chopped

1 purple onion, finely sliced

1 bunch watercress, leaves picked

1 cup frisée lettuce

⅔ cup black olives

salt

½ teaspoon fresh black pepper

PEEL THE PEARS and cut them into halves (or quarters if they are quite thick) and cut out the cores. In a small pot, warm the honey, cardamom seeds, orange-blossom water, and sherry.

In a heavy frying pan, melt together the butter and 2 tablespoons of the extra-virgin olive oil until bubbling, then sear the pears for 1 minute on each side. Add honey mixture and sauté for a further 2 minutes, until it is a warm caramel color.

To roast the walnuts, place them in a very hot oven for 5 minutes. Rub away some of the papery brown skin in a tea towel and cut them into quarters.

To grill the haloumi cheese, dust the slices in flour. Heat the ¼ cup of olive oil in a frying pan over high heat and cook the cheese slices until they are golden brown. Turn them and color the other side. Pour the lemon juice over the cheese and sprinkle with the thyme leaves.

Slice the onion finely and rinse it under cold running water for 5 minutes to reduce its sharpness.

In a large bowl, gently mix together the pears and haloumi cheese with the watercress leaves, olives, onion, and two-thirds of the walnuts. In a separate bowl, gently whisk together the remaining olive oil and the lemon juice and season with the salt and pepper. Pour the dressing over the salad and gently combine.

To serve, place a mound of salad on each plate and sprinkle the remaining walnuts over the top.

HONEY-GARLIC AÏOLI

If you find that aïoli is often just too garlicky, then you might prefer this version, which tempers the pungency of garlic with a softer, sweeter flavor from a mild-flavored honey.

3 whole heads garlic
1 tablespoon honey
2 egg yolks
1 teaspoon Dijon mustard
¼ cup champagne vinegar

⅔ cup olive oil, combined with
   ½ cup vegetable oil
juice of 1 lemon
salt and pepper

CUT THE GARLIC HEADS in half crossways and drizzle them with honey. Wrap them in foil and roast them in a preheated 350°F oven for about 20 minutes, or until they are very soft.

Squeeze out the garlic into a blender and process with the egg yolks, mustard, and half the vinegar before adding the oil, drop by drop, until the mixture emulsifies.

Loosen with the remaining vinegar and lemon juice, then add the remaining oil and season with salt and pepper.

BURNT HONEY ICE CREAM

Caramelizing honey just to the point of burning takes it from super sweetness to the very edge of bitterness. It makes a very rich ice cream and is delicious served with puffy Almond Fritters (page 6), Sweet Nut-Stuffed Quinces (page 251), or alongside a slice of Sticky Ginger Cake (page 146).

~~~~~~

1 cup sugar

6 tablespoons water

6 tablespoons honey

2 cups milk

1 quart cream

8 egg yolks

DISSOLVE ½ CUP OF THE SUGAR with the water and boil until it reaches the soft-ball stage – that is, 234°F on a sugar thermometer. This takes approximately 8 minutes. Then add the honey and cook to a dark caramel, which will take an additional 8–10 minutes. Be careful it doesn't burn, and remember that residual heat will continue to cook it once you remove it from the heat.

Meanwhile, bring the milk and cream to the boil. In a mixing bowl, whisk the egg yolks with the remaining sugar. Pour the hot cream onto the eggs, whisking vigorously, then return the mix to the saucepan. Mix in the caramel and stir over a very gentle heat until it thickens. You should be able to draw a clear line in the custard on the back of a spoon.

Remove the pan from the heat and cool it in a sink of cold water or ice, stirring from time to time. When the custard is completely cold, pour it into an ice-cream maker and churn according to the manufacturer's instructions.

SERVES FOUR TO SIX.

HONEY MOUSSE WITH PINE-NUT PRALINE

In this light-as-air dessert, sweet honey mousse is spiked with nutty, earthy Pine-Nut Praline (page 231), which also adds a very pleasing crunch to the smooth creaminess.

2 teaspoons unflavored gelatin

4 tablespoons mild honey

1⅔ cups cream

4 egg whites

1 teaspoon Cointreau

1 cup Pine Nut Praline (page 231)

DISSOLVE THE GELATIN in ¼ cup cold water and let stand for a few minutes. In a saucepan heat the honey, then add the gelatin and allow to cool down to room temperature (don't refrigerate).

Whip the cream and egg whites in two separate bowls.

Fold the honey, Cointreau, and Pine-Nut Praline into the cream. Then fold in the egg whites and chill until ready to serve.

lamb

When it comes to meat, there is little doubt that in the wealthy West we are well and truly spoilt for choice. Whether it is the ham in our lunchtime sandwich, the minced beef in our takeout burger, or our Sunday roast, many people are used to eating meat in one form or another virtually every day. The vegetables, salads, grains, and legumes which accompany it are often eaten only in a grudging nod to nutritional balance or as mere stomach filler-uppers. Consumption of meat, once upon a time an expensive treat and a symbol of wealth and extravagance, has now become the norm.

This is certainly not the case in most developing countries (and this means for the majority of the world's population), where meat is still considered something of a luxury, eaten more as a condiment to flavor starchy staples, and often only on religious feast days and special family celebrations. Many countries around the Middle East and Mediterranean are in this category, even though times are changing and different types of meat are more freely available. What little meat is eaten, however, is almost certain to be lamb. In fact, older Arab cookbooks often vaguely refer to "meat" without specifying from which animal it should come. This is because traditionally the term *meat* was virtually synonymous with lamb or mutton (or sometimes kid or goat), as they were the only meats readily available.

Sheep were one of the very first animals to be domesticated, as early as 9,000 BC, by the nomads of the Central Asian steppes, who reared them as much for their woolly coats and milk and their tallow fat as for their meat. Sheep were easy to tame, having a strong herd instinct and being quick to breed and easy to graze on scrubby hillsides and grasslands. By the time cattle were domesticated, several thousand years later, they were generally considered far too valuable as draft animals to be eaten, and to this day, much of the terrain around the eastern Mediterranean and Levant countries is too poor for cattle breeding and dairy farming.

In the hot Middle East, pig farming was not viable, as pigs are temperamental animals, generally resistant to herding, and greedy scavengers rather than grass grazers. Although pork was widely eaten and enjoyed by most early civilizations, the annoying tendency of pigs to roam, coupled with their reputation for spreading disease and parasites, eventually led to taboos surrounding their consumption among two of the major religions of the Middle East, Judaism and Islam.

Lamb, on the other hand, has become strongly associated with many different cultural and religious festivities around the world, and particularly in the Middle East. For Christians, a paschal lamb has a deep spiritual significance at Easter as the symbol of Christ. Lamb is also the meat of choice at Jewish and Muslim feast days. The Jewish celebrations of Passover and Rosh Hashanah would be unthinkable without lamb, and Muslim countries ritually slaughter and feast on whole roasted lambs on religious holidays and at wedding feasts or other family celebrations.

SELECTING AND STORING LAMB

Lamb is eaten at every age from a few weeks to several years old. The animal that we eat most of the year around is generally between 3 months and a year old. New-season spring lamb is also available – usually at a higher price – and is tender and juicy, although its flavor is often milder.

Two other extremes are baby milk-fed lambs (2–4 weeks old), weighing 9–13 pounds, which are available from some specialist butchers and are a special delicacy in the Arab world. Their meat is sweet, delicate, and buttery soft, as befits an animal which has not yet tasted a blade of grass. At the other end of the age spectrum is mutton, which is hard to find. At least two years old, it has a strong, pungent flavor, which some people adore, and its mature meat requires really slow, long cooking to tenderize.

Young lamb is a vivid rosy pink, whereas the older animals and mutton turn a deeper, more purple red. Avoid meat which looks brown and tired. The fat should be white and dry, not yellow and wet.

USING LAMB

There are myriad different cuts available to consumers these days, and you need to choose the appropriate cut for each particular dish.

In the Middle East, whole lambs roasted on a spit for festive occasions are often baby or milk-fed lambs, which are greatly enjoyed for their delicate and very tender meat. Cuts from older lambs also lend themselves very well to roasting. The European tradition is usually to roast the leg, shoulder, or racks. These are often flavored with garlic and rosemary and eaten with roasted vegetables and gravy. In the Middle East, lamb is more likely to be stuffed with rice, fruit, and nuts.

Braised dishes are often simmered long and slowly, using cheaper cuts from the shoulder, neck, or shank and eked out with lots of vegetables and beans or lentils.

Much of the thrill of these dishes comes from the elaborate and subtle combinations of many different spices and herbs, or from simmering with fruits such as apricots, dates, or quinces.

And then there are minced-meat dishes, which are a mainstay of Arab, Jewish, and Turkish cooking. These offer an economical way of using tougher cuts of meat, by pounding or grinding them into a fine paste, adding a generous pinch of carefully selected spices, and then rolling into tiny meatballs for frying or for cooking in a thick sauce or casserole. Spicy minced lamb is also shaped into long sausages around skewers for grilling over hot coals. It is the main ingredient for the legendary Lebanese dish kibbeh, which can be fried or eaten raw.

All around the Middle East and eastern Mediterranean the air is filled with the savory aroma of sizzling grilled lamb, known as *meshwi*, which is sold from humble street stalls and kiosks everywhere. The technique of packing tender, tasty little morsels of meat onto skewers or spits, and then grilling them over flames or glowing charcoal, was reputedly first used by Ottoman soldiers during their long battle campaigns. Being constantly on the move, camping out of doors, and having only small amounts of fuel led to this practice of quickly grilling tiny pieces of meat over intense heat.

This style of quick grilling over fierce heat is perfectly suited to the most tender cuts of lamb. These days they are marketed as lean, with much of the fat removed to suit the antifat brigade. They are usually fillets, cut from the loin or leg. Because the meat is lean, it needs to be brushed with oil to keep it moist and to stop it from sticking.

LAMB KIFTA TAGINE WITH EGGS

Meatballs with a difference! This makes a tasty supper dish and, with its spicy tomato sauce and rich, runny eggs, is bound to become a firm favorite.

~~~~~~

MEATBALLS
1 pound lamb, finely ground
1 medium onion, finely chopped
3 tablespoons parsley, finely chopped
¼ teaspoon cayenne pepper
salt and pepper
2 tablespoons olive oil for frying

SAUCE
2 tablespoons olive oil
2 medium onions, finely chopped

1 clove garlic, finely chopped
2 cans tomatoes (14 ounces each),
   drained and chopped
1 teaspoon cumin powder
1 teaspoon cinnamon
½ teaspoon cayenne pepper
salt and pepper
2 cups water
⅓ cup parsley leaves, finely chopped
⅓ cup cilantro leaves, finely chopped
6 eggs

TO MAKE THE MEATBALLS, combine all the ingredients well and, with wet hands, form into walnut-sized balls. Heat the oil and brown the meatballs all over. Drain well on kitchen paper.

For the sauce, heat the oil in a heavy-based casserole dish and lightly sauté the onions and garlic until they are translucent. Add the remaining ingredients (except the water, fresh herbs, and eggs) and stir well. Then add the water, stir again, and bring to the boil. Lower the heat and simmer the sauce, uncovered, for around 30 minutes, or until it has reduced to a very thick gravy.

Add the meatballs to the sauce and continue cooking for a further 8 minutes. Carefully break the eggs into the sauce, cover it with a lid, and cook until the eggs are just set, which will take around 5 minutes.

Serve at once, straight from the pot, liberally garnished with the fresh herbs and with plenty of pita bread to mop up the runny egg yolks. Alternatively, accompany with a dish of plain Buttered Couscous (page 96) and a dollop of thick natural yogurt.

Those who enjoy a more piquant dish may add one finely chopped hot chili while sautéing the onion and garlic.

STICKY LAMB-SHANK SOUP WITH
FRESH FENUGREEK AND MOLTEN MOZZARELLA

This amazingly fragrant soup is really more of a meal. Fresh fenugreek can be hard to find – try an Asian or Middle Eastern grocer.

¼ cup olive oil

6 lamb shanks

salt and pepper

2 medium yellow onions, coarsely
  chopped

3 celery sticks, coarsely chopped

2 medium carrots, scraped and halved
  lengthways

2 medium leeks, washed and halved
  lengthways

4 cloves garlic, peeled

½ cup sherry

2 quarts chicken stock or water

1 tablespoon fenugreek seeds, rinsed
  and lightly cracked

1 teaspoon cumin seeds

2 sticks cinnamon

1 teaspoon allspice berries, lightly
  cracked

1 small butternut squash, peeled,
  deseeded, and cut into ½-inch dice

2 medium turnips, peeled and cut into
  ½-inch dice

2 medium potatoes, peeled and cut into
  ½-inch dice

¾ cup fresh cilantro, roughly chopped

1 bunch fenugreek leaves (or flat-leaf
  parsley)

7 ounces mozzarella cheese, sliced

HEAT OLIVE OIL in a heavy-based casserole dish and season lamb shanks with salt and pepper. Brown all over. Remove from pan and drain on kitchen paper.

To the casserole dish add onions, celery, carrots, leeks, and garlic and sauté over low heat for 5 minutes. Return the lamb to the pan, add the sherry and stock, and bring to the boil. Skim, then lower the heat.

To make a spice bag, combine the fenugreek seeds, cumin seeds, cinnamon sticks, and allspice in a small muslin cloth and tie with string. Submerge the bag among the vegetables and shanks. Place the casserole on the middle shelf of a preheated 350°F oven for 1¾ hours, until the lamb is falling from the bones.

Remove the casserole from the oven and strain the mixture through a sieve, pressing on the vegetables to extract maximum flavor. Discard the vegetables and spice bag, remove the meat from the bones, and shred it coarsely.

Cook the squash, turnips, and potatoes in the strained stock until tender, then strain and reserve with the meat. Bring the stock to the boil and reduce it by one-third, skimming constantly.

Return the meat and vegetables to the pan and heat through, then add the cilantro leaves and adjust the seasoning. To serve, ladle the soup into serving bowls, top with mozzarella slices, and sprinkle with fenugreek leaves.

Serve with crusty bread.

SERVES TEN.

MARINATED BABY LAMB WITH LEBANESE NUT RICE

This is a traditional favorite at Easter time, when a whole baby lamb is stuffed with a rice and nut mixture and barbecued or spit-roasted for a real family feast. If you can procure a baby lamb, and your oven or barbecue can accommodate it, go for it. Otherwise try this adaptation, which is equally delicious, if not quite as spectacular.

MARINADE

4 cloves garlic, crushed with
   1 teaspoon salt
juice of 2 lemons
1 teaspoon pepper
1 teaspoon ground allspice
2 teaspoons fresh thyme,
   finely chopped
1 cup olive oil

RICE

3 tablespoons olive oil
1 large onion, finely diced
5 ounces lamb mince
3 cups short-grain rice
1 quart chicken stock
1 cinnamon stick
salt
1 teaspoon pepper

LAMB

1 small lamb shoulder (3–4½ pounds)
   with shank, cut at ball joint
two 6-point lamb racks (bones trimmed
   and scraped back to the meat)
salt and freshly ground black pepper

TO SERVE

⅔ cup pine nuts
⅔ cup pistachio nuts (shelled)
⅔ cup blanched whole almonds
½ cup olive oil
2 cloves garlic, crushed with
   ½ teaspoon salt
juice of 1 lemon
1½ cups fresh cilantro leaves and stalks

FOR THE MARINADE, blend the garlic paste, lemon juice, pepper, allspice, and thyme with the olive oil. Marinate lamb pieces overnight.

Preheat the oven to 425°F. Remove the lamb from its marinade and brown it all over in a heavy-based baking pan (there will be enough oil in the marinade). Sprinkle it with salt and black pepper and place it in the oven. Roast the shoulder for 50 minutes to 1 hour, and the racks for 30 minutes, then remove them from the oven and allow them to rest in a warm place, covered with foil.

Prepare the rice while the lamb is roasting. Heat the olive oil in a large heavy-based pot and sauté the onion and minced lamb until the onion is soft and the meat has browned. After about 4 minutes, add the rice and boiling chicken stock. Turn the heat down to a simmer and add the cinnamon stick, salt, and pepper. Cover and cook for 16 minutes.

Fry the nuts separately in ½ cup olive oil until they are golden brown.

To serve, turn the rice out onto a large serving platter and sprinkle it with the nuts. Cut the lamb racks into three and carve shoulder meat for each person, arranging the pieces around the rice. Pour the juices from roasting into a small pan, bring quickly to the boil, and add the garlic paste and lemon juice. Pour over the lamb and garnish the whole platter with fresh cilantro. Accompany with thick Greek-style yogurt and a fresh green salad.

SERVES SIX.

DEVILED LAMB LOIN

4 whole lamb loins (approx. 7 ounces each)   3 teaspoons hot English mustard
freshly ground black pepper   3 teaspoons Chermoula (page 72)

CAREFULLY SLICE AWAY any excess fat on the lamb loins, then grind the fresh black pepper onto both sides. On one side, spread a little mustard, and then over that a little Chermoula. Turn over onto a piece of plastic wrap and repeat on the other side.

Grill or barbecue the lamb for 2 minutes on each side for medium-rare, turning twice to stop it from burning. Serve with creamy Harissa-Potato Salad (page 71) or Preserved-Lemon Guacamole (page 171) and Garlic Yorkshire Pudding (page 140).

lemons

When we were first married, we lived in an inner-city district of Melbourne that sported all the signs of a neighborhood on the up-and-up. The streets were crowded with dumpsters full to the brim with cast-off furniture, and the noise of builders' drills filled the air. Although bright young things are flocking to areas such as this, they are still peopled, in the main, by the same Greek and Italian families who moved in during the 1950s. Many still live in the same old workers' cottages: some have renovated or added grand extensions, but the one thing they have in common is a lemon tree in the garden.

For our Greek neighbors, it is inconceivable that they could live without a lemon tree close at hand. It is easy to understand why. The lemon must surely be the most indispensable item for any cook. Lemon is one of the most popular flavors for desserts: both its juice and its zest add a refreshing zing to cakes, tarts, puddings, sorbets, and refreshing summer drinks. Lemon juice adds a piquant tang to salad dressings and brings grilled meat and poultry to life, while fried fish and seafood are unthinkable without an accompanying lemon wedge. As well as bringing out the flavors of most foods, lemon juice is also useful as a tenderizer and color preserver. Rubbing the cut surface of an avocado with lemon juice will stop it from going brown, and, similarly, fruits and vegetables such as apple and artichoke can be prevented from discoloring by keeping them in acidulated water.

We tend to think of lemons as being quintessentially Mediterranean, but it seems likely that the lemon and its forebear, the citron, originated in northern India and from there spread to Mesopotamia and Persia. But lemons and other citrus fruits (apart from the thickly pithed bitter citron, which was widely cultivated by Jews for use in religious ceremonies) were not widely known in the Mediterranean until the spread of Islam in the seventh century.

The Arabs loved citrus trees not just for their fruit but also for their fragrant blossoms and leaves. They treated their empire in Spain as a big citrus orchard: it was they who planted the courtyards of the Alhambra with orange and lemon trees, and who filled the *patios de los naranjos* outside the great mosques in Cordoba and Seville.

The Arab and Persian penchant for sour flavorings is evident in their use of ingredients such as verjuice, tamarind, pomegranate, and, of course, lemon in many dishes. A lemony tang is the unifying characteristic of most Middle Eastern dips: baba ghanoush, hummus, skordalia, and taramasalata all have a distinctive lemon flavor. This preference also underpins many of their fruit and meat combinations. The strong, fatty mutton which is the basis of most meat dishes benefits enormously from sharpening with fruits like apricots, pomegranates, and lemons. One of the characteristics of Moroccan cuisine – learned from the Arabs – is the use of whole preserved lemons in meat stews known as tagines.

SELECTING AND STORING LEMONS

If you have had the foresight to plant a lemon tree in your backyard, you are very fortunate. The rest of us have to make do with lemons from the local market, green-grocer, or supermarket, and there are a couple of things to bear in mind. Firstly, choose organically grown fruit if you can. Most commercially grown lemons are picked green, when they are most acid; this is also what makes them keep so well. Once picked, though, lemons do not ripen any more, so to make them that bright, sunshiny yellow we all love, lemons are treated with ethylene gas. This destroys the chlorophyll and leaves behind only the yellow pigment.

Thin-skinned lemons tend to be juicier and are ideal for preserving. Thick-skinned lemons are good for zesting. However, any lemon you buy should feel weighty, an indication of its juiciness. Lemons should be wiped dry, as they have a tendency to go moldy if damp. They can sit happily in a bowl on the kitchen table, where they will cheer up the room with their sunny hue. In a humid climate, though, they will last better if refrigerated.

Lemons, and indeed other citrus fruits, are often waxed to a shiny gloss before they are stored. So if you are planning to use the zest, make sure you wash and dry the skins very well before zesting.

USING LEMONS

To improve the yield of juice from lemons, soak them in warm water for 20 minutes or so before squeezing. Lemon juice will keep for 4–5 days in the refrigerator and can also be frozen. To maximize the lemony flavor, add lemon zest to a dish, as it is the skin of the lemon that contains the intense essential lemon oil. To zest a lemon, carefully remove the yellow skin (avoid the pith, which is bitter) with a zester. This will peel away long, thin threads of lemon skin, which usually need to be chopped more finely with a sharp knife. If you don't possess a lemon zester, then a vegetable peeler will also do for removing thin slices of peel, which, again, will need to be chopped finely. A grater will also work, but it tends to get clogged up with a wet, sticky mess.

PRESERVED LEMONS WITH HONEY

Preserving lemons in salt, Moroccan style, adds complex, spicy undertones to the sourness of the lemons. The addition of honey, cinnamon, and coriander seeds gives further depth and a more rounded sweetness. This version uses a trick learned from Claudia Roden, which involves freezing the lemons first to speed up the whole maturing process. For a delightful change you can try the same recipe using limes.

Use only the rind of preserved lemons and discard the flesh. Add the finely chopped skin of ½ a preserved lemon to 6 tablespoons of butter and use it to stuff a chicken under the skin before roasting, or rub over skewers of prawns before barbecuing. Thinly sliced, it adds a piquancy to tagines and other braises and fricassees. Use it to make a sensational Preserved-Lemon Oil (page 192) for vinaigrettes and salad dressings. Or finely chop it and add to mayonnaise, hollandaise sauce, or even guacamole.

---

3 pounds thin-skinned lemons
1½ cups salt
1 tablespoon coriander seeds,
   lightly crushed
2 cinnamon sticks

2 lemon leaves or bay leaves
¼ cup honey
1 cup lemon juice
3 cups warm water

WASH AND DRY THE LEMONS. Cut them lengthways into quarters from the point of the lemon to three-quarters of the way down, but leave them joined together at the base. Place them in a plastic bag in the freezer for 24 hours.

Remove the lemons from the freezer and allow them to defrost. Stuff the center of each lemon with a heaped teaspoon of salt. Arrange them neatly in a 2-quart jar, sprinkling each layer of lemons with salt and crushed coriander seeds.

Place the sticks of cinnamon down the sides of the jar, along with the lemon leaves or bay leaves. Mix together the honey and lemon juice with the warm water until the honey dissolves. Pour into the jar, covering the lemons entirely, and screw the lid on tightly. Place a piece of cardboard on the bottom of a large pot and sit the jar on top. This stops it from vibrating. Add warm water to cover the jar completely, and slowly bring it to the boil. Boil for 6 minutes, then remove from the heat. Gently lift the jar from the pot.

Store in a dry, cool place a month before opening. Once opened, keep refrigerated. If the lemons are not frozen first, the maturation process will take at least 3 months.

PRESERVED-LEMON GUACAMOLE WITH
SMOKED EEL AND PINE-NUT WAFERS

GUACAMOLE

1 large, ripe but firm avocado,
 cut into ¼-inch dice
1 small tomato, skinned, deseeded,
 and cut into ¼-inch dice
⅓ cup cilantro leaves, chopped
1 fresh green chili, deseeded, scraped,
 and finely chopped
juice of 1 lime
1 clove garlic, crushed with
 ½ teaspoon salt

½ Preserved Lemon with Honey (page
 170), skin only, finely chopped
½ medium purple onion, finely chopped

1 small smoked eel, skinned
8 Pine-Nut Wafers (page 230)
2 tablespoons extra-virgin olive oil for
 sprinkling
1 teaspoon sumac (optional)
salt and pepper

GENTLY COMBINE all guacamole ingredients in a large mixing bowl.

Carefully divide the eel into two long fillets. Depending on the size of the eel, you will probably only need to use one of these. Cut it into strips about 2 inches long, and cut each piece in half lengthways to give a total of 12 strips.

Spoon a generous mound of guacamole onto each plate and serve with 3 strips of eel and 2 wafers.

Drizzle a little extra-virgin olive oil around the plate and sprinkle with sumac and salt and pepper, if desired.

PRESERVED-LEMON BUTTER

Use this tangy, salty butter to stuff under the skin of a chicken before roasting.

¾ cup (1½ sticks) softened butter
1 Preserved Lemon with Honey (page 170), skin only, finely chopped
2 shallots, finely chopped
½ clove garlic, finely chopped

1 tablespoon parsley, finely chopped
1 teaspoon thyme leaves, finely chopped
½ teaspoon sumac

ADD ALL THE INGREDIENTS to the softened butter and mix thoroughly.

Shape into a rough sausage and place onto a square of waxed paper. Roll into a smooth log and then wrap in plastic wrap and refrigerate until needed.

It will keep in the freezer for 3–4 weeks. Cut off slices and use as required.

LEMON-CURD FOOL

Serve this lemony fool with Sesame-Honey Wafers (page 280), or to accompany the Sticky Lemon-Yogurt Cake (page 322), or any other nutty citrusy-syrup cake. The curd can also be folded into an ice-cream base for a stunning lemon ice cream.

juice and zest of 2 lemons
6 tablespoons (¾ stick) butter
1 cup sugar

3 eggs, beaten
2 cups cream
¼ cup caramel

TO MAKE THE LEMON CURD, finely chop the lemon zest and place it with the juice, butter, and sugar in the top of a double boiler. Heat and stir until the sugar is completely dissolved, then pour in the eggs. Continue to heat gently, stirring all the time, until the mixture thickens. Do not allow it to boil.

Strain and chill. When ready to serve, whip the cream to soft peaks and swirl in the lemon curd and caramel. Serve in a glass bowl or individual glass dishes for the full effect.

AVGOLEMONO

This egg and lemon combination is a Greek favorite sauce and soup. But it is also considered a cornerstone of Sephardic cooking. Claudia Roden's fascinating book of Jewish food has several recipes for this as a sauce, and she suggests that it was probably Portuguese or Spanish in origin. Made like a custard, it is similar in flavor to a hollandaise, but much lighter and fresher in the absence of large amounts of butter.

2 whole eggs
1 egg yolk
juice of 1 lemon

½ cup chicken stock
a pinch sumac

IN A SMALL PAN, whisk together the whole eggs and egg yolk with the lemon juice. In a separate pot, bring the stock to the boil and add one tablespoon of it to the egg mixture. Mix in well, then pour the eggs back into the hot stock, stirring well.

Cook gently over very low heat, stirring constantly with a wooden spoon. Mixture will gradually start to thicken. Continue cooking and stirring until the sauce is thick enough to hold a line drawn across the back of a wooden spoon.

Remove from the heat and straightaway pour the sauce into a clean bowl.

It can be served hot or cold and is a light, tangy accompaniment to most seafood and fish, oysters, brains, or even simply steamed vegetables.

lentils

As with so many of the world's subsistence foods, lentils have received bad press through the ages. Sneered at by the wealthy and moaned about by the poor, who have so often depended upon them as their staple diet, they are also considered dull and bland and, worse still, suffer a disturbing reputation for causing flatulence.

And yet, despite all this, people have been stolidly munching away on lentils for many thousands of years. Their place of origin is believed to be somewhere in the Middle East, and archaeologists have found evidence of their cultivation as early as the seventh century BC, in sites ranging from Iraq, Turkey, and Egypt to China.

The reason for the lentil's unpopularity really has little to do with its taste but rather its relentless availability. Through long, dark winters, when other fresh vegetables were lacking, families could always rely upon their store of lentils for the cooking pot. Similarly, when meat is scarce – as indeed it has been for most of the world's population since the beginning of time – lentils and other legumes have always been cheap and easy to grow.

Furthermore, in the world of legumes, lentils are second only to soybeans for their high protein content, and, when combined with other grains, cereals, or nuts, they provide us with nearly all our necessary daily proteins. Lentils are also high in fiber and a variety of minerals, low in fat – and very politically correct!

The combining of various plant foods to boost the protein value of a dish is a common practice throughout the Middle East. Lentil and rice dishes feature everywhere: the Lebanese have their mjaddarah (lentils and rice), while the Egyptians call a similar dish *megadarra*. In Iran they enjoy *addas polow*, a creamy lentil-rice dish enlivened with chopped dates and raisins. In India they pour dal on rice and scoop it up with flat breads. Lentil soups around the Arab world also usually include cracked wheat, noodles, or rice.

Although many people think lentils are dull and flavorless, it is this same soothing blandness which makes them the perfect vehicle for herbs, spices, and other aromatics. Think of spicy Indian dal and Moroccan *harira* soup, or lentil and spinach soup, tangy with lemon and a favorite all around the Middle East. Gently braised with a piece of smoked bacon, in the northern European tradition, lentils are deliciously earthy and comforting and act as the perfect foil to rich smoked meats and sausages.

SELECTING AND STORING LENTILS

Most lentils are readily available from supermarkets, health food stores, and Middle Eastern and Indian specialist stores. They can be divided into three broad color groups: brown/green, red, and the green Puy lentils from France. These last lentils are available from fancy delicatessens and specialist food stores.

There are several different varieties of the large brown and green lentils, which taste very similar and can be used more or less interchangeably. They are whole and unskinned, so they keep their shape and texture when cooked.

Red lentils are also sold as Egyptian lentils. They are small, skinned, and split, so they cook down rapidly to a soft purée and are best used for soups and dips.

Puy lentils are currently the darlings of the foodie world. These tiny blue-green lentils have become ultrafashionable, as they have an excellent flavor and, though small, maintain their shape and texture well. They are ideal for salads or as a simple lentil braise to accompany meaty sausages or smoked pork dishes.

As with all legumes, store lentils in an airtight container in a cool, dark cupboard. They will keep well for about a year, but will begin to age and deteriorate from then, losing their shape and texture in cooking.

USING LENTILS

Most of the prepackaged varieties of lentil have been thoroughly washed and checked over for grit and gravel. If you buy them loose, though, you should certainly give them a good wash in several changes of water and check them carefully.

Unlike many other legumes, lentils don't need to be soaked. After washing and draining, they should be cooked in plenty of stock or plain water. The cooking time for lentils will vary depending on their type and on the dish: for example, in salads they need to be tender but still retain their shape, whereas for soups and purées they can be cooked down to a creamy mush.

GREEN LENTIL SOUP WITH SAFFRON SCRAMBLED EGGS

This is one of the best soups we can think of for a cold winter's night. It is deliciously warming and subtly spiced, and the creamy scramble of eggs makes it comforting and filling.

1 medium onion, finely chopped
⅓ cup olive oil
1 clove garlic, finely chopped
2 green chilis, deseeded, scraped, and finely chopped
2 cups green lentils
1 teaspoon allspice
1 teaspoon honey
juice and zest of 1 lemon
1¾ quarts vegetable stock or water

salt and pepper
1½ cups fresh cilantro leaves
5 eggs
10 saffron strands, lightly roasted and crushed
⅓ cup cream
salt and pepper
3 tablespoons butter
extra-virgin olive oil
fresh cilantro leaves to garnish

HEAT THE OIL in a heavy pan and sweat the onion for 2 minutes, until it is softened. Add the garlic and green chilis, and cook a further minute. Add the lentils, allspice, honey, lemon juice, and zest, and then the vegetable stock or water. Season with salt and pepper and bring to the boil. Skim, lower the heat, and simmer for 45 minutes, until the lentils are very tender. Add the cilantro and remove from the heat. Allow to rest uncovered for 10 minutes before blending to a purée in a blender or food processor.

Taste and adjust seasoning and thin with a little more stock if necessary.

Lightly combine the eggs with the saffron, cream, and a little salt and pepper. Melt the butter and cook the eggs over a very gentle heat until they are very softly scrambled.

To serve, bring the lentil soup to the boil, skim, and pour into serving bowls. Top with a spoonful of the scrambled eggs, drizzle with a little extra-virgin olive oil, and garnish with fresh cilantro leaves.

SERVES SIX.

CHICKEN IN PARCHMENT WITH
MOROCCAN AROMATICS AND LENTILS

This is an ideal dinner-party dish. Everything can be prepared ahead of time and needs simply to be reheated for serving. Served in individual parchment parcels, it also brings a touch of drama to the dinner table.

½ cup French Puy lentils
½ medium onion
1 cinnamon stick
4 sprigs thyme
3 pounds chicken pieces on the bone
1 cup plain flour
1 teaspoon sweet paprika
1 teaspoon salt
¼ cup olive oil
1 large brown onion, finely chopped
1 pound potatoes, peeled and cut into ¾-inch dice

½ pound carrots, scraped and cut into ¾-inch dice
2 tablespoons Chermoula (page 72)
1 can crushed tomatoes (14 ounces)
½ Preserved Lemon with Honey (page 170), skin only, finely chopped
1 quart chicken stock
¾ pound squash or pumpkin, peeled and cut into ¾-inch dice
salt and pepper
¼ cup parsley leaves, finely chopped
¼ cup cilantro leaves, finely chopped

PLACE THE LENTILS in three times their volume of cold water with the onion half, cinnamon stick, and thyme. Bring to the boil, then lower the heat and simmer uncovered for 20 minutes, or until they are just tender. Strain.

Mix the flour and paprika. Dust the chicken pieces in the spiced flour. Heat the olive oil in a large, heavy-based pan, add the chicken pieces, and sauté until they are golden all over. Add the onion, potatoes, and carrots and mix well. Add the Chermoula, coating all the ingredients, then add the crushed tomatoes, the chopped preserved lemon, and the chicken stock. Bring to the boil, then lower the heat, cover, and simmer for 8 minutes. Add the lentils and squash and cook uncovered for a further 5 minutes, by which time the vegetables should all be just tender and the chicken just cooked. Remove the pan from the heat. Allow to cool and then refrigerate overnight.

To serve, preheat the oven to 350°F. Using nonstick baking parchment, cut four 16-inch lengths to make four squares. Fold each square into sixteenths, trim around the ends, then open up to form the rough circle. Place the circle into a fairly deep bowl and heap in a quarter of the mixture, ensuring even amounts of chicken, vegetables, and sauce. Sprinkle with the chopped parsley and cilantro. Gather the edges of the paper together above the mixture and tie with kitchen string so you have a little bag. Place the parcels on a baking tray and cover with foil (this stops the tops from getting crispy and the string from burning).

Cook for half an hour and serve individual parcels for each person to open up and release the delicious, aromatic braise within.

Serve with Buttered Couscous (page 96), Cracked-Wheat Pilaf (page 38), or even Fried Pine-Nut Gnocchi (page 229).

MJADDARAH

Just about every country and region of the Middle East has its own lentil and rice dish. The Turks have their lentil pilafs, the Persians their *addas polow*, and everywhere there are versions of Mjaddarah (Lebanon and Syria), *moudjendar* (Cyprus), or *megadarra* (Egypt). It must be said that this homely dish doesn't look very special – just a brown sort of mush. But it is fantastic comfort food – sweet and earthy, and topped with heaps of caramelized onions. It is a great home-cooked favorite in Lebanese and Syrian families, and is often eaten during Lent, or on Fridays and other meat-free days, with a sharp, lemony salad such as Fattouche (page 289).

⁓⁓⁓⁓⁓⁓⁓⁓⁓⁓⁓⁓⁓⁓⁓⁓⁓⁓⁓⁓⁓⁓⁓⁓⁓⁓⁓⁓⁓⁓⁓⁓⁓⁓⁓⁓⁓⁓

⅓ cup olive oil
1 medium brown onion, diced small
2 cups brown lentils
5 cups water

⅓ cup long-grain rice, washed well
  and drained
½ teaspoon cumin
2 medium onions, sliced

HEAT HALF THE OIL and sauté the diced onion until soft. Add the lentils and half the water, cover, and cook for 15 minutes (or until lentils are just cooked). Add the rice, mix well, and continue cooking for a further 15 minutes, stirring every now and then and gradually adding more of the water as it is absorbed.

The dish is ready when the lentils have broken down almost to a purée and the rice grains have swelled and almost burst – in fact, it looks rather like an unappetizing khaki brown porridge! Add the cumin and stir well. Heat the remaining oil and cook the sliced onions over low to medium heat for 5–8 minutes until they have caramelized.

Serve the Mjaddarah at room temperature, garnished with the onions.

SERVES FOUR TO SIX.

mint

Minty things are all around us, from breath-freshening toothpastes and chewing gums to palate-cleansing after-dinner sweets. Yet in Western kitchens, not nearly enough is made of the humble mint. The most exciting thing that many of us do with mint is to chop and scatter a handful on new-season potatoes and garden peas, or drown it in vinegar to serve with roast lamb.

Why this reluctance to use one of the most readily available herbs? Mint must surely be the easiest herb in the whole world to grow. Unless vigorously pruned, it runs rampant in most backyards. It is ideally suited to a window box, which contains its aggressive root system better. Even if you have no patch of earth in which to plant a few mint cuttings, these days neat little bunches of the fresh herb are available from supermarkets pretty much all year round.

In the Levant countries and all around the Mediterranean, people buy great armfuls of all kinds of fresh herbs and use them lavishly. Mint is certainly one of the most popular, loved for its cleansing, fresh flavor during the long, hot summer months. In Lebanon, Syria, Iraq, and Iran, freshly picked mint leaves are tossed into mixed-leaf salads. Mint is also a key ingredient in the Lebanese favorites tabbouleh and fattouche. Fresh mint is often eaten with soft white cheeses and fresh bread, perhaps with a dish of olives or a drizzle of olive oil. Small bunches of mint are a classic garnish for all kinds of mezze dishes, in particular the Lebanese national dish, kibbeh nayeh. Often fresh mint and other herbs are set on the table in a small jug to be nibbled during the meal.

In Morocco, fresh mint is essential for the sweet green tea served endlessly throughout the day and night. Although it is traditionally served very sweet, its mintiness makes it surprisingly refreshing. Mint, with its sharp, clean taste, is an ideal palate cleanser, and is frequently partnered with cucumber or yogurt to make dressings, chilled soups, and cooling relishes, which make a terrific foil for hot and spicy dishes. This combination is used throughout the Middle East and eastern Mediterranean (and also in India, where raitas are a popular accompaniment to spicy curries). Fresh mint is also used to add a characteristic sweet flavor to a number of hot savory dishes – either mixed into rice and meat stuffings or packed on top of braised dishes, such as vine leaves or koussa, while cooking.

Mint is one of the few herbs which retain their flavor when dried. All around the Middle East and in countries like Turkey and Greece, many households dry their own mint and use it even more than the fresh herb. Dried mint works particularly well with fresh white cheeses such as feta and is often added to flavor little cheese pies. In Cyprus dried mint is used to flavor haloumi, and you can see little flecks in the surrounding brine. Egg dishes are commonly flavored with a sprinkle of dried mint. A great Lebanese favorite is *eggah* – a classic flat omelet, colored bright green from the mint. The Lebanese version of tzatziki, *khiyar bi laban*, also uses dried mint rather than fresh.

SELECTING AND STORING MINT

If you grow your own mint, you will need to pick it constantly to keep it at bay. But this shouldn't be too burdensome: even if you can't face eating it at every meal, its fragrance fills the kitchen delightfully. Growing it at home also means you have the luxury of choosing different varieties – not just common old spearmint (or garden mint) but also peppermint (cultivated commercially for pharmaceuticals and food flavorings), apple mint, lemon mint, and pineapple mint.

If you buy mint in the shops, it is likely you will get spearmint, which is the most common variety grown commercially. This is available all year from supermarkets and greengrocers, but it is most abundant in summer. When purchasing, try to avoid bunches with wilted, drooping leaves, especially if they appear to be turning black. Don't wash mint until you are ready to use it, as water makes the leaves blacken and rot more quickly. Store it in the refrigerator and use it within a few days. A sprig of mint in a glass on the windowsill won't last very long but will make the kitchen smell fresh, sweet, and clean for a day or so.

As for dried mint, you can find little packets at the supermarket, which are fine, but drying it yourself is even better. Strip the leaves from the stalks and lay them on waxed paper to dry over several days – or place them outside in the sun until completely dry.

USING MINT

Wash and dry fresh mint well before using. If you need it chopped, do so at the last minute with a sharp knife – using a blunt knife only bruises it. If you must use mint as a garnish, don't use timid, little individual leaves, but big, generous bunches.

MINTED SPLIT-PEA SOUP

This is a fabulously minty soup – a kind of variation on a classic fresh-pea version – but using split peas means you can enjoy it all year round. Of course, you could also make it in the summer when fresh peas are plentiful, which makes for a slightly lighter-textured soup. If you make it ahead of time, it will thicken up, and you may like to thin it with a little extra stock or water before serving.

1½ cups green split peas or fresh peas
¼ cup olive oil
1 medium onion, finely sliced
1 clove garlic, finely chopped
2 cups butter or romaine lettuce,
   roughly shredded
½ teaspoon dried mint

1½ quarts vegetable or light chicken
   stock
½ cup fresh mint leaves, roughly
   chopped
salt and pepper
watercress to garnish
whipped cream to garnish

PICK OVER THE SPLIT PEAS and remove any stones, dirt, and yellow peas.

Heat the oil in a pan and add the onion, garlic, and lettuce. Sauté gently for a few minutes, then add the dried mint and split peas. Stir well. Add the stock and bring to the boil. Then lower the heat and simmer uncovered for about 40 minutes, or until the peas are soft. Add the roughly chopped fresh mint and cook a further 3–4 minutes to soften.

Taste and season with salt and pepper. Purée until very smooth, then strain to remove any bits.

Garnish with Hot Mint Oil (opposite), watercress, and lightly whipped cream.

SERVES FOUR TO SIX.

HOT MINT OIL

A classic Persian recipe, hot mint oil is used a little like French pistou, for drizzling over all kinds of soups. You could also splash a little on fresh white cheese and eat it with hot, fluffy Turkish bread.

2 teaspoons olive oil
2 cloves garlic, finely chopped
1 teaspoon dried mint

HEAT THE OIL, then add the garlic and stir. Add the mint and immediately remove from the heat, as it burns quickly. Allow to infuse overnight. Strain and use sparingly.

MINTED CABBAGE SALAD

Cabbage salad is a popular Lebanese dish, often eaten as an accompaniment to kibbeh. This version includes both fresh and dried mint and is delightfully refreshing.

½ pound Savoy cabbage, core removed and very finely shredded
⅓ cup watercress leaves
⅓ cup mint leaves
juice of 1 lemon

1 large clove garlic, crushed with 1 teaspoon salt
3 tablespoons extra-virgin olive oil
1 teaspoon dried mint
salt and pepper

IN A LARGE BOWL, mix together the cabbage with the watercress and mint leaves. In a separate bowl, blend the lemon juice with the crushed garlic, extra-virgin olive oil, and dried mint. Pour the dressing over the salad ingredients and toss lightly. To serve, twist small handfuls of the cabbage in the palm of your hand to form little turbans.

HOT MUSSEL SALAD WITH FETA AND FENNEL

This is a delightful salad full of clean, refreshing flavors like the salty feta and aniseedy fennel. The juices from the mussels blend beautifully with the minty-lemon dressing and make the whole dish taste of the sea. Eat as a salad with plenty of hot, crusty bread, or top each serving with a little turban of egg noodles, briefly sautéed in lemon butter.

2½ pounds fresh mussels
2 tablespoons olive oil
1 onion, roughly chopped
1 celery stick, roughly chopped
2 cloves garlic, roughly chopped
½ cup white wine
1 large purple onion
½ pound fennel
acidulated water
6 ounce good-quality feta cheese
½ cup radicchio leaves, roughly torn
2 Belgian endives, leaves separated
⅔ cup watercress or parsley leaves

DRESSING
½ cup extra-virgin olive oil
juice of 2 lemons
1 clove garlic, crushed with
    1 teaspoon salt
1 teaspoon dried mint
freshly ground black pepper

TO SERVE
¾ pound egg noodles
1 tablespoon butter
juice of ½ lemon
salt and pepper

SCRUB THE MUSSELS clean of any sand and dirt and pull away the beards. In a heavy-based pot, heat the olive oil and sauté the onion, celery, and garlic. Add the wine and mussels. Cover and steam on high heat for 3 minutes. Uncover and stir them around well, then steam for a further 2 minutes. Remove from the heat and leave covered to steam for another minute or so. Then strain off the liquor, reserving for future use. Discard the aromatics and any unopened mussels.

Slice the whole onion into rings as finely as possible, then rinse it under cold running water for about 4 minutes. This crisps it up and softens the sharp flavor. Slice the fennel in half, remove the core, slice it very thinly lengthways, and cover it with acidulated water until it is required.

For the dressing, whisk the oil and lemon together, then add the garlic paste, 2 tablespoons of the mussel liquor, the dried mint, and a grinding of black pepper.

To serve, place the fennel, onions, crumbled feta, radicchio, endive, and watercress in a mixing bowl. Add the mussels and dressing and mix carefully.

Cook and drain the egg noodles, then sauté them briefly in butter and add the lemon juice, salt, and pepper. Use a fork to twist into six little turbans and arrange on top of salad.

SERVES SIX AS A STARTER OR LIGHT LUNCH.

olive oil

We both maintain, to differing degrees, butter-free households. Greg must avoid butter because he has to be careful with his cholesterol levels, but both of us also tend to prefer the underlying flavor olive oil imparts to many dishes. We use olive oil to cook with and as a condiment at mealtimes. In our view, there is virtually nothing which is not improved by a splash of fruity extra-virgin olive oil, whether it be a rich soup, a simple pasta, steamed crisp vegetables, grilled meats, chicken, and fish, or a few humble leaves of lettuce.

Olive oil is the universal cooking medium of the Middle East and Mediterranean, and there is a wealth of literature praising its nutritional virtues, which we briefly touch on here. Beware of fanaticism, though; some dishes simply have to be made from butter. In Middle Eastern cooking, these tend to be elaborate dishes like pastries, cookies, and cakes, which are eaten sparingly on special occasions.

Choosing a good extra-virgin olive oil has become a little like choosing a fine wine. Whether you choose a peppery Tuscan oil, a sweet, fruity Spanish, a bold, pungent Greek, a lighter, floral French, or a boutique Australian or California oil will depend on your personal preference. It makes sense to experiment and try all kinds of different oils.

OLIVE OIL AND CHOLESTEROL

It is universally acknowledged that replacing part of the animal-fat content of our diet with olive oil can radically reduce levels of cholesterol. Current research centers on two main types of lipoproteins: low-density lipoproteins and high-density lipoproteins. The low-density ones (the bad guys) move cholesterol around the body and leave deposits in the arteries and body tissue. They increase with our consumption of saturated animal fats. However, high-density lipoproteins (the good guys) have actually been shown to eliminate cholesterol from cells.

Polyunsaturated fats (found in sunflower and vegetable oils) have been shown to reduce both kinds of lipoprotein, whereas only monounsaturated fats reduce the level of the bad cholesterol and actually increase the good. Oils such as canola, peanut, sunflower, and nut oils all contain varying small levels of monounsaturated fats, but olive oil has the highest percentage of all, by far (55–83 percent).

As well as being good for the heart, olive oil also contains small levels of a range of other nutrients and antioxidants, which are thought to play a part in reducing the risk of developing cancers. Extra-virgin olive oil, the purest form, has the widest range of all these.

A word of caution, however: despite its good qualities, olive oil is still a fat, and therefore high in calories. If you are concerned about your weight, it makes sense to limit your consumption of all oils and fats. However, you might choose to use extra-virgin olive oil, as its stronger flavor means that you will be inclined to use only small amounts.

SELECTING AND STORING OLIVE OIL

LIGHT OLIVE OIL This is not light in terms of calories, as the labeling might lead us to think, but rather in terms of flavor. This type of oil is a blend of lesser-quality oils, which have been refined to give a mild, neutral flavor.

"PURE" OLIVE OIL This is a blend of refined oils with lesser-quality unrefined virgin olive oil to give it some flavor. It is best used for general cooking purposes.

VIRGIN OLIVE OIL Virgin olive oil is extracted from the fruit by means which do not alter it in any way. This essentially means that no solvents and only minimal heat are used in the extraction process. The oil is not refined in any way and is not blended with other oils. Virgin olive oil is graded by its acidity: the lower the better. Less-expensive virgin olive oils have an acidity of 1.5–3 percent.

EXTRA-VIRGIN OLIVE OIL This is the purest form of the oil, with the best flavor and lowest levels of acidity (below 1 percent). It is also the most expensive. Some extra-virgin olive oils are labelled "first pressed" or "cold pressed," which mean little when used by the big brand-name commercial manufacturers – most olive oil these days is extracted using megapresses, which extract the maximum amount of oil from just one press.

Small estates that press their own extra-virgin olive oils are a different matter. They fall under the same classification system, but are hugely superior. These oils may be extracted from organically grown olives using old-fashioned stone-milling techniques and minimal filtering. If they are labelled "cold pressed," it really does mean that no heat has been used to enhance the extraction process. "First pressed" means that the bottle contains only oil from the initial pressing.

When buying extra-virgin olive oils, there are all manner of fancy-shaped bottles and names to choose from, particularly in trendy food stores and delicatessens. If you live near an olive-growing area, you may find some locally produced single-estate oils which are excellent; otherwise, try selecting from the large range of imported oils from small producers in Italy, France, Spain, and Greece. These can be very pricey, but the aroma, depth, and complexity of flavor will knock your socks off!

It is best to buy expensive oils in small quantities, so experiment and choose a different one each time. Olive oil deteriorates with age and in light, so store it in a cool cupboard or larder, and try to use it within a year of purchase.

USING OLIVE OIL

For all-purpose frying and cooking, it is best to choose a mild-flavored, good-quality "pure" olive oil, and this is what we mean in all recipes when we refer to "olive oil." Most supermarkets sell their own house brands as well as a range of imported Spanish, Greek, and Italian oils. As a rule, most major brands will have a consistent and reasonably acceptable flavor.

Extra-virgin olive oil – especially the really expensive stuff – is better used in dishes in which you can appreciate its fine flavor. Use it liberally as a condiment: drizzle onto soups or braised dishes just before serving; sprinkle over your favorite pasta dish; brush it on grilled fish, poultry, and meats; make a little well in the surface of dips and purées and fill with oil; always dress salad leaves with a home-made olive-oil dressing; and splash it over fresh sun-ripened tomatoes with freshly torn basil leaves.

Olive oil is a very good choice for deep-fried dishes. You might think that it is more expensive than a polyunsaturated oil such as corn or sunflower oil, but these can only be used once. Leading Australian nutritionist Rosemary Stanton says that olive oil may be used up to 40 times, if strained after each use, whereas polyunsaturated oils develop dangerous chemical compounds if reheated. She also advocates deep-frying, as food which is deep-fried at hotter temperatures actually absorbs less fat than food that is shallow-fried.

PRESERVED-LEMON OIL

The variety of flavored oils is really only limited by your imagination. Preserved-Lemon Oil is a firm favorite of ours. It should be used to add flavor to dishes, not for frying or cooking. It makes a surprising tangy change in vinaigrettes and salad dressings. Or drizzle it straight onto fish or poultry after grilling.

2 Preserved Lemons with Honey (page 170), skin only

2 lemons, cut into quarters

1 teaspoon coriander seeds, crushed

½ teaspoon black peppercorns, crushed

1 cup olive oil

SCRAPE THE FLESH OUT of the preserved lemons and discard. Finely dice the skins and place into a 1-pint jar with the fresh lemon quarters, the coriander seeds, and the black peppercorns. In a saucepan, gently warm the oil to blood temperature and pour over the lemons. Seal the jar tightly and allow to sit, undisturbed, for 3 days.

Strain the oil through a tea towel, allowing it to drain naturally. Don't be tempted to push it through, as this will cloud the oil. Pour it into a sterilized bottle, reseal, and use as desired.

This infused oil will keep up to a month in a cool, dark cupboard.

GREEN-OLIVE MAYONNAISE

2 egg yolks
1 teaspoon Dijon mustard
1 teaspoon white wine vinegar
1 cup olive oil
juice of ½ lemon

1 tablespoon green olives, chopped
  very fine
1 tablespoon baby capers
salt and pepper

WHISK THE EGG YOLKS with the mustard and vinegar until they are light and creamy. Gradually add the olive oil, drop by drop, ensuring each amount is incorporated before adding more. When about half has been added, you should have a very thick, glossy paste. Loosen the mixture with the lemon juice and then continue to add the olive oil in a slow trickle.

Mix the olives and capers and add to the mayonnaise, taste and adjust seasoning, and serve.

olives

We twenty-first-century folk consider ourselves pretty clever, with the sophisticated food-processing techniques we have at hand to help us manufacture and manipulate all sorts of fancy new foodstuffs. And yet consider the miracle wrought by our forebears on one of the most ancient trees we know: it seems barely credible that early cultures were able to develop ways of extracting oil from the hard little fruit of the olive tree, let alone work out a way to make these same fruit edible.

The olive tree is inextricably entwined with the history and development of Mediterranean civilizations. The olive tree has been cultivated for over 6,000 years, beginning in Palestine and Syria. It was here that the wild tree developed into a sturdy, compact, oil-rich variety which quickly spread westward to flourish all around the rocky coastlines of the Mediterranean. The great ancient civilizations of Crete, Egypt, Greece, and Rome revered the olive's oil. It was used in ritual and religion, to light their temples, to anoint their bodies, and also to work a more mundane transformation on their daily bread. Through the ages the olive branch has become a symbol of peace, constancy, and wisdom — one might almost say of civilization itself.

It remains a mystery when the discovery was first made that the small, bitter berries of the olive tree could be made edible by a complex curing process. Soaking in lye, rinsing, salting, and preserving in oil or brine with herbs and other aromatics results in a unique, complex taste sensation — at once salty, bitter, and pungent, with a hint of ripe sweetness. It is hardly surprising that cured olives quickly became a staple of the Mediterranean and Middle Eastern diet.

Each olive-growing country produces its own style of olive, the variations depending on soil, climate, and local tradition. Green olives are young fruit, harvested when they are still rock-hard and unripe. Left on the tree, they slowly ripen to a soft purple, and finally to rich black. From here, the curing process complete, there is a bewildering range of sizes, shapes, textures, and flavors: big, juicy kalamata olives from Greece; small, intensely flavored niçoise olives; garlicky, chili-spiced olives found in the souks of Morocco; and plump, almond-stuffed green olives from Spain.

Different regions also eat olives in very different ways. Countries to the east, such as Egypt, Greece, Turkey, Lebanon, and Syria, don't really use olives in cooked dishes. They eat predominantly black olives as appetizers, side dishes, snacks, and garnishes. To the west, countries like Morocco, Tunisia, Spain, Portugal, Italy, and France make more use of green olives. They also like to use olives, both green and black, as an ingredient in many cooked dishes.

SELECTING AND STORING OLIVES

In the souks of the Middle East, you are absolutely expected to taste before you buy, and the best advice we can give for choosing olives anywhere in the world is to do just this. There are so many different sorts to choose from, and they vary in flavor and quality so much, that it really is important to taste them first. For these reasons too, it is much better to buy olives where they are sold loose rather than bottled.

As a very general rule, green olives tend to have a lighter, grassier flavor, with firmer flesh, which clings to the stone. Softer and juicier, black olives tend to have a stronger and more complex flavor. Olives are often sold flavored with all sorts of herbs and aromatics – bay leaves, rosemary, fennel, lemon, and orange peel are all popular.

Olives do not have to be kept refrigerated as long as they are stored in an airtight container in a cool, dark cupboard. If you do prefer to keep them in the refrigerator, make sure you allow them to return to room temperature before serving, to bring out their flavor.

USING OLIVES

If you intend to use olives in cooking, you run across the unavoidable chore of having to stone them. It is a fiddly job, but it has to be done. Ready-stoned olives tend to be poorer-quality rejects which may have been damaged during the harvesting or curing process. As a rule, the soft, squishy black olives are much easier to stone than green olives, which often leave a lot of their flesh behind on the stone. The quickest, but least delicate, way of stoning them is to give them a good, sharp bash with a rolling pin, which splits them open. It should then be quite easy to pull the stone away. If you want to do a neater job, then carefully slice them lengthways with a sharp knife, twist them apart, and pry the stone out with your fingernails.

As a rule, it is best to add olives to hot dishes, like braises and stews, at the end of cooking. This will ensure that they retain their shape and texture, and that their strong, salty flavor doesn't overpower the dish.

COARSE TAPENADE SALAD

A robust salad full of strong salty flavors. Serve it with grilled lamb or beef.

~~~~~~

juice of 1 lemon

3 tablespoons extra-virgin olive oil

1 cup black olives, stoned and diced

1 strip bacon, finely chopped and
   sautéed until crisp

1 small purple onion, roughly diced

1 clove garlic, finely sliced

6 anchovies, rinsed and cut into thirds

1 red bell pepper, roasted, peeled,
   and cut into ½-inch dice

freshly ground black pepper

1 tablespoon fresh thyme leaves,
   chopped

1 tablespoon baby capers, rinsed

1 serrano chili, deseeded and finely
   chopped

1 cup parsley leaves, shredded

WHISK TOGETHER the lemon juice and olive oil. Thoroughly combine all ingredients and serve.

BLACK-OLIVE CREAM

Light, lemony, and with a sweet honey undertone, this delicate cream is delicious with any robust white fish. Serve a big blob of it with grilled or sautéed snapper or John Dory. It is also good swirled into thick bean or lentil soups. Choose a good-flavored fleshy olive, such as kalamata.

~~~~~~

½ cup black kalamata olives, stoned

3 tablespoons olive oil

⅔ cup cream

zest of ½ lemon

1 teaspoon honey

PLACE THE OLIVES in a saucepan with the oil, cream, lemon zest, and honey. Bring them to the boil, then lower the heat and simmer for 15 minutes. Remove them from the heat and allow them to cool completely. Purée. Chill.

GREEN-OLIVE AND LENTIL DIP

This sludgy green lentil dip is fabulous with garlicky pork sausages or smoked ham. Serve it with a drizzle of extra-virgin olive oil.

~~~~~~

½ cup brown lentils

1 tablespoon brandy

¾ cup pitted green olives

1 tablespoon small capers

2 anchovies

2 cloves garlic

½ teaspoon chili flakes

1 tablespoon dried oregano

juice of 1 lemon

3 tablespoons extra-virgin olive oil

salt

freshly ground black pepper

COOK THE LENTILS in twice their volume of water at a rapid boil for 30 minutes, then strain them, reserving half a cup of the liquid. Place the lentils in a blender with the brandy and purée while warm.

Cover the olives in warm water and soak for 20 minutes, then drain. Rinse the capers and anchovies. In a heavy saucepan, cook the olives, garlic, chili, and oregano with the reserved cooking liquid and boil for 5 minutes, until the liquid has evaporated.

Purée with the capers, anchovies, and lemon juice. With the motor running, add the oil very slowly, then tip into the lentil mixture and fold in well.

Check seasoning, adding salt and a grinding of pepper if needed.

orange-blossom water

One of the best holidays we had together was one enchanted late summer, when we spent a glorious few weeks pottering around Andalusia in southern Spain. We were there to explore the rich cultural heritage of the Moors – in the region's architecture, its gardens, and, naturally enough, its cuisine. During those two weeks, a benign sun shone down on us from a brilliant blue sky, and wherever we went, from the sun-dappled, elegant city squares of Jerez to the shady, winding alleyways of Seville's Jewish quarter, the scent of orange blossom enveloped us, perfuming the air with its heady magic.

When Moorish invaders conquered Spain in the eighth century, they planted their new lands extensively with citrus trees from Persia, at the eastern end of their empire. In Andalusia's southern cities they constructed grand mosques, each of which had a *patio de los naranjos* alongside, the fragrant orange trees planted in austerely elegant lines. These were the bitter Seville oranges we favor today for jams and marmalades. The Arabs loved them not just for their bittersweet fruit, but also for their fragrant blossoms, leaves, and twigs.

For many thousands of years, Persian and Arabic cooking has made liberal use of flower waters, such as rose-petal and orange-blossom. A splash or two in an elaborate meat and fruit *khoresht* will lift it to another dimension. Orange-blossom water is frequently added to thirst-quenching fruit syrups and cooling sherbets, or sprinkled over simple summer fruit salads.

In Morocco, too, they love the complex perfume of orange-blossom water and sprinkle it over the traditional salad of grated carrot, which is served in just about every Moroccan restaurant to cleanse the palate after a rich tagine. All across the Maghreb and Levant, and even in parts of Provence, a few drops of orange-blossom water flavor cookies and cakes, almond pastries and sweetmeats, milky puddings and refreshing fruit salads. It seems only natural that orange-blossom water should have a particular affinity with orangey things – and indeed just about any sweet orange dish, from a simple dish of sliced oranges to orange jellies, mousses, cakes, and cookies, is enhanced by a drop of its flower water.

In Lebanon, orange-blossom water is even added to sweetened boiling water to make *cafe blanc*. This has nothing at all to do with coffee beans but is a soothing, fragrant digestive drink, often enjoyed at bedtime to ensure a sound night's sleep.

SELECTING, STORING, AND USING ORANGE-BLOSSOM WATER

Orange-blossom water is distilled from the flowers of orange trees. In the Middle East and North Africa you can often find concentrated floral essences, which are far stronger than the diluted flower waters available in the West. You will probably have to go to a specialist Middle Eastern or Asian store to find orange-blossom water.

Orange-blossom water has a fairly intense perfume and taste: too heavy a hand will result in food tasting of soap! Start with just a few drops – some people don't like their food overly perfumed, although they are happy with the gentlest suggestion of fragrance.

PERFUMED SQUASH COUSCOUS

This is an oven-baked couscous dish with a surprise hidden layer of sweetly spiced squash. It is good served with rich braises or stews.

⁓⁓⁓

⅔ cup couscous
1 cup butternut squash, peeled
   and cut into ½-inch dice
1 teaspoon melted butter
salt and pepper
¼ teaspoon cinnamon

2 tablespoons currants, soaked in water
   for 10 minutes
1 tablespoon water
½ tablespoon butter
orange-blossom water for sprinkling

PREPARE THE COUSCOUS according to the instructions on the box, or use the quick-cook method on page 95.

Steam the squash for 5 minutes and then drain well. Brush a 7- x 10-inch baking dish with the melted butter and line the bottom with the squash. Season lightly with salt, pepper, and cinnamon.

Sprinkle the currants over the squash and then cover them with a layer of couscous. Lightly pack down and smooth the surface. Again, season lightly with salt and pepper. Drizzle a tablespoon of cold water around the edge of the dish and dot a few knobs of butter over the top of the couscous. Cover with foil and bake in a preheated 400°F oven for 15–20 minutes. Remove and sprinkle with orange-blossom water to serve.

ORANGE-BLOSSOM CLOTTED CREAM

This perfumed cream is delicious served alongside almond, orange, and lemon cakes, or with hot fruit tarts, roasted peaches, or even Sweet Nut-Stuffed Quinces (page 251).

~~~~~~

1 cup cream

¼ cup sour cream

2 tablespoons mild-flavored honey

zest of 1 orange, finely grated

1 teaspoon orange-blossom water

COMBINE ALL THE INGREDIENTS in a saucepan and very, very slowly bring them to the boil. As soon as the cream boils, lower the heat and keep it at a low simmer for 5 minutes. Tip it into a glass bowl and leave it overnight, outside the refrigerator, wrapped in a blanket.

Refrigerate until required.

ORANGE-BLOSSOM TART

This sweet, citrusy tart makes a pleasing change from plain lemon once in a while. Orange-blossom jam is available from Middle Eastern grocers. The quantities below are enough to line one deep 8-inch tart ring or one shallow 9-inch tart ring.

PASTRY	FILLING
1¼ cups plain flour	3 eggs, plus 1 yolk
¼ cup sugar	½ cup sugar
5 tablespoons butter, chilled	juice and zest of 1 orange
zest of ½ orange	juice and zest of 1 lemon
zest of ½ lemon	½ teaspoon orange-blossom water
1 egg, chilled	½ tablespoon orange-blossom jam
1–2 tablespoons cold milk	2¼ cups cream

PLACE THE FLOUR, SUGAR, AND BUTTER in the bowl of your food processor. Place the whole bowl, blade too, in the freezer for 10 minutes. Remove, and quickly process the ingredients to the texture of fine sand. Add the orange and lemon zest and egg and process again. Then add 1 tablespoon of the milk and process, adding the rest if required. The mix will probably still look like buttery crumbs, but if you squeeze a little in your hand, it should come together as a dough. Tip out and shape into a round. Wrap in plastic wrap and refrigerate for an hour.

After an hour, roll out the pastry fairly thinly on a well-floured work surface, then lift onto a well-greased tart pan. Trim the edges and return to the refrigerator for another hour. When you are ready to blind-bake the tart, preheat the oven to 350°F. Line the tart with foil, fill with dried beans, and bake for 10 minutes. Remove the foil and beans and cook for a further 10 minutes, or until the pastry is pale golden.

To make the filling, whisk the eggs and egg yolk with the sugar until well combined. Add the juice and zest, the orange-blossom water, and jam and stir. Pour in the cream and whisk together.

To fill the tart, simply pull out the oven tray halfway and carefully pour the filling straight into the tart shell. Gently push the shelf back in and bake for 30–40 minutes, or until just set.

Allow the tart to cool, and serve with slices of chilled fresh mangoes or peaches and a dollop of crème fraîche.

MIDDLE EASTERN LEMONADE

This is an extremely simple lemonade, requiring no sugar syrup. The gritty action of the sugar against the lemon skins releases the essential oils. They should then be left to infuse for as many hours as you can wait. Make sure you use unwaxed fruit if possible, or at the very least scrub them well before you start. Serve the lemonade with plenty of crushed ice in tall glasses, with a drop of orange-blossom water to taste. Mixed with vodka and a few shredded mint leaves, this lemonade also makes a delicious cocktail for a hot summer's day.

5 whole lemons

1 cup superfine sugar

3½ cups water

orange-blossom water to taste

WASH THE LEMONS very well, then cut them into eighths and place them in a large mixing bowl. Pour the sugar over the top and massage the lemons. The idea is to rub the sugar into the skins, so that the abrasive action releases the lemon oils, and at the same time squeeze out as much juice as possible from the flesh. After about 5 minutes, the sugar should have dissolved into a thick, sticky syrup.

Cover the bowl with plastic wrap and chill in the refrigerator for 4 hours or so.

Then add the water and return the bowl to the refrigerator to chill overnight.

Strain and serve with lots of crushed ice and a few drops of orange-blossom water to taste.

parsley

Preserved-Lemon Gremolata **209**
Natural Oysters with Parsley-Bastourma Salad **210**
Parsley Salad with Parmesan-Crumbed Brains
  and Tomato-Pomegranate Dressing **211**

Parsley is such a familiar and universal ingredient that even the most timid cook is happy to fling it about with gay abandon. We debated whether to include it in this book, as it is so commonplace – that is to say, its distinctive, vital flavor is included in just about every savory recipe you can think of, in many different cuisines. But just because something is commonplace doesn't mean it is not worth a mention!

Herbs have always been everyday ingredients for everyday folk – and not just in the kitchen, either. As early as 5,000 years ago, the Sumerians and then the Egyptians were using them to concoct healing potions and remedies. Greek, Roman, and Arab civilizations all contributed to the large body of herbal literature. Even today, a strong interest in herbalism and the healing power of plants persists. But on the whole, the medical and magical uses of herbs have dwindled, and their main role is to brighten up our food with their pungent, lively flavors.

Of all the herbs, parsley is probably the favorite, loved the world over for its abundant, vivid green leaves and its vigorous, almost peppery flavor. In classical French cuisine, parsley stalks are the backbone of the bouquet garni (with thyme and a bay leaf), which is used to flavor stocks, soups, and casseroles. Finely chopped, parsley's flavor is restrained enough to be used as a garnish for all kinds of savory dishes, either on its own or combined with equal quantities of finely chopped chervil, chives, and tarragon to make fines herbes. Italian cooks sprinkle it over pasta and risotto dishes and combine it with lemon zest and garlic to make gremolata, the classic zesty garnish for rich, sticky osso buco and other hearty soups and stews. It tempers the stronger, salty flavors of anchovy and capers in salsa verde, which accompanies poached chicken, fish, and offal or boiled meats, such as the favorite bollito misto.

Middle Eastern food is almost unthinkable without parsley. All sorts of dips and mezze dishes are garnished with roughly chopped parsley – never finely chopped, as in classical French cooking. The raw leaves are torn and tossed through countless refreshing salads, not just the ever-popular tabbouleh and fattouche. Parsley is often combined with lemon juice and garlic in dressings and marinades, which work particularly well with grilled poultry. It may also be combined with garlic and onion and other spices as a base for minced-meat dishes such as kifta, or rice stuffings for vegetables.

SELECTING AND STORING PARSLEY

Large bundles of flat-leaf parsley look a bit daunting next to those neat little posies of the curly sort, but the latter is barely known in the Middle East. Flat-leaf or Italian parsley has a much better flavor than the curly type. It is stronger and sweeter and perfectly suited to scattering around salads. Thankfully, these days it is widely available all year round.

Parsley is one herb which is totally unsatisfactory when dried. You really have to buy it fresh, but it keeps pretty well in the refrigerator. We store it in the refrigerator in a jug of water, with its head neatly tucked away in a plastic bag. If you remember to change the water every now and then, parsley lasts like this for up to a week. Alternatively, you can strip the leaves off, wash and dry them carefully, and keep them in a plastic container in the refrigerator.

USING PARSLEY

There is often grit and sand sticking to parsley leaves and stalks, so it is a good idea to wash it at least twice before picking the leaves from the stalks. A salad spinner is useful for drying them.

Parsley can be added to and will improve just about every dish imaginable, so don't reserve it for use as a garnish. Middle Easterners buy herbs such as parsley in such dauntingly large quantities because they recognize the need to use lots and lots, not just a few dainty sprigs. Remember this particularly when it comes to making herb butters and sauces, which should be bright green and thick with the herb, not pale and speckled.

PRESERVED-LEMON GREMOLATA

Gremolata is traditionally used to finish off the Italian dish osso buco, adding a sharp, tangy counterpoint to the marrow-rich, sticky dish. It can be used equally well with winter braises and stews.

1 Preserved Lemon with Honey
    (page 170), skin only, finely chopped
1 cup parsley leaves, finely chopped

1 teaspoon sumac
2 cloves garlic, finely chopped

MIX ALL THE INGREDIENTS together and use as soon as possible for the freshest flavor.

NATURAL OYSTERS WITH PARSLEY-BASTOURMA SALAD

Bastourma is a Turkish air-dried beef, which has first been rubbed with fenugreek, chili, and sugar. You can find it at Turkish butchers and some Continental delicatessens. It is strongly flavored and pungent, and very addictive. Slivers of the beef with vital, metallic parsley work as a terrific counterfoil to the briny tannin flavors of natural oysters.

6 ripe tomatoes
¼ cup sugar
¼ cup water
2 tablespoons olive oil for sautéing
½ pound bastourma, thinly sliced, then
    cut into ⅛-inch batons
1½ cups parsley leaves, shredded

1 cup artichoke leaves
7 tablespoons red wine vinegar
1 clove garlic, finely minced
7 tablespoons extra-virgin olive oil
salt and freshly ground black pepper
36 oysters, freshly opened

CUT THE TOMATOES IN HALF and scoop out the flesh and seeds.

In a heavy pan, dissolve the sugar in 2 tablespoons water. Once it is fully dissolved, simmer gently for 8 minutes, or until the syrup turns a deep golden color. Add the remaining 2 tablespoons of warm water, stir, and bring back to a simmer for 2 minutes more, until the caramel thickens.

Place the tomatoes on a rack, skin side down, and drizzle the caramel over them. Leave them to dry in a preheated 275°F oven for 6–8 hours.

Heat the olive oil in a heavy-based pan and sauté the bastourma over high heat until it is crisp (around 3–4 minutes).

Cut the caramelized tomatoes into thick strips. In a large bowl, mix together the tomatoes, bastourma, parsley, artichoke leaves, red wine vinegar, garlic, and extra-virgin olive oil. Season lightly.

For each person, arrange 6 oysters in their shells on a plate and place a heaped spoonful of the parsley salad on top of each oyster. Serve straightaway.

SERVES SIX PEOPLE AS A STARTER.

PARSLEY SALAD WITH PARMESAN-CRUMBED BRAINS AND TOMATO-POMEGRANATE DRESSING

This makes a lovely light lunch for six people. The creamy brains in their crunchy crumb are perfectly offset by the peppery, bitter leaves and tangy sweet-sour Tomato-Pomegranate Dressing (page 242).

6 sets lamb's brains, cleaned and
   soaked overnight in milk
½ lemon
1 cinnamon stick
½ onion, quartered
½ celery stick, roughly chopped
1 bay leaf
salt and pepper
2 tablespoons grated parmesan cheese
1¼ cups fresh bread crumbs
flour for dusting
1 egg
¾ cup canola oil for shallow-frying

SALAD
1½ cups parsley leaves
1½ cups watercress sprigs
1 head radicchio, leaves roughly torn
1 purple onion, sliced finely
pepper
6 small strips bacon, cut into batons and
   fried crisp
⅔ cup Tomato-Pomegranate Dressing
   (page 242)

RINSE THE BRAINS and place them in a saucepan. Cover them with cold water and add the lemon half, juice squeezed in first, with the cinnamon, onion, celery, and bay leaf. Bring slowly to the boil, then lower the heat and simmer for 3 minutes. Remove from the heat and allow the brains to cool down in the poaching liquor.

Dry each set of brains and cut it into quarters. Lightly season with salt and pepper. Combine the parmesan with the bread crumbs and begin to flour, egg, and crumb each portion of brain. Heat the oil in a wok, which is ideal for shallow-frying. Fry 6 pieces at a time for about 5 minutes, or until golden brown.

To assemble the salad, combine the parsley, watercress, and radicchio leaves in a large bowl with the onion and bacon. Season lightly with pepper and add half the Tomato-Pomegranate Dressing. Toss the leaves gently. Mound a portion in the center of each plate and carefully arrange 4 pieces of crumbed brains on the top. Drizzle extra dressing around and serve straightaway.

pastry

Most people go somewhere romantic for their honeymoon: Fiji, Venice, or Paris all fit the bill nicely. We, on the other hand, went to Beirut, with its checkered reputation for kidnapping, bullets, and bombs. But so much for preconceived notions and worries. Beirut, and indeed the rest of Lebanon, proved to be a constant delight and endless fascination during that two-week stay, and indeed on subsequent visits.

Despite the ravages of seventeen years of civil war, one thing which seems to survive, miraculously intact, is the irrepressible and overwhelming warmth of Arab hospitality. Every home we visited seemed to be mysteriously prepared for guests – their coffee tables were always set with little dishes of pistachio nuts, Turkish delight, or other exotic sweets. Our arrival would cause a flurry of excitement, kisses, and questions and, of course, instant refreshments. As if from nowhere, cardamom-scented coffee would appear, poured from exquisitely engraved brass pots into tiny cups, always accompanied by sweet nut-stuffed biscuits or elaborate sticky pastries.

Both the Arab and Ottoman empires excelled in the art of making pastries, cakes, and cookies. Their influence can be seen right across the Mediterranean in an endless variety of sweet and savory pastries, ranging from the universally popular baklava and kataifi to savory phyllo pies, such as Greek spanakopita and bisteeya, the extraordinary cinnamon-spiced pigeon pie from Morocco, to Lebanese phyllow "cigars," Turkish boreks, and Tunisian briks à l'oeuf.

SELECTING, STORING, AND USING PASTRY

Many of the Middle Eastern–style recipes that follow, both sweet and savory, require special kinds of pastry which are virtually impossible to make at home. What a bonus for the weary home cook!

There are many different brands of commercially available phyllo, and a few of kataifi, many of which are frozen. However, quality is variable, and they are often not stored well, which means you can end up with a packet of torn, sticky phyllo sheets with crumpled corners, or kataifi which is too crushed to unravel. If you buy your pastry frozen, do not refreeze it, but wrap and seal it carefully and store it in the refrigerator, where it will keep for a few days. If you have the inclination, it is worthwhile tracking down good-quality Greek or Lebanese freshly made versions.

As far as preparation goes, the same rules apply for phyllo and kataifi, in both savory and sweet dishes. Only take from the packet as much pastry as you think you'll need. Carefully wrap and seal the remainder and put it back into the refrigerator. These pastries really must be used immediately, as they dry out and harden surprisingly quickly in the air. If you are assembling individual pastries, one at a time, place one sheet of phyllo or a small bundle of kataifi on the work surface and cover the rest with a damp cloth. Both phyllo and kataifi need to be liberally brushed with butter or ghee to get the required golden crunchiness. This is no time to be worrying about cholesterol!

Techniques for other home-made pastry doughs are explained as appropriate.

SAVORY PASTRY

Savory pastries are enormously popular throughout the Middle East. As with their sweet cousins, there is a huge and varied repertoire of different shapes, sizes, and fillings found all around the Middle East and eastern Mediterranean. They are believed to have been spread by the Arabs and the Ottoman Turks, and are also a specialty of the Sephardic Jewish tradition, probably learned in Spain under Moorish rule.

Each region, community, and family has its own favorites. Pastries can be made from crisp, wafer-thin phyllo or a flaky type of puff pastry or a denser yeast dough. They can be deep-fried or baked. Fillings can be anything from spicy minced meat, poultry, or offal to lemony spinach, meltingly soft eggplant, or tangy, salty cheese. Some are tried and tested combinations, while others are just a good way of using up leftover bits and pieces. Favourite shapes are little triangles, cigars, crescents, rectangular parcels, and little round, raised pies.

Smaller pastries, such as Lebanese fatayer, Syrian sambusek, Tunisian briks, Turkish boreks, and even Spanish empanadas, are eaten as snacks or as part of a mezze selection. Other, larger pies, such as the Greek spanakopita or Moroccan bisteeya, can be more substantial dishes.

Overall, savory pastries are an important part of the mezze culture. This idea is central to the Arab tradition of hospitality, friendship, and generosity. A mezze selection can be as simple as a dish of olives and some freshly cut-up vegetables and dips, or it can be a range of elaborately made bite-sized morsels which tempt the eye far beyond the stomach's capacity. If you are ever lucky enough to be invited to an Arab home for a special occasion, you will almost certainly not have enough room left for the main course once you have succumbed to the temptation of tasting every mezze dish on the table.

Many of these little parcels can be fairly labor-intensive and time-consuming to prepare, especially in the large quantities which are required for special occasions and parties. There is still a tradition among some of our Egyptian friends and our Lebanese in-laws for several generations of women to get together to make big batches of little savory pies like sambusek for a family party.

Savory Arab pastries make a deliciously different starter, or the perfect light lunch accompanied by a simple green salad. They make a terrific alternative to quiches and can be very easy to make. After all, the concept is pretty straightforward – crisp pastry parcels with some kind of tasty filling. The options are endless.

TUNISIAN BRIKS WITH BRAINS

Briks are probably the best-known Tunisian snack food and are sold just about everywhere in Tunisia. They are traditionally made from the same type of paper-thin pastry as the *warka* pastry used in bisteeya. This is often sold as brik pastry, but it is hard to find, and phyllo will do just as well, or, at a pinch, Chinese spring-roll wrappers. The fillings are numerous, but mashed tuna fish, spinach and cheese, or creamy brains are favorites. Briks nearly always include an egg, which is broken onto the filling. The pastry is then carefully wrapped up and the whole parcel quickly deep-fried. The idea is to eat them immediately, so the egg yolk is still runny when you bite into the crispy pastry.

---

6 sets of lamb's brains, cleaned
   and soaked overnight in milk
½ lemon
1 stick cinnamon
½ onion, quartered
½ stick celery
a few parsley sprigs

1 bay leaf
salt and pepper
4 tablespoons melted butter
6 sheets phyllo pastry
12 large mint leaves
3 teaspoons Chermoula (page 72)
6 egg yolks

SOAK THE BRAINS OVERNIGHT, and when you are ready to cook, rinse them well and place them in a saucepan. Cover with cold water and add the half lemon – squeeze in the juice first – and the cinnamon stick, onion, celery stick, parsley, and bay leaf. Bring the water slowly to the boil, then lower the heat and simmer for 3 minutes. Remove the pan from the heat and allow the brains to cool down in the poaching liquor. When they are completely cold, remove the brains from the liquor, pat them dry, and lightly season them with salt and pepper.

Take a round soufflé or ramekin dish (3 inches diameter) and brush inside with melted butter. Take one sheet of phyllo pastry and brush it with melted butter. Fold it in half and brush it with butter again, then fold it in half again. Carefully place the phyllo pastry square inside the ramekin so that it covers the base and comes up the sides.

Lay a mint leaf on the bottom and place one set of brains upside down, on top. Carefully smear a scant teaspoon of Chermoula over the surface and then gently spoon an egg yolk into the hollow at the center of the brains. Season lightly with salt and pepper, then lay a second mint leaf over the top of the egg yolk and fold the pastry sides up and over to completely cover the filling.

Repeat for the remaining 5 briks.

Bake in a preheated 425°F oven for 8 minutes, or until the briks are golden brown. Remove from the oven and carefully turn each brik out. Put back into the ramekin, right side up, and return to the oven for another 4–5 minutes at 400°F, or until the top is golden brown.

Serve straightaway.

MAKES SIX BRIKS.

CILANTRO AND PRAWN BRIOUATS

Serve these deliciously flaky fragrant pastries with a blob of Preserved-Lemon Guacamole (page 171), a splash of Green Harissa (page 87), or even a creamy Cilantro and Soft-Boiled-Egg Vinaigrette (page 88).

½ pound raw prawn meat
1 tablespoon olive oil
2 shallots, finely sliced
1 tablespoon Chermoula (page 72)
½ cup fresh cilantro leaves and stalks, roughly chopped
½ cup fresh mint leaves, roughly chopped

1 egg yolk
salt and pepper
3 sheets phyllo pastry
egg wash, made from 1 egg and 1 teaspoon water
¾ cup vegetable oil for shallow frying

PEEL THE PRAWNS and chop into smallish pieces, about ¼ inch.

Heat a tablespoon of olive oil in a frying pan, then add the shallots and Chermoula and stir for a minute to bring out the flavor of the spices. Remove from the heat and add to the prawn meat. Then add the cilantro, mint, and egg yolk, season with salt and pepper, and mix together lightly.

Lay a sheet of phyllo out and cut it into thirds lengthways. Each strip makes one briouat. Take one strip and brush with egg wash. Place 1 tablespoon of prawn mixture across the corner of one end. Fold this corner up and over on the diagonal, to make a triangle shape. Fold the triangle over, and continue in this fashion all along the pastry strip. Trim any extra little pieces of pastry. You should end up with a nice triangle-shaped pastry parcel. Seal any open edges with egg wash. Repeat to make 7 more pastries.

Shallow-fry these pastries – a wok is ideal – two at a time until they are golden brown. It should take about 2 minutes on each side. If they brown too quickly, then lower the temperature, wait a few minutes, and try again.

Remove them from the oil and drain them on absorbent paper.

SERVES FOUR PEOPLE (TWO EACH) AS A STARTER.

PRAWNS WRAPPED IN ALMOND KATAIFI

Don't think that kataifi is used only for sweet pastries. It works just as well for many savory pies. Serve these as a spectacularly simple starter, with a sprinkle of Preserved-Lemon Gremolata (page 209), a drizzle of extra-virgin olive oil, and a big dollop of Saffron Yogurt Cheese (page 320).

~~~~~~

12 king prawns
salt and pepper
1 Preserved Lemon with Honey (page 170)
½ package kataifi pastry
⅔ cup melted butter

⅔ cup sliced almonds, fried in 1 tablespoon olive oil
1 tablespoon Preserved-Lemon Gremolata (page 209)
extra-virgin olive oil
1 cup Saffron Yogurt Cheese (page 320)

REMOVE THE BODY SHELLS and legs from the prawns, keeping the heads and tails intact. Cut carefully along the back and remove any black intestines. Lightly season with salt and pepper. Scrape away the flesh from the preserved lemon and cut the skin into ⅛-inch strips. Lay a strip of lemon along the groove in each prawn's back.

Carefully unfold the kataifi pastry into one "skein" and ease away one half. (Return the rest to the package, seal tightly, and refrigerate or freeze for future use.)

Trim the pastry to 8 inches and carefully divide it into 12 long sections. Take one section (cover the rest with a damp tea towel), bunch the strands together tightly, and lay out in a strip along the work surface. Brush all down the length of the pastry strands with the melted butter and then sprinkle with the sliced almonds.

Lay a prawn, head touching tail, at one end of the pastry, and roll it up tightly to make a fat pastry cocoon around the body. Trim so any excess pastry is tucked underneath the prawn. Repeat with the remaining prawns. Cover them with a damp tea towel and refrigerate for at least half an hour before baking.

Preheat the oven to 350°F. Place the prawns on an oven tray lined with baking paper and cook until the pastry is golden brown and crisp.

SERVES SIX PEOPLE (TWO EACH) OR FOUR HUNGRY PEOPLE (THREE EACH).

SAMBUSEK

These crescent-shaped pastries are very similar to Turkish boreks. Our Egyptian friend Denise and her mother, Rachel, make a version which is legendary among her friends. She uses ordinary cheddar cheese for a filling, which sounds banal, but they are absolutely delicious. This version, however, uses the classic Middle Eastern combination of spinach (you could also use Swiss chard) and feta cheese, lifted with a dash of pomegranate essence. The crunch comes from hazelnuts, although traditionalists would probably use pine nuts, which are pricier. Serve them as party snacks or as a mezze dish. Sambusek are also good as a starter drizzled with a tangy Avgolemono sauce (page 173) or the creamy Cilantro and Soft-Boiled-Egg Vinaigrette (page 88).

The dough for Sambusek is easy to make – we favor a mixture of oil and butter and self-raising flour. To make the little crescent shapes, pinch off a walnut-sized piece of dough and roll it into a thin round circle (approx. 3 inches in diameter) using a well-oiled glass bottle. Place a heaped teaspoon of your choice of filling into the middle, fold the dough over, and shape the pie into a crescent. Traditionally the edges are then pinched and twisted to seal.

PASTRY
2 cups self-raising flour
2 tablespoons butter, chilled
¼ teaspoon salt
a pinch sugar
¼–½ cup warm water

FILLING
2 tablespoons olive oil
2 shallots, finely chopped
1 clove garlic, crushed with
    ¼ teaspoon salt
2 bunches spinach, leaves picked and
    washed twice
¾ cup toasted hazelnuts, skin rubbed
    away
¼ cup feta cheese
¼ teaspoon ground allspice
juice and finely chopped zest of 1 lemon
1 tablespoon hazelnut oil (or any other
    nut oil)
1 teaspoon pomegranate molasses
egg wash, made from 1 egg and
    1 teaspoon water

PLACE THE FLOUR, chilled butter, salt, and sugar in a food processor, and process until the mixture is the consistency of fine bread crumbs. Gradually add enough lukewarm water for the mixture to just come together in a dough. Allow to rest for half an hour before using.

Heat the oil in a pan and sauté the shallots and garlic for 3–4 minutes, until they have softened. Throw in the spinach leaves, turning them as they wilt down. When all the spinach has collapsed and softened, tip it into a colander and press out the moisture well.

Lightly crush the hazelnuts in a mortar and pestle.

Put the spinach into a mixing bowl and add the hazelnuts, feta, allspice, lemon juice and zest, hazelnut oil, and pomegranate molasses and mix together thoroughly.

Preheat the oven to 400°F. To make the Sambusek, roll out the pastry on a floured surface to around ⅛-inch thickness. Cut out pastry circles using a 3-inch pastry cutter and brush half of each with the egg wash. Place a tablespoon of the mixture in the center of each circle. Fold the pastry over to make a half-moon shape and pinch or crimp the edges to seal. Brush with more egg wash and place the pastries on a nonstick baking sheet.

Bake on the middle shelf for 10 minutes, or until golden brown.

MAKES AROUND 15 SAMBUSEK.

SWEET PASTRY

In the Middle East, desserts tend to revolve around fresh fruit. Sweet pastries are considered something of a luxury and are reserved for special occasions and entertaining. There are countless varieties of these honeyed golden pastries, with all sorts of suggestive shapes and names – ladies' fingers, sweethearts' lips, lovers' navels, to name a few. Many of these appear all around the Middle East and eastern Mediterranean, sporting different names and slightly different fillings depending on the region.

Sweet pastries are part of the Arab tradition of hospitality and friendship. A beautifully wrapped box of these sweetmeats is quite the correct gift to take when visiting, and, in turn, no self-respecting Arab hostess would be without a selection of goodies in her pantry to offer guests. However, most Middle Eastern women no longer have the time to spend making their own pastries – except, maybe, for a family celebration or party. These days, they are more likely to buy their selection from a specialist pastry shop which bakes its own, where the variety can be mind-boggling, and where they can be assured of excellent quality.

Of the huge range of Middle Eastern pastries, baklava are probably the best known to us in the West, as they are served in just about every Greek and Lebanese restaurant around the world. These are the small lozenge-shaped pastries made from layers of phyllo pastry, which sandwich a filling of ground pistachio nuts, walnuts, or almonds, perhaps flavored with a touch of cinnamon, and are drenched in an orange-blossom syrup.

Kataifi (or konafi) are the pastries made from the special dough which looks remarkably like shredded wheat. They too are made with a range of different fillings, such as walnuts, pistachios, and even soft cream cheese. Then there are the long cigar-shaped pastries or the snail-like spirals or the ones which look like little birds' nests – the list goes on and on!

The recipes below are decidedly nontraditional. For authentic Middle Eastern pastries, we suggest you do what most Middle Eastern home cooks would do, and seek out a really good Middle Eastern pastry shop. This will allow you to sample many more pastries than you could ever make at home.

CARAMEL-PEAR KATAIFI WITH
PINE-NUT PRALINE AND GINGER CREAM

These are warm, rich flavors for the autumn: sticky, caramelized slices of pear, buttery, crisp birds' nests of pastry, and a spicy whipped Ginger Cream (page 147).

8 Bartlett pears
¾ cup sugar
½ cup (1 stick) melted butter
¼ cup apple juice

½ package kataifi pastry
Ginger Cream (page 147) to serve
½ cup Pine-Nut Praline (page 231)

PEEL THE PEARS, cut them in half, and remove the cores. Then cut each piece into ½-inch slices. Place the sugar in a pan and heat gently until it dissolves and just begins to color. Add the pears and 2 tablespoons of the butter. Sauté until the pears are well coated with caramel. Add the apple juice and cook for another minute until the caramel thickens.

Unravel the kataifi into a straight, long piece and divide it into 8 equal portions. Keep the remaining portions covered as you work. Take one section and curl it into a 2½-inch pastry cutter to form a perfectly round "birds' nest." Lift the cutter away and drizzle the pastry with melted butter. Repeat with remaining sections. Brush a baking sheet with butter and gently place the nests on the sheet. Bake them in a preheated 400°F oven for 6–8 minutes until they are golden brown. Remove them from the oven and dry them on kitchen paper.

When ready to serve, place a kataifi nest in the center of each plate. Spoon the pears on top, then add a dollop of the Ginger Cream and a sprinkling of the Pine-Nut Praline. Place another kataifi nest on the top and sprinkle extra praline around the plate. Drizzle extra caramel around.

SERVES EIGHT.

HONEY-CURD PIES WITH ROSE-SCENTED FIGS

These little raised pies are made from fresh ricotta cheese, flavored with honey, orange zest, and sherry-soaked currants. They are similar to many Jewish cream-cheese desserts, but not nearly as sweet as you might imagine. Serve them with rose-scented fresh figs, fresh white peaches in caramel, mixed summer berries, or simply a drizzle of maple syrup.

1 cup ricotta cheese
2 tablespoons currants, soaked for
    10 minutes in 2 tablespoons sherry
4 tablespoons sliced almonds
zest of 1 lemon, finely chopped
1 teaspoon cinnamon
1 egg
4 tablespoons mild honey

2 tablespoons butter
6 sheets phyllo pastry
12 fresh ripe figs
6 teaspoons rose water
1 cup sugar
4 pounds ice cubes
confectioner's sugar to dust

PREHEAT THE OVEN to 400°F. Then, in a large bowl, mix together the cheese, currants and any excess sherry, almonds, zest, cinnamon, egg, and 1 tablespoon of the honey until they are well blended. Melt the butter.

Lay a sheet of phyllo on your work surface and brush it with melted butter and fold. Repeat the folding and brushing twice more. Place a heaped teaspoon of the cheese mixture in the center of each pastry square. Brush the sides with more butter, then gather up the corners and sides over the mixture and flatten slightly to form a little ball-shaped pie. Repeat with the remaining pastry and filling to make a total of 6 pies.

Place the pies on a lightly greased baking sheet, brush them all over with butter, and cook them on the top shelf of the oven for 8–10 minutes until golden brown.

Meanwhile, cut the figs in half and lay them, cut side up, in a flat dish. Sprinkle with the rose water and sugar. Then pour ice cubes into a deep metal tray and lay the dish of figs on top of them (this ensures the figs don't cook through). Place the tray under a very hot preheated broiler for 1–2 minutes until the figs caramelize.

To serve, remove the pastries from the oven and dust them with a little confectioner's sugar. Serve immediately with the rose-flavored figs and cream.

SERVES SIX.

ARAB PANCAKES WITH FRESH MANGOES
AND ORANGE-BLOSSOM CLOTTED CREAM

These thick, fluffy little pancakes are traditionally made with a yeast batter. If you want a lighter, airier version, you can use baking powder to raise them or, as in this recipe, egg whites. Like their counterparts in the West, these pancakes are a great favorite all over the Middle East, where they are often bought ready-made from the bakery and stuffed with Arab clotted cream (*eishta*), chopped pistachios, and rose-petal jam, and drizzled with syrup. The following pancakes are a lighter version, delicious on their own with whipped cream or butter and maple syrup. But layered with slices of luscious mango and rich Orange-Blossom Clotted Cream (page 203), they are out of this world.

~~~~~~

3 egg yolks

⅓ cup sugar

2 cups self-raising flour

zest of 1 orange, finely chopped

2 drops vanilla essence

1 cup milk

3 egg whites

2 mangoes, cheeks sliced off, peeled, and cut into thick slices

Orange-Blossom Clotted Cream

WHISK THE EGG YOLKS with half the sugar. Mix in the flour, orange zest, and vanilla, and then add the milk slowly, ensuring there are no lumps. The batter should be like a thick pouring cream.

Whip the egg whites with the remaining sugar until they form soft peaks, and carefully fold them into the batter. Fry spoonfuls of batter in a nonstick pan.

Fold the pancakes over and stuff with a generous dollop of Orange-Blossom Clotted Cream and a few slices of mango. Drizzle with a little caramel or maple syrup, or a little dried-lime sugar syrup (page 313), and eat straightaway.

MAKES AROUND 12 PANCAKES.

pine nuts

On warm summer days, when the heady aroma of basil perfumes the air, many a young cook's fancy turns to pesto. If you have experienced the pleasure of making your own vivid green pesto sauce, you will have also experienced the pain associated with the pine nut's hefty price tag.

These tiny golden kernels come from the cones of the stone pine tree, which is native to the southern Mediterranean. Their harvest is a long and labor-intensive business, and the yield is proportionally extremely small. But their rich, creamy texture and sweet, piney flavor make them well worth the effort.

All around the Mediterranean and in the Middle East, the legacy of the Arabs is clearly visible in the number of different dishes which combine pine nuts with fruit, such as currants or raisins, often in a tangy sweet-sour base. Spinach salads with pine nuts and currants can be found in many different Mediterranean regions, from Portugal and Spain through to Provence and Italy. In Sicily they are crushed into a kind of sweet-sour salsa, also with currants, and served as an accompaniment to grilled sardines. In fact there are countless dressings and sauces made thick with crushed pine nuts, of which the best known is undoubtedly the Genovese favorite, pesto. In Lebanon, pine nuts are often ground with bread, lemon juice, and olive oil to make the dressing called *tarator*.

Pine nuts are also dearly loved for the flavor and crunch they add to many dishes, ranging from hot savory pilafs and rice stuffings to refreshing cool salads. They are also used in more extravagant sweet cookies and cakes as a special treat.

SELECTING AND STORING PINE NUTS

In North America, the most readily available pine nuts come from the western United States and Mexico. Harder to find, but worth seeking out, are the long, elegant Lebanese pine nuts. You will probably be able to find them in a specialist nut shop or Middle Eastern store, and they are well worth tracking down for their creamy-soft texture and buttery flavor, with complex, piney overtones.

Like all nuts, pine nuts are high in fat (mostly unsaturated), which means they should be stored in the refrigerator and used quickly.

USING PINE NUTS

Many dishes around the Middle East and Mediterranean use pine nuts as a pleasing, crunchy garnish for salads and rice dishes. As with most nuts, toasting or frying intensifies and mellows their flavor. But watch them carefully so that they don't burn. It is probably wise to toast them in a dry frying pan, rather than roast them in the oven, as this gives you far greater control. It only takes a few minutes of gentle tossing over low to medium heat. Don't get impatient and leave them to sit still, as they burn surprisingly quickly.

Like many other nuts, pine nuts are also a sublime ingredient in confectionery and are a firm favorite in Mediterranean countries. The Italians make them into a praline, *croccante di pignoli*, which is often scented with lemon or orange peel, and they work equally well in buttery, sweet cookies and in almondy tarts, such as the Provençal *tarte aux pignons*.

FRIED PINE-NUT GNOCCHI

Finely ground semolina sometimes replaces flour in Middle Eastern countries, particularly for desserts. Here it is cooked a little like an Italian polenta and enlivened with cheese and a pine-nut crunch. You can make these gnocchi a day ahead.

~~~~~~

1 quart milk
2 cups fine semolina
2 egg yolks
3½ tablespoons butter
1½ cups pine nuts, fried in oil
   until golden brown

½ cup parmesan cheese, grated
1 teaspoon salt
½ teaspoon pepper
flour for dusting
vegetable oil for frying

BRING THE MILK TO THE BOIL, then slowly add the semolina, whisking as you go, until it is all incorporated into a stiff paste. Lower the heat and cook at a gentle bubble for about 15–20 minutes, stirring from time to time. When cooked, the semolina grains should have dissolved into the paste. The best way to test this is to taste a little: if the mix feels grainy in your mouth, it needs further cooking.

Remove the pan from the heat and add the egg yolks, butter, fried pine nuts, and cheese, and season with salt and pepper. Pour into a buttered pan (approximately 11 x 19 inches and at least 1½ inches deep) and smooth the surface with a spatula. You should then allow the mix to rest and cool completely, for a minimum of 6 hours or even a day.

When you are ready to cook, turn the slab out onto a work surface and cut it into the desired shapes with a wet knife. These can be any shape you like, but they shouldn't be too big – 2 inches square is about right. Dust the shapes lightly in flour and deep-fry them in oil heated to 350°F for 4 minutes, or until they are golden brown. They can also be shallow-fried: it will take about 3 minutes on each side for them to color evenly.

PINE-NUT WAFERS

Surely nothing could be simpler than these cheesy little wafers. They keep for
2–3 days in an airtight container and are delicious served with predinner drinks –
a good chilled amontillado sherry would be ideal – or as an accompaniment to a
Preserved-Lemon Guacamole with Smoked Eel (page 171).

¾ cup pine nuts, roughly chopped
½ cup parmesan cheese, grated

1 teaspoon fennel seeds, roasted
and lightly crushed

IN A MIXING BOWL, combine the ingredients well.

Line a baking sheet with baking paper and sprinkle the mixture into circles
about 2½ inches in diameter and ¼ inch thick. Use an egg ring or cookie cutter
as a mold if you have one.

Bake the circles in a preheated 350°F oven for 8–10 minutes.

Remove them from the oven and allow them to cool on the baking tray, then,
using a metal spatula, carefully remove them to a cake rack and leave to cool
completely.

Store them in an airtight container.

MAKES ABOUT 12 WAFERS.

PINE-NUT PRALINE

Praline has endless uses in desserts and cakes. It works with all flavors, from chocolate to fruits, and is particularly useful for adding a bit of crunch to creamy-smooth desserts. Don't think of it just as a garnish, to sprinkle over desserts, but fold it into whipped cream to accompany rich chocolate cakes, or mix it into all sorts of ice creams, custards, and mousses to add a sweet crunch.

¾ cup sugar
2 tablespoons water
1½ cups pine nuts

PLACE THE SUGAR AND WATER in a saucepan and heat slowly to dissolve the sugar. Bring to the boil and cook for about 5 minutes until the syrup reaches the thread stage (when a drop of the syrup falls from a wooden spoon in a long thread) at about 230°F.

Stir in the pine nuts, which will make the sugar mixture crystallize as the oils come out of the nuts. Don't panic! Turn the heat down a little and stir gently until the crystallized sugar redissolves to a caramel. This will take 10–15 minutes.

Carefully (as it's hot) pour the syrup onto a baking pan lined with baking paper or greased foil. Smooth it with the back of a fork and allow it to cool down and harden.

When it is completely cold, bash it with a rolling pin to break it into chunks, and then pound it to crumbs in a mortar and pestle. The praline should be the consistency of coarse bread crumbs. It can be frozen and used as required.

MAKES 1 GOOD-SIZE CUP OF PRALINE.

PINE-NUT PRALINE ICE CREAM

This is made using the Italian method rather than the French custard-based method. It is quick and easy, virtually foolproof, and results in a luscious, creamy ice cream. To make airy, velvety-smooth ice cream at home, you really do need an ice-cream maker. Making it in the freezer compartment of the refrigerator requires constant stirring and scraping, and the result is a hard, solid block rather than the soft, airy creaminess we all love.

¾ cup water

1⅓ cups sugar

1 vanilla bean, split lengthways
   and scraped

8 egg yolks

3½ cups cream

½ cup Pine-Nut Praline (page 231)

PUT THE WATER, SUGAR, AND VANILLA BEAN in a saucepan and bring to the boil, stirring so the sugar is fully dissolved. Lower the heat and simmer for 5 minutes.

Meanwhile, place the egg yolks in an electric mixer and whisk them for about 5 minutes, until they are light and fluffy. Reduce the speed of the mixer and pour the boiling syrup in. Add the cream, mixing quickly to incorporate, then turn off the mixer.

Allow the mixture to cool for about 5 minutes, then pour it into your ice-cream maker and churn according to the manufacturer's instructions. Just before it is ready to be transferred to the freezer, add the Pine-Nut Praline and let the machine work it through the mixture. Move it to the freezer and let it firm up before serving.

SERVES FOUR TO SIX.

pistachios

We are all familiar with the pistachio nut, lightly roasted and salted, as a stylish preprandial snack. Greg's family – and indeed most Lebanese families – always seems to have a huge dish of pistachios on offer for guests, which everyone from the youngest child to the oldest grandparent eagerly scoops up by the handful. And then begins the fun of prizing open the polished shells – some stubborn ones need to be carefully cracked between the teeth – to get at the tasty morsel within.

The pistachio tree is thought to be a native of Persia, and its name derives from the Persian word *pesteh*. In their homeland, pistachio nuts grow into plump beauties with a delicious sweet flavor, worlds away from the older, shriveled-up little nuts we are more familiar with in the West. In autumn, however, freshly harvested pistachios are available, although you will have to hunt them out. These boast a vivid red-pink skin (which fades to a duller brown with age) around a bright green, juicy nut.

Sweetened and ground to a paste, pistachios impart a delicate pastel hue to ice creams. Studded into galantines, pâtés, and terrines, they add a delightful visual surprise and pleasing textural counterpoint. Finely chopped and sprinkled over Middle Eastern pastries, they add a gaudy, almost vulgar final touch.

SELECTING AND STORING PISTACHIOS
Roasted, salted pistachio nuts should be reserved for snacks. For cooking, always buy unsalted pistachios, which can be bought ready-shelled but will usually still be shrouded in their rough red-brown skin. The older they are, the darker the skin will be: fresh pistachios have a vibrant, blushing red skin. Regardless of age, the nuts need to be soaked for 5–10 minutes in boiling water – longer for older nuts – and the skin should then slip off easily. Always ensure that they are well dried before use or storage. The simplest way is to scatter them on a baking sheet and dry them in a cool oven for 10 minutes or so.

USING PISTACHIOS
Cut into slivers or finely chopped, pistachio nuts are used around the Middle East as a garnish for both savory and sweet dishes. They are a key addition to many

Persian pilafs and other Middle Eastern rice dishes, and are also delicious in meat dishes. Mixed with rice and herbs, for example, they can be stuffed into a whole boned chicken, which is then roasted and sliced to reveal the bright green nuts within.

Naturally, their delicate sweetness makes them ideal for desserts and pastries. Coarsely ground pistachio nuts are a popular festive stuffing for special-occasion sweet pastries such as baklava or the Easter cookie *ma'amoul*. Chopped pistachios are also used to garnish numerous different types of creamy desserts and rice puddings, usually with a drizzle of flowery sugar syrup. Even a humble fresh fruit salad will benefit from a sprinkling of pistachio dust, made by crushing the nuts finely in a food processor and mixing them with confectioner's sugar and perhaps a splash of lemon or lime sugar syrup.

SQUID STUFFED WITH PORK AND PISTACHIOS

Ideally, you need fresh, medium-sized squid tubes for this dish. Stuffed with a spicy ground-pork filling and studded with pretty green pistachios, they make an attractive and very tasty starter. Serve with a handful of salad leaves and warm, crusty bread.

4 medium squid tubes, about 3–4
   ounces each
⅓ cup pistachio nuts, shelled
¾ pound ground pork
1 clove garlic, finely chopped
1 shallot, finely chopped
1 teaspoon sweet paprika
½ teaspoon ginger powder

1 large green chili, deseeded and
   finely shredded
1 tablespoon extra-virgin olive oil
1 egg
salt and pepper
1 tablespoon olive oil
1 lemon, cut into 4 wedges

CLEAN THE SQUID TUBES thoroughly and pat them dry.

Soak the pistachios in cold water for 5 minutes to get rid of any extra salt. Mix the pork, nuts, garlic, shallots, spices, chili, extra-virgin olive oil, and egg until they are thoroughly combined. Preheat the oven to 400°F.

Stuff a quarter of the stuffing into each tube, making sure you work it right down to the very bottom and that no air is trapped inside. Leave about ½ inch at the open end. If you like, use a pastry bag for this step. Close the ends with a toothpick. Lightly season the tubes with salt and pepper.

Heat olive oil in an ovenproof pan and sear the squid tubes on medium-high heat, rolling them around like sausages, until they are a nice golden color all over.

Move the pan to the middle shelf of the oven and cook for 12 minutes.

Remove the squid tubes from the oven and allow them to rest for a couple of minutes on a wire rack until ready to serve.

Slice each tube into 4 even pieces and arrange them on a plate. Drizzle a little extra-virgin olive oil over the top and serve with lemon wedges and a generous dollop of preserved-lemon mayonnaise.

LAMB RUMP WITH PISTACHIOS AND PEPPERCORNS

This is a great way of jazzing up lamb rumps or lamb rounds. To serve, slice each rump into 3 thick slices and accompany with a big bowl of Goat-Cheese Mashed Potatoes (page 54), cheesy Pease Pudding with Goat Cheese (page 51), garlicky Parsnip Skordalia (page 141), or a robust Coarse Tapenade Salad (page 197).

½ cup unsalted, shelled pistachio nuts
3 tablespoons white peppercorns
1 tablespoon whole allspice berries
1⅔ cups fresh bread crumbs

4 lamb rumps (8-ounce portions)
1 tablespoon grainy mustard
salt and pepper

IN A SPICE GRINDER or mortar and pestle, grind the pistachio nuts, then the peppercorns and the allspice berries, and mix them together with the bread crumbs.

Brush each lamb rump evenly with a little mustard and then roll in the crumbing mixture.

Preheat the oven to 400°F and roast the lamb rumps for 12 minutes for medium-rare or a little longer for medium. Remove them from the oven and allow them to rest for another 12 minutes in a warm place.

Reheat in a hot oven for 1–2 minutes when ready to serve.

DRIED-FIG AND PISTACHIO CHOCOLATE TRUFFLES

Squidgy, fudgy and chocolaty, with a pleasing crunch from the nuts, these chocolate goodies are irresistible. This makes quite a large quantity, but they freeze well and will keep for 3–4 weeks in the refrigerator, although it is unlikely they will last that long!

¾ cup condensed milk

1 pound good-quality dark chocolate

1 tablespoon vanilla extract

1 cup dried figs, finely diced

2 cups unsalted, shelled pistachio nuts

best-quality cocoa powder for dusting

MELT THE CONDENSED MILK, chocolate, and vanilla over a pan of simmering water.
   Mix in the figs and pistachio nuts and pour into a pan lined with waxed paper. Leave to set, then turn out, cut into squares, and dust with cocoa powder.

pomegranates

One of nature's most challenging fruits, for many people pomegranates fall into the "too hard" basket. However, all you really need is a good, sharp knife, and maybe a little patience, to pierce the leathery skin and pry loose the delicious seeds lodged in the thick membrane. But it's well worth the effort: gloomy winter days are immeasurably cheered by these glorious ruby red seeds, bursting with sour-sweet juice.

In many cultures, pomegranates are considered a symbol of fertility and abundance, no doubt because of their prolific number of seeds. At Rosh Hashanah, Jewish traditionalists will set out a dish of pomegranates as an omen for fertility. In Greek legend, the pomegranate is forever linked to the change of seasons: Persephone, daughter of Demeter, the goddess of agriculture, was condemned to spend half the year in the underworld because she ate six seeds of the fruit.

In the Middle East, where they are believed to originate, pomegranates are consumed avidly. The refreshingly tart-sweet juice is squeezed into both savory and sweet dishes, and the fruit's jewel-like seeds add a divinely opulent touch when sprinkled like sparkling rubies over a humble dish of baba ghanoush, the odd salad, or even rice dishes.

Out of season, imported pomegranates here rarely warrant the effort in terms of flavor. They may certainly be used as an exotic addition to fancy flower arrangements and table decorations, but they are likely to be a big disappointment on the culinary front. If you also believe that life is too short to spend digging away at pomegranate seeds, you could consider pomegranate molasses. We are big fans of this lusciously dark and mysterious syrup. It is very concentrated and shouldn't be substituted directly for fresh pomegranate juice without being diluted, or it will overwhelm a dish. But used with a light touch, pomegranate molasses adds that exotic sweet-sour tartness so favored in many Persian and Arab dishes.

SELECTING AND STORING POMEGRANATES

Choosing fresh pomegranates can be a bit of a hit-and-miss affair. The usual rules apply, though: select fruit which appear to be unblemished and with a smooth, dusky, golden red skin. If they feel heavy for their size, this is a good sign: they are more likely to be fresh and juicy. Pomegranates can be stored at room temperature for a couple of weeks before they dry out.

USING POMEGRANATES

To remove the seeds from their pithy cocoon requires a little patience. Cut the fruit in half and, using a teaspoon or a very small skewer, dig out the top layer of seeds. A more brutal approach involves whacking the back of the fruit with a rolling pin a few times, which can dislodge more seeds. Do this over a bowl to avoid making a mess.

If you are lucky enough to get a juicy pomegranate, you can squeeze the fresh juice out using a normal lemon squeezer. Be warned, though, that it will take several pomegranates to obtain a decent amount of juice. Far better, we think, to buy a bottle of Middle Eastern pomegranate molasses, which will give you the desired ruby red juice (when diluted with water) with no effort at all.

OYSTERS WITH TOMATO-POMEGRANATE DRESSING

Pomegranate molasses adds an indefinable tart sweetness to a vinaigrette when used instead of balsamic vinegar. This dressing works well with cooked-vegetable salads such as spinach, zucchini, or eggplant, as well as salad leaves, and is good drizzled over barbecued fish or poultry. It works brilliantly with creamy offal, such as the Parsley Salad with Parmesan-Crumbed Brains (page 211). We love it spooned on natural oysters as a change from all those Thai-inspired dressings and dipping sauces.

1 teaspoon pomegranate molasses
4 shallots, finely chopped
1 clove garlic, finely chopped
2 ripe tomatoes, deseeded and cut
   into ¼-inch dice

juice of 1 lemon
¾ extra-virgin olive oil
salt and pepper
24 freshly shucked oysters

PLACE ALL THE INGREDIENTS except for the salt, pepper, and oysters in a bowl and whisk well. Season with salt and pepper. Spoon a little dressing onto each oyster and serve.

SERVES FOUR (SIX EACH) AS A STARTER.

POMEGRANATE BUTTER

Use discs of this tangy butter on top of all kinds of grilled and barbecued dishes, or stuff it under the skin of a whole chicken before roasting.

~~~~~~

¾ cup (1½ sticks) softened butter
1 teaspoon pomegranate molasses
½ teaspoon sumac

2 shallots, very finely chopped
½ clove garlic, very finely chopped
zest of ½ lemon

ADD ALL THE INGREDIENTS to the softened butter and mix thoroughly.

Shape into a rough sausage and place onto a square of waxed paper. Roll to a smooth log and then wrap in plastic wrap and refrigerate until needed. It will keep in the freezer for 3–4 weeks.

Cut off discs and use as required.

LEBANESE PIZZA WITH PINE NUTS AND POMEGRANATE

A splash of pomegranate molasses added to all kinds of ground meats will lift them to another dimension. These Lebanese "pizzas" are a firm favorite. Serve them hot from the oven with a squeeze of lemon juice and, if you like your food spicy, a sprinkling of dried chili flakes.

PIZZA DOUGH
3 cups plain flour
½ teaspoon salt
¾ teaspoon sugar
1 tablespoon dried yeast
3 tablespoons warm water
1¼ cups yogurt
3 tablespoons extra-virgin olive oil

MEAT TOPPING
3 tablespoons olive oil

⅓ cup pine nuts
1 small onion, finely chopped
1 clove garlic, finely chopped
6 ounces ground lamb
1 tomato, deseeded and finely chopped
1 teaspoon pomegranate molasses
½ teaspoon allspice
½ teaspoon cinnamon
¼ teaspoon fresh black pepper
½ teaspoon salt
½ teaspoon sumac

SIFT THE FLOUR into a large mixing bowl and add the salt. Dissolve the sugar and yeast in the warm water. In another small bowl, whisk together the yogurt and olive oil. Pour the bubbling yeast into the flour with the yogurt mix. Knead for about 10 minutes, until the dough is smooth and silky. Lightly oil the ball of dough and put it into a bowl. Cover and leave in a warm place to rise for 2 hours, by which time it should have at least doubled in size.

Fry the pine nuts over medium heat until they are golden brown, then remove them and drain them on kitchen paper.

Fry the onion until it is soft and then add the garlic and ground lamb. Cook until the meat is browned all over. Add the pine nuts, tomato, pomegranate molasses, and spices and stir well. Remove from the heat and check seasoning.

Preheat the oven to 400°F and heat a heavy baking sheet. Knock the air out of the dough, then spread it out on a floured work surface. Roll it out into rounds of around 8 inches in diameter and ¼ inch thick. Brush lightly with a little olive oil. Spread the meat topping evenly over each round and bake on the preheated sheet for 5–10 minutes, or until the pastry is a nice golden brown.

Serve hot from the oven with a squeeze of lemon and a big dollop of yogurt.

quinces

The quince is a strange, old-fashioned kind of fruit, with a delightful sibilant name. Its fall from grace in our kitchens is something of a mystery, as, despite its ordinary appearance, rather like an overgrown apple, it is deliciously fragrant. A bowl of quinces will perfume a whole house – well, a small one, anyway. Even more bewitching is the transformation of its flesh, on cooking, from an unremarkable pasty white into a beautiful rosy amber hue.

According to American food writer Waverley Root, a key reason for the demise of the quince is its startlingly astringent flavor. He suggests that because sugar is now such a dominant flavor preference in Western diets, we reject foods which lack it. Less prosperous regions, like the Middle East or the southern Mediterranean, are traditionally more dependent on natural sweeteners such as honey, date syrup, and fresh fruits than on bland old sugar cane. Their palates are more likely to accept sour, tart, and bitter flavors than our lazy Western ones!

However, the quince in temperate areas is a very different fruit from that of the hotter countries of the Middle East, where it has been widely cultivated for over 4,000 years. In those climates, the fruit becomes softer and juicier and can even be eaten raw. Quince trees do not fruit as well in cooler climates, where the lack of sunshine means the fruit has a disappointing tendency to rot on the tree rather than ripen.

As they have a very high pectin content, the most obvious use for quinces is to make jams, jellies, and pastes. French *cotignac*, Italian *cotognata*, and Spanish or Portuguese *marmelado* are all different sorts of quince paste, the last in fact being the origin of our English word *marmalade*. The curious word *quince* is itself derived from a French word, *coing*, recalling the ancient city of Kydonia on Crete, where the best quinces were said to grow in ancient times.

In Middle Eastern countries like Iran, Syria, and Turkey, quinces are commonly used in both sweet and savory dishes. They make a delicious fruit compote, poached with a little honey and lime syrup and served with whipped cream or yogurt. They can be stuffed with a mixture of chopped nuts and spices and slowly oven-baked until their aroma fills the kitchen. Other Persian recipes favor stuffing them like a vegetable, with a mixture of ground meat and split peas. They are also the fruit par excellence to use in a Moroccan lamb tagine, enlivened with paprika, saffron, and ginger.

SELECTING AND STORING QUINCES

In terms of finding quinces, you have to seize them when you can. If you know someone with a quince tree in their garden, make sure you become their best friend! The season for quinces is startlingly short, and they are rarely grown commercially. However, they are becoming a more common sight in specialty greengrocers and markets, and in a true sign of increased acceptance, stewed quinces are returning to the breakfast menus of lots of chic little bistros, while quince paste has become a common accompaniment to the cheese board.

Choose fruit which are firm and free from wrinkly bits and insect damage. The color of the fruit will give some clue to its ripeness: as quinces mature, they lighten from a sharp, pale green to a Golden Delicious yellow. Fully ripe quinces are a deeper, brighter yellow, and the real giveaway is the bewitching honeyed fragrance, which is at its most intense in the ripe fruit. Don't reject the less ripe fruit, though. They have a higher pectin content, which makes them ideal for making jams and jellies. Riper fruit is better suited to poaching or baking.

Quinces should not be kept in the refrigerator. They have a naturally long shelf life and are very slow to rot. And, more obviously, one of the very best things about quinces is their extraordinary scent – leave them in a bowl on the kitchen table and allow them to work their magic!

USING QUINCES

To prepare the fruit for poaching, it first needs to be well washed to get rid of the gray down on its skin. Then comes the hard work. Quinces are usually rock hard, so use a very strong knife to cut, core, and peel them. Include the cores and peelings when cooking the slices of fruit, as they also contribute flavor, especially when making jellies or pastes. A great deal of the fruit's pectin is to be found in the skin and the pits.

Like apples, quinces discolor very quickly, which may or may not matter to you, and will in most cases depend on the recipe you are using. Some people recommend dropping them in acidulated water until you are ready to cook, which will certainly slow the browning process. However, quinces undergo a fairly dramatic color change on cooking: poaching them transforms them to a glowing pink, and if you are simmering the fruit for a long time to make jam or jelly, then the individual slices will collapse down to a deep amber hue, and a little surface discoloration won't really matter.

When poaching quinces, the key thing to remember is that they take a long, long time – sometimes as much as an hour, or even more – to soften to an acceptable texture. As they are very tart, they require a lot of sugar, especially in sweet dishes. They also benefit from the addition of a vanilla pod or some orange, lemon, or even lime zest to the cooking syrup.

A few wafer-thin slices of quince added to an apple pie will impart a delicious scent to the whole dish. You might also like to develop the Eastern theme by adding a few grains of cardamom.

SPICED QUINCES

Quinces, with their aromatic tart-sweet perfume, are the ideal fruit to balance rich, fatty cuts of lamb in a Persian or Moroccan braise. Many traditional recipes are overly sweet to Western palates, though, and the addition of even one quince will easily sweeten an entire dish. If you are partial to savory-sweet combinations, add a few slices of these pickled quinces to a spicy Lamb Kifta Tagine (page 161), or serve them with terrines and pâtés and cold meats such as honey-roasted ham or even leftover slices from a roast.

4 quinces, peeled, cored, and cut into
    8 pieces
1 cup white wine or cider vinegar
2 cups water
6 tablespoons mild honey
1 teaspoon black peppercorns
1 teaspoon coriander seeds

1 teaspoon cardamom seeds,
    crushed and sieved
½ teaspoon allspice berries
½ teaspoon whole cloves
1 cinnamon stick
2 bay leaves

PLACE THE QUINCES in acidulated water until you are ready to cook them – you do not want them to discolor.

Place them in a large pan and cover with the liquids, honey, and spices. Bring slowly to the boil, stirring gently to ensure the honey dissolves. Then lower the heat and simmer for 25–45 minutes until the quinces are soft and tender. Be careful not to overcook them, or they will start to disintegrate.

Using a slotted spoon, carefully lift the quince slices into warm, sterilized jars and pour the poaching liquor over them so that the fruit is completely covered.

Seal and store in a cool, dark place for at least 4 weeks before using.

QUINCE TURKISH DELIGHT

There are many types of quince paste or cheese to be found all around the Mediterranean. These are delicious eaten as a sweetmeat, or, as in Spain, with a slice of Manchego cheese. Softer versions are delicious spread on toast like jam, or as a glaze for grilled meats. The idea inspired Greg to use quince as a flavor for Turkish delight, finding out only later that traditional recipes used it as well. The tart-sweet quince flavor is a thrilling change from the very sweet rose-water and vanilla versions usually on offer in Middle Eastern stores and restaurants. Turkish delight is time-consuming to make, requiring plenty of patience and a strong arm for stirring. It is a fickle sweet, and the addition of different fruits requires constant slight variations to the basic recipe. The recipe below is a simple adaptation, using shop-bought quince paste to provide the flavor and color.

4 cups sugar

1¼ quarts water

1 teaspoon lemon juice

1 cup cornstarch

1 teaspoon cream of tartar

7 ounces quince paste, cut into ¼-inch dice

1½ cups confectioner's sugar

¾ cup cornstarch

PLACE THE SUGAR in a heavy-based pot with 1½ cups of the water and the teaspoon of lemon juice and bring to the boil.

In a separate bowl, gradually mix together the cornstarch and cream of tartar with the remaining water, ensuring there are no lumps. As soon as the syrup reaches 240°F on a sugar thermometer, quickly pour in the cornstarch mixture, stir well, and lower the heat to a bare simmer.

Cook on this very gentle heat for about 2 hours, stirring constantly so that the mixture does not stick to the bottom of the pan and burn. It will gradually thicken, become transparent, and deepen in color to a soft amber hue.

Eventually the mixture will be thick enough for you to draw a distinct channel across the bottom of the pan with your spoon. At this point, add the diced quince paste and stir in evenly.

Quickly pour into a deep baking sheet, 12 x 10 x 1½ inches, lined with waxed paper. Allow to cool overnight, but do not refrigerate.

Turn out, and peel away the waxed paper. Cut into ¾-inch cubes and roll them in a mixture of the confectioner's sugar and cornstarch before serving with strong black coffee.

SWEET NUT-STUFFED QUINCES

Oven-bake quinces as you would apples. Stuff them with a buttery mixture of chopped toasted nuts and honey and serve them with Burnt Honey Ice Cream (page 155), Ginger Cream (page 147), Orange-Blossom Clotted Cream (page 203), or generous dollops of softly whipped cream.

~~~~~~

NUT STUFFING
⅓ cup ground almonds
¼ cup unsalted pistachio nuts, finely
   chopped
¼ teaspoon cardamom seeds, ground
⅓ cup soft brown sugar
¼ cup softened butter

QUINCES
2 large or 4 small quinces
2 tablespoons honey
3 tablespoons butter
juice and zest of 1 orange
zest of ½ lemon
½ vanilla bean, split and scraped
1 cup water

COMBINE THE INGREDIENTS to make the Nut Stuffing and reserve.

Cut the quinces in half and hollow out the cores. Pack the quinces, cut side up, into a lightly buttered gratin dish. Drizzle with the honey and add the remaining ingredients.

Bake in a preheated 350°F oven for 1–2 hours until the quinces are tender. About 20 minutes before the end of the cooking time, stuff the central hollows of the quinces with the nut mixture. Raise the heat to 400°F and return to the oven until the nut topping is golden brown.

rice

In the West — by which, rather ethnocentrically, we mean Australia, North America, England, and most of Western Europe — people traditionally have not eaten much rice. Rice is, at best, a starchy, stomach-filling accompaniment to Chinese or Indian takeout and, at worst, bland, pappy baby food.

It is hard for us to grasp, then, that rice is the main sustenance of nearly three-quarters of the world's population, largely because of economic necessity but also through choice. All around West Africa, India, China, and Southeast Asia, people have developed a fierce devotion to this grain, each community preferring its own particular local variety for its unique texture, aroma, and flavor — differences which most of us in the West would be hard-pressed to distinguish. But even those Mediterranean countries which grow their own small (in world terms) rice crops prefer the home-grown variety: for northern Italians, there is only Arborio, ideally a *superfino* such as Carnaroli or Vialone Nano; for Spaniards, a paella can only be made with their very own *arroz de Valencia*.

In the Middle East, rice is also a serious business. Like bread, it is often referred to as *aishi* (the Arabic word for "life") and forms the basis of most daily meals. However, it is not native to the Middle East. The first grain of choice in this region was wheat, which originated and flourished in the area between the Tigris and Euphrates rivers known as the Fertile Crescent. The origins of rice are somewhat less clear. Primitive strains of numerous different varieties are believed to have evolved independently all through Asia, but its earliest cultivation is thought to have centered on the hot, humid foothills of the mountainous region between China and India. Its spread from there was comparatively slow, for rice cultivation requires sophisticated farming and irrigation techniques.

Rice is though to have reached ancient Persia via northern India about 2,000 years ago. The Persians, with their farming know-how and advanced irrigation systems, farmed it quite happily for several hundred years. It was virtually unknown in Europe, though, until the Arabs started cultivating it in their new territories. They took it with them as they forged a trail west from Persia, introducing it on the way to Turkey, Sicily, and Spain, until by the tenth century the secrets of irrigation and rice cultivation were known throughout the Muslim world and began to influence local cuisines in ways that endure to this day.

SELECTING, STORING AND USING RICE

There are many thousands of different varieties of rice cultivated around the world. If you would like to know more about rice, *The Rice Book* by Sri Owen (see the bibliography at the end of this book for publication details) makes compelling reading. On the whole, though, Middle Easterners use long-grain rice, unless making a stuffing or pudding, in which case short-grain rice is preferred.

Below is an overview of the main types of rice: long-, medium-, and short-grain.

LONG-GRAIN As a general rule, long-grain rices are the least starchy, so the individual grains remain separate, dry, and fluffy after cooking. For this reason, they are ideally suited to savory dishes and pilafs. Good-quality long-grain rices include the aromatic basmati rice and fragrant jasmine rice, although the latter's very distinct flavor is probably better suited to Thai dishes. For many Middle Eastern rice dishes we use a good basmati rice, which swells up to three times its length on cooking but retains its elegant slimness.

MEDIUM- AND SHORT-GRAIN Medium-grain rices are plumper and shorter than long-grain varieties and are ideal for the Chinese style of cooking. Short-grain rices are the plumpest and shortest of all, and tend to be starchier and quite sticky when cooked. They are good for Middle Eastern stuffing mixtures and other dishes for which the rice is required to clump together, such as Japanese sushi and Spanish paella. Their propensity to break down to a soothing, creamy mass also makes short-grain rices perfect for puddings.

Risotto rice, known as Arborio, is probably better defined as round-grain. Its grains are larger, with a firm, chalky center. Risotto rice is never washed before cooking, as the surface starchiness is essential for making creamy, rich risottos. Our favourite risotto rices are Vialone Nano and Carnaroli.

OTHER RICE Other varieties of rice, outside the scope of this book, are Southeast Asian varieties such as glutinous rice and black rice. Then there is red rice from the Camargue in France, and brown rice, which has its bran still attached and is enjoyed by the virtuous and nutrition-conscious. Wild rice is not rice at all, but the strong-flavored grain from a species of North American wild grass.

As far as storing rice goes, the same rule applies to them all: once the package is opened, the rice should be kept in an airtight container. Most refined rices available in the West keep fairly well for up to three years, although aromatic rices gradually lose their fragrance. Cooked rice has a surprisingly short life span. Harmful bacteria will grow very quickly above 39°F, and will even grow slowly in the refrigerator. Cooked rice should therefore be refrigerated and eaten within two days.

USING RICE

In the Middle East, rice cooking is almost an art form, and different regions and even different families swear by their own particular method. At its most straightforward, long-grain rice (which is preferred for most occasions) is cooked by a simple absorption method, so that each perfect spoonful is light and fluffy, never sticky, each grain firm and separate.

From here the variations are endless: some people like to sauté the rice in a little oil or butter first; others add this afterward. Some people soak; others don't even wash the rice first. Many people cover the rice with a tight-fitting lid; others only partly cover the pan. Even the amount of cooking water used and the cooking time will be endlessly disputed.

We have included in this book a number of risotto dishes, which are of course not at all Middle Eastern. Greg did part of his training in Italy, where he cooked risotto every day. As a result, he is quite passionate about it: he always includes a risotto dish on his menus, and we cook it at home as a regular treat. Risottos work beautifully with many Middle Eastern ingredients and make a terrific accompaniment to many Middle Eastern and Mediterranean dishes.

RISOTTO – THE BASIC PRINCIPLES

To make risotto, the first thing to know is that you should never wash the rice – you definitely want all the starchiness you can get. There is nothing hard about making risotto; it simply requires supervision and constant stirring to create the proper creamy texture. Risotto is ready when the individual grains are tender but with some residual bite. The overall consistency of the dish should be a little like a porridge – creamy and starchy, and definitely not swimming in liquid. One other thing: risotto is not for those watching their cholesterol and calories. The final compulsory touch is a healthy handful of grated parmesan and a big knob of butter, which help to thicken the final dish, enrich it, and add a lovely glossy sheen.

The following is a basic four-stage technique. Stock is added in three stages to make a base, with a little reserved until the fourth stage. Other ingredients are added halfway through the third stage. In the fourth stage, the risotto is enriched with butter and cheese.

¼ cup olive oil
1 small onion, quartered
2 cups Vialone Nano rice
Up to 1 quart chicken stock, simmering

7 tablespoons butter, chilled and cut into small cubes
⅓ cup parmesan, grated
salt and pepper

STAGE 1 Fry the onion for a few minutes to flavor the oil, then discard it. Add the rice and stir for 2 minutes to coat each grain of rice with the oil. Next, add enough hot stock to cover the rice by a finger width. Cook on medium heat, stirring with a wooden spoon from time to time, until most of the stock has been absorbed.

STAGE 2 Add the same quantity of stock. Again, cook on medium heat, stirring with a wooden spoon from time to time, until most of the stock has been absorbed.

STAGE 3 Add a third amount of stock (reserving ½ cup for the last stage), and when half the liquid has been absorbed, add your choice of vegetables, spices, etc. Stir gently until the stock is absorbed.

STAGE 4 Stir in the butter and parmesan and season with salt and pepper. Add the last ½ cup of stock and stir until the butter has been incorporated. Cover and allow to rest off the heat for a minute.

RISOTTO WITH ZUCCHINI, PRAWNS, AND PRESERVED LEMON

This is a brightly colored, flavorful risotto which makes an ideal light lunch with a simple salad.

~~~~~~

2 large zucchini
½ pound raw prawn meat
¼ cup olive oil, flavored with
   1 small onion, quartered
2 cups Vialone Nano rice
up to 1 quart chicken stock,
   simmering

½ cup olive oil
2 shallots, finely sliced
1 clove garlic, finely sliced
salt and pepper
1 Preserved Lemon with Honey (page
   170), skin only, washed and diced small
2 cups mixed baby salad leaves
7 tablespoons butter, chilled and cut
   into small cubes
1 tablespoon parsley, chopped

SHRED ZUCCHINI into small batons. Cut prawns into thirds.

Prepare risotto according to basic four-stage method.

Meanwhile, in a separate frying pan, heat 2 tablespoons of the oil, until it is smoking hot. Add the zucchini and shallots. Do not stir, but let sit for 30 seconds. Then stir well, remove from the heat, and drain in a colander or sieve. Place the frying pan back on the heat, add the remaining 2 tablespoons of the oil, and heat again until it is smoking hot. Add the prawns and again, do not stir, but let sit for 30 seconds. Then add the garlic, season with salt and pepper, and stir well. Remove the pan from the heat.

Halfway through the third stage of making the risotto, add the prawns, zucchini, preserved-lemon dice, and parsley with the cold butter. Add the last ½ cup of stock and stir well until the butter is incorporated. Cover and let sit for a minute. Adjust seasoning.

To serve, divide the risotto into 4 shallow bowls and top with a small handful of lightly dressed mixed salad leaves.

FAVA-BEAN PILAF, LEBANESE STYLE

Beans and rice are an almost universal favorite. This is an adaptation of two traditional Lebanese dishes: rice with beans, and rice with chicken. It is quite rich and, served with a bitter-leaf salad, makes an ideal lunch or supper dish.

¼ cup olive oil
½ small onion, finely chopped
½ pound ground chicken
salt and pepper
½ teaspoon allspice
2 cups basmati rice
½ cup squash, cut into ¼-inch dice

1 cup fresh fava beans, blanched
   and peeled
2½ cups chicken stock, simmering
1 clove garlic, crushed with
   ½ teaspoon salt
juice of 1 lemon
½ cup fresh cilantro leaves

HEAT THE OIL IN A PAN and sauté the onion for a few minutes until it has softened. Add the chicken and cook on high for 2–3 minutes, until the juices start to run out. Season with a little salt and pepper and the allspice. Then add the rice, squash, fava beans, and chicken stock. Lower the heat, cover, and cook for 15 minutes without disturbing.

Turn off the heat and fork through a mixture of the garlic paste and lemon juice. Cover again and rest for a further 5 minutes. Turn out onto a large, shallow dish and garnish with cilantro.

Serve with dollops of satiny-smooth yogurt.

SPRING VEGETABLE PAELLA

This paella is cooked more like a risotto so that the rice becomes creamy. It has no cheese, though, in order to maintain the fresh, intense flavors of the vegetables.

¼ cup olive oil, flavored with 1 small onion, quartered, and 2 cloves garlic

2 cups Vialone Nano rice

Up to 1 quart chicken stock, simmering

15 saffron strands, roasted and crushed to powder

⅔ cup shelled peas, blanched for 2 minutes

⅔ cup fresh fava beans, blanched and peeled

8 artichokes cooked à la niçoise (page 19), or good-quality purchased artichokes preserved in oil

2 medium tomatoes, deseeded and diced

2 small red bell peppers, roasted, skinned, and diced

7 tablespoons butter, chilled and cut into small cubes

salt and pepper

PREPARE THE RISOTTO according to the basic four-stage method.

Prepare the peas and fava beans and cut the artichokes in quarters.

Halfway through the third stage, add the saffron, blanched peas and beans, and artichokes. Stir gently and then add the tomato, red pepper, salt, and pepper.

Remove from the heat, cover the pan, and let sit for 3 minutes. Return the pan to the heat and add the cold diced butter and the last ½ cup of stock, and stir gently until the butter has been incorporated.

Adjust seasoning and serve with a fresh green salad.

RICE AND CHORIZO STUFFING

Use this to stuff chicken or any other game birds. Rub the skin with crushed garlic, thyme, and lemon zest, and roast. This quantity will stuff a 4½-pound chicken, roasted for 50 minutes at 375°F, or 12 quail, roasted for 15 minutes at 400°F.

1 tablespoon olive oil
1 shallot, finely chopped
1 small clove garlic, finely chopped
2 ounces semidried chorizo sausage,
    finely shredded

½ cup medium-grain rice
¾ cup stock or water, simmering
zest of 1 lemon, finely chopped
1 tablespoon parsley, chopped
1 egg yolk

HEAT THE OIL in a pan and gently sauté the shallot and garlic until they have softened. Add the chorizo and rice and stir well to combine ingredients. Add the simmering stock, cover, and cook over a low heat for 12 minutes. Remove the pan from the heat but leave the lid on and allow to steam a further 5 minutes. Tip into a bowl and allow to cool. Add the lemon zest, chopped parsley, and egg yolk to bind.

rose water

Roses have been enjoyed since ancient times for their beauty and perfume – from the lush gardens of Persia, where they were first cultivated, to Roman times, when they were strewn extravagantly about the floors and tables at banquets and used to scent bathing water. Early civilizations macerated rose petals in hot oil to make pomades, which were used for anointing the body as a kind of primitive perfume. But it was not until the tenth century that the Arab doctor Avicenna discovered the process of extracting the rose's essential oil by distillation. The intensely concentrated perfume could then be diluted to make rose water for use in medicine, perfume, cosmetics, and even cooking.

With their heady, sweet fragrance it is hardly surprising that rose petals and rose water were also enjoyed by the ancients in their food, as indeed they are today in parts of the Eastern world. Iranian cooks like to sprinkle crushed dried rose petals onto rice pilafs or desserts and add them to complex spice mixes, to which they contribute a musty-sweet undertone. Nearly all Middle Eastern and eastern Mediterranean countries have a tradition of rose-petal preserves, which are eaten as jam with bread for breakfast, or enjoyed eaten in tiny spoonfuls as an accompaniment to a cup of strong black coffee and a glass of icy cold water.

At the other end of the Arab world, the Maghreb countries of North Africa also use rosebuds in cooking. Huge sacks of tiny dried rosebuds are to be found in every spice shop in Morocco. They are mixed with other sweet spices, like cinnamon, to add an exotic dimension to both sweet and savory dishes. They are also a common ingredient in stronger North African spice mixes, like the Moroccan ras el hanout or the Tunisian four-spice mix.

Rose water, too, is used at mealtimes all around the Middle East, both as a perfumed hand wash and to add a touch of edible luxury to nearly every dessert and sweet pastry imaginable. It is used to flavor honey and sugar syrups and poured lavishly over all kinds of sweet pastries. Rose water is used to flavor buttery ground-almond cookies and to moisten delicate nut pastes for stuffing into little shortbread biscuits, like ma'amoul. Creamy milk puddings, thickened with ground rice, cornstarch, or ground almonds, are a favorite dessert treat in Middle Eastern countries. These too are nearly always enhanced with a few drops of fragrant rose water or orange-blossom water.

Rose petals and rose water featured quite prominently in the cooking of medieval England. They were used extensively in candies, preserves, desserts, and syrups, as well as in more exotic game and fish dishes, but by the nineteenth century they had fallen from favor. It is true that, used with too heavy a hand, flower waters can become cloying and overpowering, yet a delicate touch can add an exotic dimension to many European desserts, too. Rose water can be added to cakes and cookies and splashed into sorbets and ice creams, mousses, fools, and cooked creams, or even added to a humble rice pudding for an exquisitely different sweet flavor.

Rose water marries particularly well with fresh fruit. A favorite Moroccan dessert, for instance, is devastatingly simple: fresh orange segments are dusted with cinnamon and sugar and then sprinkled with rose water. At home we often drizzle a little rose water over fresh strawberries or a mixed-berry compote and serve them with thick, creamy yogurt for a deliciously easy summer dessert.

SELECTING, STORING, AND USING ROSE WATER

Rose water can be found in Middle Eastern and Indian stores and in some upmarket food shops and delicatessens, but usually in a diluted form compared with the full-strength distillations available in Asia. Our favorite is the Lebanese Cortas brand, but there are several other Lebanese, Syrian, and even Indian varieties available.

Rose water and orange-blossom water are often used interchangeably, particularly in sugar syrups poured over fresh fruit salads, sticky pastries, and almond-thickened milk puddings. However, rose water tends to be less overpowering than orange-blossom water. Surprisingly, it is also quite robust and can be heated quite happily without an alteration in its flavor.

PERSIAN-STYLE ROSE-SCENTED PLUM JELLY

We used to have a relentlessly productive plum tree in our garden and created this gorgeous, jewel-like jam in desperation one summer when faced with the annual glut of fruit. Plums are high in pectin, and this jelly practically makes itself. It is good on fresh white bread with lots of butter, but we like it particularly on nutty whole-wheat or even savory rye toast.

5 pounds plums
3 tablespoons rose water
sugar

PLACE THE PLUMS in a large, heavy-based pan and boil for about 10 minutes, until they are soft and pulpy and have released a lot of juice.

Strain them overnight through a jelly bag (a piece of muslin or cheesecloth or even a heavy-duty paper towel will do just as well). Do not force the pulp through, as this will make the jelly cloudy, but allow it to drip through naturally. The amount of juice yielded will vary, depending on the fruit, but you should have about 2 quarts.

Pour the juice into the pan, and for every cup of juice add a generous cup of sugar. Stir well over low heat until the sugar has completely dissolved, then bring to the boil.

Boil for 20–25 minutes, until the jelly reaches the setting point. To test, spoon a small amount onto a cold plate and place it in the refrigerator to cool. The jelly is at the setting point if it forms a skin which wrinkles when you push your finger through it. When it reaches the setting point, remove the pan from the heat and skim the froth from the surface.

Stir in the rose water and then carefully ladle the jelly into sterilized jars and seal.

ROSE-FLAVORED BERRY FOOL WITH MASCARPONE

2 pints strawberries, hulled and halved

2 pints blueberries

2 pints raspberries

(reserve a few of each berry to garnish)

1 cup powdered instant coffee

2 tablespoons rose water

½ cup sugar

½ cup cold water

1 cup cream

1½ cups mascarpone

a sprinkling of Pine-Nut Praline (page 231)

MAKE A BERRY PURÉE using 1 pint of each of the fruits. Cook with the instant coffee for 10 minutes, then allow to cool slightly and pass through a sieve to remove the seeds. Stir in half the rose water and allow to cool.

Heat the sugar with ¼ cup of the cold water until the sugar is dissolved. Bring the water to the boil, then lower the heat and simmer until the syrup thickens and darkens to a caramel. Remove it from the heat and carefully add the remaining cold water. Stir in well and allow it to cool.

Whip the cream with the mascarpone and remaining rose water until stiff. Loosely fold in the whole berries with half the purée and half the caramel to give a marbled effect.

Place a big blob on each plate and swirl with extra purée and caramel.

Garnish with the fresh whole berries and a sprinkling of Pine-Nut Praline.

SERVES SIX TO EIGHT.

APPLE–ROSE WATER SORBET

This fragrant sorbet makes a lovely light dessert. As the apples discolor slightly in cooking, the purée needs a splash of color to give it a rosy blush: add a few puréed raspberries, a drop of black-currant or grenadine syrup, or even beetroot juice.

~~~~~~

6 green apples, peeled, cored, and diced
1 cup apple juice
juice and zest of 1 lemon
1¼ cups sugar
1 stick cinnamon

3 juniper berries
2 cloves
2 cups water
2 teaspoons rose water
1 teaspoon grenadine (optional)

GENTLY SIMMER THE APPLES in the apple juice with the lemon juice and zest until they are soft and starting to collapse.

Place the sugar, cinnamon stick, juniper berries, and cloves in a pan with the water and bring to the boil. Lower the heat and simmer for 5 minutes to make a syrup. Allow to cool a little and then strain to remove the spices.

Purée the apple mixture and then pass it through a sieve. Allow it to cool and then add the rose water and grenadine. Mix together the syrup and apple purée, pour into an ice-cream maker, and churn according to the manufacturer's instructions.

Serve with fresh berries or other fresh fruits.

saffron

A rummage for saffron in the kitchen cupboard at home revealed the following: one plastic package of fake saffron threads purchased for novelty value from the souks of Marrakesh (it is really safflower); one small square glass bottle of La Mancha saffron threads brought back from a holiday in Spain; and one tiny jar of brick red, ferociously expensive saffron powder from Iran. Neither version of the real thing looks like much for the money, but even the tiniest pinch results in an explosion of bright yellow sunshine through your food and contributes an indescribable bittersweet flavor that leaves you longing for more.

True saffron threads are the orangey-red stigmas of a type of crocus flower (*Crocus sativus linnaeus*) which is thought to be native to the Fertile Crescent. Archaeological remains in Sumerian burial grounds suggest that saffron was used as a natural yellow dye as early as 5,000 BC. The yellow color comes from crocin, an intensely potent natural pigment: 1 part crocin will turn 150,000 parts water bright yellow! This characteristic meant it was much in demand in ancient times as a dye for textile and carpet weavers.

Saffron has always been adored by the aristocracy as a symbol of opulence and refinement. The Greeks and Romans used it to dye their clothes and to tint their bathing water. They believed it had cleansing qualities and used it to perfume their houses and public meeting places. Saffron was also used medicinally, to relieve depression and as a tonic for the heart, and stuffing it into bedding was thought to aid sleep. In the kitchen, saffron was used to gild all manner of pastries, meat, and seafood dishes, as well as contributing its own indefinable flavor.

The Romans spread saffron all around their empire – even as far west as England – but with the decline of Rome, trading networks in Europe collapsed, and the supply of spices from the East dried up. The violent peoples responsible for the chaos of Europe's Dark Ages had no interest in subtlety and refinement – least of all in their food – so it was not until the emergence of the Arab empire in the eighth century that relative calm returned to the region. Gradually, the Arabs reemerged as a significant trading power. Many spices were reintroduced to European cities, and refinement returned to local customs and, in particular, foods. The word for saffron in most European languages is strikingly similar, and they all derive from the Arabic (from *sahafarn*, meaning "thread," and *za'faran*, meaning "yellow").

The use of saffron in many cuisines can be traced back along common cultural threads. In Spain, for instance, the Arabs planted fields of both rice and saffron, the ingredients for the best-known Spanish dish, paella. Saffron is also added to rice dishes in countries as far apart as Iran, Turkey, the Balkan countries, Lebanon, Syria, Italy, and Morocco. Another significant cross-cultural use of saffron is in the baking of special cakes and breads for religious celebrations.

Saffron adds a magic touch to both savory and sweet dishes. It is often combined with seafood, as in the classic Mediterranean *bourrides* and bouillabaisse, and it adds a spicy pungency to Moroccan tagines. Saffron also works in sweet dishes, transforming milky custards, brûlées, and ice creams. In Northern Europe it is favored in baking and yeast cookery, tinting breads, tea cakes, batters, and pastries a glorious yellow.

SELECTING AND STORING SAFFRON

The rule with saffron is that if it isn't expensive, it probably isn't real saffron, and you should give it a miss. This rule applies particularly if you are a traveler in a strange land. In Morocco, for instance, many vendors in the spice markets offer vividly appealing mounds of a deep orange-yellow powder which they insist is saffron. In fact it is turmeric (often called Indian saffron), which is not at all the same thing. Turmeric is used a great deal in Moroccan cooking to add color, but it has nothing like the pungent, distinctive flavor of real saffron, and the two are certainly not interchangeable. At other stalls, you might be offered "saffron threads," which look genuine and are again offered at an enticingly cheap price. These, too, are likely to be imposters, probably tasteless safflower or, worse still, shredded marigold petals. There is no getting away from the fact that because of the labor-intensive process of its cultivation and harvest, real saffron is expensive, and the better the quality, the costlier it will be. But the rewards are great and the effect is huge relative to the amount needed.

On the whole, we recommend using saffron threads rather than saffron powder, as the latter is too easily adulterated (although there are exceptions, like the very pricey powder from Iran). In the West, however, you are likely to buy saffron from an upmarket food store or delicatessen. They pretty much only have the real thing, imported from Spain, Iran, Turkey, or Greece, reassuringly packaged in neat little containers, and often sealed with a label giving information about the brand, packing date, weight, and even quality.

Good-quality saffron threads should be densely entwined, long, fine filaments of a deep orangey-red hue. Most will probably also contain a small number of whitish-yellow styles – which are removed from the top-grade stuff – but these don't affect the aroma or flavor. Top-quality saffron powder usually comes in packets or tiny plastic jars, and should be as dark as brick dust. It is also more expensive than the whole threads, as the moisture is extracted before it is ground to a fine powder. Having spent so much money, you will naturally want to store your saffron correctly – away from the light, in a cool, dry cupboard, where it should last for 3–5 years.

USING SAFFRON

When using saffron, the first thing to work out is how much to use. Many recipes are decidedly unhelpful, suggesting only a vague "pinch." Weighing saffron is nigh impossible, given the tiny quantities used. In our view, it is more appropriate to count out the threads. You will probably find that once you start using saffron and become used to its bewitching flavor, you will want to use more and more, but a good starting point is four threads per person, plus a few for luck. In other words, for a dish serving four people, use 16–20 threads.

Saffron needs to be heat-activated before use, or its effect will be disappointing. One option is to dry-roast saffron threads gently and grind them to a powder before use (powdered saffron has already undergone this process). The alternative is to make a saffron infusion in a hot liquid, which should be made ahead of time and added during the cooking process. Some cuisines employ a combination of these techniques, gently roasting the saffron threads before infusing.

To roast saffron, toss the threads in a totally dry pan over a moderate heat for around 30 seconds. The last thing you want to do is burn them, but they must be completely dry before grinding. Once they have crisped up and begun to release their pungent aroma, tip the threads into a mortar and allow them to cool before crushing them with a pestle.

To make an infusion of saffron, measure out the threads and dry-roast them if desired. Next, place them in a cup and add just enough hot water to cover them – start with a tablespoon. The threads will immediately start to release their color into the water, and this will deepen and intensify over time. A minimum infusing time of 30 minutes is essential, but the saffron will continue to develop for about 12 hours. Some people like to store a saffron infusion in a tightly sealed jar for use over several weeks, in which case you should infuse the threads in boiling water.

When using saffron, either as a powder or as an infusion, the general rule is that you should add it at the start of the cooking process for maximum color and at the end for maximum flavor. Some people like to have the best of both worlds by adding most of it early and reserving a little to add at the very last minute before serving.

GOLDEN MUSSEL CHOWDER

In this glorious, creamy soup, plump, salty mussels and sweet, candied bacon rub up against soft, starchy potatoes in a golden broth. It needs only hot, crusty bread to make a satisfying lunch dish or a soul-restoring starter on a cold, gray day.

2 pounds black rope mussels,
  debearded and scrubbed
1 onion, sliced
2 sticks celery, sliced
2 cloves garlic, chopped
2 tablespoons olive oil
1 cup white wine
2 medium potatoes, peeled and diced
2 small leeks
1 cup cream

10 strands saffron, roasted and crushed
1 tablespoon fresh thyme leaves
2 medium tomatoes, deseeded and
  diced small
pepper
4 small bacon strips
soft brown sugar
watercress to garnish

IN A HEAVY-BASED POT, sauté the onion, celery, and garlic in the olive oil for about 1 minute. Then add the wine and the mussels. Cover, turn the heat up to high, and steam for 3 minutes. Turn the mussels well, replace the lid, and steam a further 2 minutes, or until the mussels have opened.

Remove the pot from the heat and allow to steam a further minute before taking off the lid and straining the liquor through a fine sieve to catch any dirt. Reserve the liquor. Throw any unopened mussels back into the pot and steam for another minute or two. Any which stubbornly refuse to open should be discarded. Allow the mussels to cool and then remove them from their shells and cut in half.

Steam the diced potatoes and whole leeks for 10–15 minutes, until they are tender. Remove them from the heat and allow them to cool for a few minutes. Split the leeks in half lengthways and then cut them into ½-inch slices.

Return the mussel liquor to the pot, add the cream, and bring it to the boil. Add the potatoes and leeks, then the saffron and thyme. Heat thoroughly. Add the diced tomatoes and mussels and warm through for a few moments. Season with pepper.

To candy the bacon, sprinkle the strips liberally with soft brown sugar and broil until golden brown. Shred and sprinkle on the soup. Garnish with watercress.

SERVES FOUR TO SIX.

À LA GRECQUE DRESSING

Greg's all-time favorite, this is a fantastically versatile saffron-infused dressing which spreads a flood of sunshine on your plate and an explosion of flavor in your mouth.

~~~~~~

10 strands saffron, roasted and crushed to a powder

⅓ cup white wine vinegar

3 tablespoons white wine

1 teaspoon honey

5 shallots, evenly and finely diced

2 cloves garlic, finely chopped

1 serrano chili, finely chopped

2 sprigs fresh thyme, leaves picked

1 teaspoon coriander seeds, roasted and crushed

½ teaspoon white peppercorns, roasted and crushed

½ teaspoon fennel seeds, roasted and crushed

juice of 1 lemon

1 cup extra-virgin olive oil

salt and fresh black pepper

IN A SAUCEPAN, mix the saffron with the vinegar, white wine, and honey. Warm the pan gently to dissolve the honey and add the shallots, garlic, chili, and thyme leaves. Pour into a large mixing bowl and allow to cool.

Roast and grind the coriander, white peppercorns, and fennel seeds. Add them to the dressing, then whisk in the lemon juice and the olive oil.

Taste for seasoning and add salt and freshly ground black pepper as required.

GRILLED-SEAFOOD BOUILLABAISSE

In traditional bouillabaisse recipes, the fish are cooked in the broth as a fish stew. Here they are broiled separately and placed in the soup as it is served. This means that oily fish like salmon may be included, and each fish retains its color and texture. You can use any white fish, such as snapper or bream.

CRAB STOCK

4 pounds crab (reserve claws for garnish)
⅔ cup olive oil
4 sticks celery, roughly chopped
2 medium onions, roughly chopped
4 cloves garlic, roughly chopped
½ teaspoon fennel seeds
1 can crushed tomatoes (14 ounces)
½ cup sherry
peel of 1 orange
15 strands saffron, roasted and crushed
2 whole bay leaves
12 sprigs thyme
4 quarts water

BOUILLABAISSE

3 large waxy potatoes, peeled and
   sliced thickly
3 leeks, sliced ¾ inch thick
2 medium fennel bulbs, cored and cut
   into 8 wedges
4 tomatoes, deseeded and diced
salt and pepper
3 pounds black mussels
1½ pounds salmon fillet, skinned and
   cut into thick slices
1½ pounds white fish fillets
12 king prawns (allow 2 per person)

REMOVE THE UNDERBODY OF THE CRAB and pull away the legs. Cut the body in half and bash the shell and claws into largish pieces. In a large, heavy pot heat the olive oil to the smoking point. Sauté the crab briefly. Add the celery, onion, garlic, and fennel seeds and sauté for a further 2 minutes. Add the remaining ingredients, bring to the boil, then skim. Lower the heat and simmer uncovered for 1 hour, skimming from time to time. Strain and reserve the stock.

   Parboil the potato slices in half the stock, then add the leek pieces and fennel wedges and cook for 4 minutes. Add the tomato dice, taste, and season lightly with salt and pepper. Remove the pan from the heat and keep to one side.

   Steam the mussels in ½ cup of the stock until all have opened. Meanwhile, broil the salmon, white fish, and prawns. To serve, ladle the broth into 6 bowls and divide the fish pieces, mussels, and prawns evenly among them. Serve with Cumin Rouille (page 105) and crusty bread.

SERVES SIX HUNGRY PEOPLE.

Sambusek **220**

Grilled-seafood bouillabaisse **274**

Egyptian eggs with dukkah **278**

sesame seeds

Sesame seeds are as familiar to us as the story of Ali Baba and his cave of treasure. They were cultivated and traded as a precious commodity by ancient civilizations, which mixed them with other grains to make a coarse flour or crushed them for their oil. Not only was sesame oil one of the first oils used in cooking around Egypt, the Middle East, the Indus Valley, and the Mediterranean, but it was also in huge demand for lighting, as an emollient, and for use in ancient medicine.

Today we tend to associate sesame oil mainly with Asian cooking, in which a few drops add a unique nutty flavor to many stir-fried dishes. In the Middle East and eastern Mediterranean, cooks use mainly sesame seeds. These are added to spice mixes such as dukkah, sprinkled as a garnish onto salads and vegetable dishes, and added to all manner of breads, cookies, and cakes. When Greg and I were honeymooning in Lebanon and Syria, we often ate crunchy sesame-encrusted bracelets of bread, known as *kahk*, for breakfast. Similar versions of these biscuit-like breads are sold by street vendors all around the region, from Lebanon and Syria to Egypt, Greece, and Turkey.

No self-respecting Middle Eastern home would be without a jar of tahini in the refrigerator. Made from crushed sesame seeds, tahini looks a little like a smooth, rather oily peanut butter and has a strong earthy, nutty flavor. Tahini is used as a base for Arab dips, like hummus and baba ghanoush. Thinned down, it is also served as an accompaniment to baked fish.

Sesame is also a favorite ingredient in confectionery. The whole seeds are used to coat sticky sweets and to make crunchy toffee brittles. Ground to a fine powder, they add flavor to the mysterious, sand-colored sweet known in the Middle East as *halawa* and in Greece as *halvah*.

SELECTING, STORING, AND USING SESAME SEEDS

Sesame seeds come in two colors, black and white, although the white seeds are far more widely available. White sesame seeds may be purchased hulled or unhulled; in the latter case they are actually a dull beige color. These may be used interchangeably, although some Asian and Middle Eastern cooks prefer the flavor of the unhulled seeds. Black sesame seeds are used for their dramatic visual effect on flat breads. They are oilier and have a more intense flavor.

Regardless of color, the flavor of all sesame seeds is greatly improved by dry-roasting. They need only a few moments' gentle tossing over medium heat, which will send them popping all around the pan. Roasting brings out a lovely toasty aroma and turns the seeds a shade or two darker. They can be stored quite well for several weeks after toasting, although that just-roasted, nutty quality fades slowly over time. The dry-roasted seeds can also be ground quickly in a spice grinder to make a coarse paste to thicken sauces, dips, and dressings.

Tahini is used with gay abandon in the Middle East. Don't confuse it with the Chinese and Japanese sesame pastes: those are made from roasted sesame seeds and are darker and stronger than tahini. Tahini may taste almost bitter straight from the jar, but diluted with lemon juice and water and whisked to make a dressing or sauce, it has a smooth creaminess and an incomparable nutty flavor.

You will probably find that your tahini separates out in the jar, and that you have a thick layer of oil floating on top. This needs to be vigorously mixed back into the paste before use, a task which requires a certain amount of muscle. Once opened, tahini will keep for 4–6 weeks in the refrigerator.

EGYPTIAN EGGS WITH DUKKAH

We were first introduced to Dukkah by our Egyptian friend Denise. Dukkah is a coarsely ground mixture of sesame seeds, hazelnuts, and heady cumin and coriander. It is delicious eaten on oil-dunked bread for breakfast or as a snack. In recent years it has also become fashionable in trendy restaurants, which offer little bowls of it for preprandial snacking. These deep-fried Egyptian eggs are delicious, but, for a simpler dish, sprinkle Dukkah on soft-boiled eggs and eat with hot buttered toast.

DUKKAH
8 tablespoons sesame seeds
4 tablespoons coriander seeds
3 tablespoons cumin seeds
½ cup hazelnuts
1 teaspoon salt
½ teaspoon pepper

EGGS
4 eggs
plain flour for dusting
vegetable oil for deep-frying

FOR THE DUKKAH, roast each ingredient separately, and rub away as much of the brown skin from the hazelnuts as you can. Pound the seeds using a mortar and pestle or process them carefully in a spice or coffee grinder. When you grind the sesame seeds and hazelnuts, be careful not to overgrind them, or they will disintegrate into an oily paste. Combine the nuts and seeds with the salt and pepper, and keep in an airtight jar in the refrigerator.

Soft-boil the eggs for 3 minutes. Cool them down under running water and peel them carefully. Dust them in plain flour and then deep-fry each egg for 1–1½ minutes, or until they are golden brown. Remove them from the oil and immediately roll them in the Dukkah.

Eat them straightaway as a snack or as a light lunch with hot buttered toast. They also make a good accompaniment to cured meats, or with a tangy goat-cheese salad or mixed green salad as a starter.

CHICKEN LIVERS PRESSED WITH DUKKAH

Ghee or clarified butter is used instead of normal butter in this recipe. Butter contains milk solids and water, which can seep out and spoil the texture of the terrine. Ghee also has a nice nutty, buttery flavor that marries well with the Dukkah and the richness of the livers.

1¼ cups ghee or clarified butter
1½ pounds chicken livers, cleaned
   of sinews
salt and pepper
¾ cup Dukkah

1 tablespoon pink peppercorns in brine
½ tablespoon fresh thyme leaves
2 large leeks, trimmed to the size of the
   terrine mold, steamed until soft

LINE A TERRINE MOLD completely with four layers of plastic wrap – a 12-inch Le Creuset cast-iron terrine mold is ideal. In a large, heavy-based pan, heat 2 tablespoons of ghee until it is almost smoking. Add a third of the chicken livers, cooking both sides to a good color, and season with salt and pepper. The livers should be cooked medium, for no more than 2 minutes. Remove them immediately onto a wire rack and repeat the process with the remaining two-thirds of the livers, using 2 tablespoons of ghee each time.

Pack half the livers into the bottom of the terrine mold and sprinkle with 1 tablespoon of the Dukkah, half the peppercorns, and half the quantity of thyme leaves. Then pour 2 tablespoons of fresh melted ghee over the top. Season with salt and pepper and place the 2 leeks down the center of the terrine, one on top of the other, flattening and pressing slightly into the livers. Cover with remaining chicken livers and sprinkle with more Dukkah, peppercorns, and fresh thyme. Pour over the remaining ghee (about ½ cup) and fold over the plastic wrap to seal.

Cut out a piece of styrofoam or a few thick pieces of cardboard just smaller than the mold and place them so they fit inside the terrine, directly on top of the livers. Press with an 8- to 10-pound weight and refrigerate for at least 6 hours.

After 6 hours, remove the weight. When you are ready to serve, unwrap the terrine and cut it into ¾-inch slices. Make a tangy dressing using ⅔ cup extra-virgin olive oil, 3 tablespoons champagne vinegar, a touch of honey, and a splash of pomegranate molasses. Brush the slices of terrine with the vinaigrette and serve with some lightly dressed salad leaves and slices of toasted buttery brioche.

MAKES TEN TO TWELVE PORTIONS.

TAHINI WHIPPED WITH YOGURT

This makes a light, creamy dressing, combining the nuttiness of tahini with the tang of lemon juice and yogurt. It is delicious with falafel and fish.

1¼ cups yogurt
3 tablespoons tahini
juice of 1 lemon

1 clove garlic, crushed with
   ¼ teaspoon salt
½ teaspoon pepper

COMBINE ALL THE INGREDIENTS in a bowl and whisk thoroughly. Taste and adjust seasoning if required.

SESAME-HONEY WAFERS

Buttery, crisp, and golden, these wafers use the classic combination of honey and sesame. Eat them with all sorts of ice creams and creamy desserts – or just on their own with a cup of strong coffee.

½ cup (1 stick) butter
1 cup sugar
4 teaspoons honey
1 cup plain flour

½ teaspoon powdered ginger
2 egg whites
⅔ cup sesame seeds

IN YOUR ELECTRIC MIXER, cream the butter and sugar at high speed. Add the honey, flour, and powdered ginger. When they are fully blended, add the egg whites and mix until all the ingredients are well combined.

Line a baking sheet with waxed paper and smear the mixture into circles about $1/_{16}$-inch thick – a wet finger is ideal for this! Sprinkle the circles liberally with sesame seeds, pouring off any excess.

Preheat the oven to 325°F and bake the cookies on the middle shelf for 7–10 minutes, or until golden brown.

Cool them on a wire rack and store in an airtight container.

MAKES ABOUT 30 WAFERS.

spinach and swiss chard

From a very young age children are exhorted to eat their greens by well-intentioned adults. Naturally, this "it's good for you" approach leaves most children cold – especially when greens such as spinach and Swiss chard can be strong-flavored or even bitter, and cook down to a distressing sliminess.

With age, of course, comes a little wisdom, and eventually most of us make that wonderful discovery that greens really are delicious. Yes, they are full of fiber, vitamins, and minerals, but instead of that being their main selling point, it becomes merely a bonus. What is more, that detested slipperiness is what suddenly makes them so desirable – steamed or braised to a luscious, glossy silkiness, or, conversely, adding a crunchy vitality to raw salads.

Spinach, chard, and many other wild greens are found throughout the Mediterranean and Middle East, where they are hugely popular. Of the two, Swiss chard is thought to have been cultivated since Neolithic times, and was certainly known and loved by the ancient Greeks and Romans. Chard is actually a type of beet, but the leaves have been developed rather than the root. In France and Italy they tend to use the stalks – the chards – which are sliced and braised or gratinéed separately, rather like celery. Middle Easterners prefer the leaves, which are sturdy enough to be stuffed, or can be shredded into soups, stuffings, and pies or braised with garlic, lemon, and allspice for a cold mezze dish.

Spinach, on the other hand, seems to have been unknown to the Greeks and Romans. Native to Persia, it is yet another vegetable that was brought west by the Arabs. By the Middle Ages, spinach had become popular in Spain, Italy, France, and even England. Its European names all derive from the Arabic *sapanekh*, which comes itself from the Persian word *espenaj*.

Spinach is rather more delicate than chard. It needs only the briefest of cooking (or can even be eaten raw) and lends itself generously to other, stronger flavors: garlic, lemon juice, and chili all complement it superbly. The Arab legacy can be seen all around the southern and eastern Mediterranean, where there are countless recipes for spinach mixed with chickpeas or lentils – often garnished with currants and crunchy pine nuts. Spinach works equally well, of course, with the smooth, softening influence of cream, yogurt, cheese, or eggs.

SELECTING AND STORING SWISS CHARD AND SPINACH

Swiss chard is a surprisingly popular home-grown vegetable. It is easy to grow, and its season is almost never-ending. Its crinkly leaves can be a deep, glossy green or tinged with bright red, orange, or yellow. When buying chard from the market or supermarket, choose small bunches, as the leaves are likely to be younger and more tender. Chard should be firm and vital, not soft and wilted. The leaves should be glossy, without sun damage, and the long stalks should be crisp.

Spinach comes in large bundles or in convenient bags of ready-washed, loose leaves. Again, choose bunches which look vibrant and healthy, not withered and drooping. If you can, select smaller leaves and avoid damaged ones. Spinach often comes with a generous covering of mud, which needs to be washed off very thoroughly.

The stalks should be torn off at the base of the leaf: the whole central stem does not need to be removed, as it does with chard.

Frozen chopped spinach is an adequate substitute for fresh spinach in soups or stuffing mixes, where the texture is less important. But if you want to serve spinach as a vegetable dish or salad, then really only fresh will do.

USING SWISS CHARD AND SPINACH

For most Middle Eastern dishes, only the chard leaves are used. After washing thoroughly, remove the stalks (they can be blanched and refrigerated for use in other recipes, if desired). If the leaves are to be used whole, blanch them for a few minutes, then refresh them in cold water. Otherwise they may be steamed until tender for around 6 minutes and tossed in butter or olive oil. Chard leaves are also good braised in olive oil with garlic, lemon juice, and a pinch of allspice.

Spinach may be steamed in its rinsing water in a large pot. It needs to be turned constantly so that the bottom leaves don't burn and the top leaves get their turn close to the heat. As soon as all the leaves have wilted down, the spinach must be very well drained, and all that is required then is a large knob of butter and a seasoning of salt and pepper. Or they may be sautéed in hot olive oil with a little garlic, or even blanched, a handful at a time, in lots of boiling salted water. Each little bundle should then be plunged into a sink of cold water and tightly squeezed of its water. This method is often better when the spinach is not to be eaten straightaway as a simple accompaniment. The leaves will be drier, so are better for stuffing mixes or for salads. The blanched leaves can even be very carefully unfurled and stuffed themselves, as a change from vine leaves.

SPINACH, PECORINO, AND POTATO PIE

Pecorino is a sharp Italian cheese made from sheep's milk. It works beautifully with the Middle Eastern combination of spinach and allspice with cubed waxy potatoes in these pies. Serve them as a starter or light lunch dish with a salad, or as an accompaniment to roast or barbecued lamb or other meats.

¼ cup olive oil

3 shallots, finely sliced

1 clove garlic, finely chopped

1 small serrano chili, deseeded, scraped, and finely shredded

½ pound spinach, destalked and finely shredded

1 large waxy potato, peeled and cut into ½-inch dice

¼ teaspoon allspice

salt and pepper

1 cup stock or water

¼ cup pecorino cheese (or parmesan or grana), grated

4 sheets phyllo pastry

1½ tablespoons melted butter, mixed with 1½ tablespoons olive oil

HEAT THE OLIVE OIL IN HEAVY-BASED POT. Add the shallots, garlic, and chili and stir over medium heat for 30 seconds. Add the shredded spinach and stir for a further minute until it collapses and softens slightly. Then add the potato dice, allspice, salt and pepper, and stock and bring to the boil. Cover the pot, lower the heat, and simmer for 4 minutes over gentle heat. Then raise the heat and cook uncovered for an additional 4 minutes to let the liquid evaporate. Remove from the heat and tip into a sieve to allow any excess moisture to drain away. Stir in the grated cheese and allow the mixture to cool.

Preheat the oven to 400°F. To make the pies, lay a sheet of phyllo out widthways and brush one half with the melted-butter mixture. Fold this half over the other. Turn this smaller rectangle 90° so it is again widthways in front of you, and brush half with the butter mixture. Again fold it in half. You should now have a rectangle of about 5½ x 8 inches. Trim off 3 inches from one side to make a 6-inch square. Brush with butter. Heap a quarter of the chard mixture into a high mound in the center of the pastry. Fold the pastry sides up and over the filling and flatten them slightly to form a raised pie. Brush the pastry edges with melted butter to help them stick together and then carefully turn the pie over. Flatten and smooth the top slightly, and then use the palms of both hands to shape into a neat, round pie. Brush the surface with butter and cook for 8 minutes on a sheet lined with baking paper.

Remove the sheet from the oven and turn the pie over. Return the sheet to the oven and cook a further 4 minutes, until the pie is a golden brown all over.

Remove it from the oven and serve it immediately.

MOORISH SPINACH AND ALMOND SALAD

Versions of this cooked spinach salad are popular throughout Portugal and Spain. The sweet-sour dressing and fruit and nut combination reveal its Moorish origins.

2 bunches spinach, picked over
   and well rinsed
4 shallots, finely sliced
2 teaspoons currants
¼ cup sherry
¼ teaspoon allspice

¼ teaspoon cinnamon
2 tablespoons sherry vinegar
3½ tablespoons extra-virgin olive oil
salt and pepper
½ cup sliced almonds, fried in olive oil
   until golden brown and crisp

BLANCH SMALL BATCHES OF THE SPINACH in plenty of boiling, salted water for 10 seconds. Refresh in cold water and then squeeze out as much moisture as possible.

Soak the currants in the sherry. Mix the shallots with the sherried currants in a large mixing bowl.

Gently pull the clumps of spinach leaves apart and place in the bowl with the spices, vinegar, and oil. Generously season with salt and pepper and sprinkle the fried almonds over the top.

SWISS CHARD STEWED WITH TUNISIAN SPICES

Swiss chard braised with lemon juice and topped with caramelized onions is a traditional Lebanese favorite. Here, in place of the usual allspice, we raise the heat level with a touch of fiery Tabil, a Tunisian spice mix.

TABIL

1½ cups cilantro leaves and stalks

1 tablespoon caraway seeds, roasted and crushed

½ head garlic, cloves peeled

1 red bell pepper, roasted and peeled

6 serrano chilis, deseeded, scraped, and finely chopped

⅓ cup olive oil

SWISS CHARD

⅓ cup olive oil

2 onions, sliced

1 teaspoon red wine vinegar

1 leek, finely diced

1 bunch Swiss chard, stems removed and roughly chopped

1 clove garlic, crushed with ½ teaspoon salt

juice of 1 lemon

salt and pepper

TO MAKE THE TABIL, blend all the ingredients together, slowly adding the oil to make a smooth paste.

Heat half the oil in a heavy-based pot and sauté the onions over a low heat for 10–15 minutes until they are darkly caramelized. Stir in the vinegar and remove the onions to a bowl.

Heat the rest of the oil and sauté the leek for 1 minute until it has softened, then add the chard and garlic. When this has wilted, add the lemon juice and season with salt and pepper. Cover, lower the heat, and braise for 10 minutes. Then raise the heat, remove the lid, and stir in 1 teaspoon of the Tabil. Remove from the heat and serve in a bowl with lemon wedges and the caramelized onions piled on top.

SERVES FOUR TO SIX.

sumac

When it comes to food, a defining characteristic of Middle Easterners is their love of sour flavors. Lemons, pomegranates, and sumac are all used extensively to add a refreshing tartness to dishes. Of these three, sumac, which has a lovely lemony flavor and is a pretty, dark-red color, is virtually unknown outside the Middle East.

Sumac is usually purchased as a coarse powder. It is ground from the dried berries of a shrub which grows widely all around the Middle East and eastern Mediterranean. Sumac is particularly popular in Lebanon and Syria, but it is also used in Iran, Iraq, and Turkey and other Middle Eastern countries.

In Iran and Iraq, sumac is used mainly as a tangy seasoning for sprinkling over kebabs: Iranian restaurants will nearly always set it on the table as a condiment to accompany grilled meats. Elsewhere, sumac is used in marinades. Its tangy flavor works well with grilled meats, poultry, and fish. It is often added to vinaigrettes and other dressings, or added to salads such as the refreshing bread salad fattouche. In Lebanon, sumac's greatest use is in the ubiquitous spice mix za'atar (page 293), in which it is combined with thyme and sesame seeds and used as a topping for fabulous freshly baked breads.

SELECTING, STORING, AND USING SUMAC

You will probably have to visit a specialist Middle Eastern grocer to find sumac, but it is worth tracking down. It is comparatively inexpensive and keeps very well in an airtight container in a cool, dark cupboard.

Sumac is a pretty, deep red-brown color, rather like rich, loamy soil, with a sour, salty flavor. When you use it in Middle Eastern recipes, it is often a good idea to wash it in a little water first: heap it into a strainer and run it under cold water for a few minutes. This helps to intensify the flavor even further.

FATTOUCHE

Fattouche is a simple garden salad and a handy way to use up stale pieces of pita bread. It is most delicious when the bread pieces are fried, but for a healthier option you can toast or grill them.

2 teaspoons sumac

¼ teaspoon allspice

¼ teaspoon pepper

1 medium purple onion, sliced

4 romaine lettuce leaves, washed and dried

4 radishes, thickly sliced

2 tomatoes, ripe but firm, roughly diced

2 Lebanese cucumbers, cut into chunky dice

⅓ cup fresh mint leaves, roughly chopped (or 1 tablespoon dried mint)

½ cup parsley leaves, roughly chopped

½ cup purslane (if available)

6 small pita breads

¼ cup olive oil

¼ cup (½ stick) butter

1 clove garlic, crushed with 1 teaspoon salt

juice of 1 lemon

3 tablespoons extra-virgin olive oil

½ tablespoon balsamic vinegar

SOAK THE SUMAC in cold water for a few minutes and remove any husks or uncrushed berries which float to the top. Add the sumac, allspice, and pepper to the sliced onion and rub it in well. Cut the lettuce leaves crossways into 1-inch strips. Place them in a large salad bowl with the radishes, tomatoes, cucumbers, and all the herb leaves.

Split the bread open and cut it into rough ¾-inch triangular shapes. Melt the butter and oil in a frying pan until they are foaming. Fry the bread in two batches until it is golden brown, remove it with a slotted spoon, and drain it on absorbent kitchen paper. Mix the garlic paste with the lemon juice. Whisk together the extra-virgin olive oil and balsamic vinegar.

When you are ready to serve, add the spiced onions to the other salad ingredients, add the lemon-garlic mix, and stir well. Finally, pour over the dressing, add the pieces of fried bread, mix everything together gently, and serve straightaway.

SERVES SIX.

QUAIL ESCABÈCHE WITH MIDDLE EASTERN SPICES

Escabèche is a traditional Spanish and Portuguese dish using fish or little game birds like quail and partridge. These are fried or poached, then cooked and allowed to cool in a spicy marinade for 24 hours or so. They are served at room temperature as a tapas dish or as a light meal. The sourness of sumac works really well with the tangy lime marinade. Serve with warm, crusty bread as a starter or a light lunch.

4 jumbo quail

2 cloves garlic

½ teaspoon salt

2 tablespoons Ras el Hanout (page 80)

7 tablespoons olive oil

1 large green chili, deseeded, scraped, and finely shredded

2 onions, finely sliced

2 medium ripe tomatoes, skinned, deseeded, and cut into large dice

juice of 2 limes plus the zest of 1

2 teaspoons sumac

salt and pepper

CUT THE QUAIL IN HALF and trim off the excess fat.

Crush the garlic with the salt and add 1 tablespoon of the Ras el Hanout and 2 tablespoons of the oil. Rub this mixture all over the quail pieces and let them sit for 1–2 hours.

Heat the remaining olive oil in a heavy-based pan and place the quail pieces in, skin side down. Cook on medium heat for about 5 minutes, until they become golden. Turn them and cook a further 5 minutes. Remove the quail from the pan with a slotted spoon.

Lower the heat and add the chili, onions, tomatoes, and lime juice and zest. Allow to sweat gently until the onions become very soft and translucent (about 10–15 minutes). Place the quail back on top of the onion mix and cook on the same low heat for a further 8–10 minutes. .

Place the quail in a serving dish and pour the hot marinade over the top.

Allow to cool, then cover and refrigerate overnight. Allow to return to room temperature before eating.

SALMON GRILLED WITH SUMAC AND FENNEL CRUMBS

These days salmon has lost its cachet as a true gourmet food, as it is widely farmed, relatively cheap, and readily available. Sadly though, the farmed variety lacks the flavor of its wild cousins, and we are always looking for interesting ways to liven it up. As salmon is a dense, oily fish, it benefits from being matched with robust flavors. Baking salmon medallions in this tangy crumb is surprisingly simple and effective. Serve them with a big bowl of Goat-Cheese Mashed Potatoes (page 54) and salad greens dressed with a sour-sweet Tomato-Pomegranate Dressing (page 242).

CRUMBING MIX

1 tablespoon sumac

1 tablespoon fennel seeds, roasted
  and crushed

zest of ½ lemon

½ cup fresh bread crumbs

SALMON

four 6-ounce pieces salmon fillet,
  skinned

¼ teaspoon salt

pepper

3 tablespoons olive oil

1 teaspoon Dijon mustard

FENNEL-MINT SALAD

1 medium fennel bulb, cored and very
  finely sliced

2 purple shallots, very finely sliced

⅓ cup mint leaves

⅓ cup parsley leaves

1 ripe tomato, deseeded and sliced

½ teaspoon dried mint

juice of ½ lemon

5 tablespoons extra-virgin olive oil

½ teaspoon sumac

salt and pepper

PREHEAT THE OVEN to the maximum heat. Mix the sumac, fennel seeds, and lemon zest with the bread crumbs and set aside.

Lightly season the salmon. In a heavy-based, ovenproof pan, heat the olive oil, and sauté the salmon pieces for 30–40 seconds, moving constantly so they don't stick. Turn and sauté for a further 30 seconds.

Remove the pan from the heat, brush each salmon fillet with the mustard, and sprinkle over a ¼-inch layer of the crumbing mix, packing it on neatly.

Place the pan on the top shelf of the oven and cook for 3 minutes for medium-rare, or longer as desired. Remove from the oven and allow to rest in a warm spot for 4–5 minutes.

To make the fennel-mint salad, put all the ingredients into a large mixing bowl and toss together. Divide the salad onto 4 plates and top with a piece of salmon.

thyme

The heady fragrance of thyme wafts through the sun-warmed air above countless rocky hillsides around the Mediterranean and in the Middle East. But it is a hardy, tenacious little plant and grows just as well in cooler climates, even thriving as far north as Iceland!

Thyme is well known because of its inclusion in those dusty little bags of herbes de Provence, and it is also one of the three essential herbs in a bouquet garni, used to make stocks, soups, and all kinds of slow-cooked savory dishes in classical French cooking. It has a special affinity with rabbit – bunnies that have fed on wild thyme are said to be particularly delicious – as well as game birds such as quail, pigeon, guinea fowl, and even partridge. Even simple lamb cutlets acquire a lovely savory flavor when grilled with a few sprigs of thyme or brushed with a honey-thyme glaze. Interestingly, the magical alliance between honey and thyme was even remarked by Virgil: the bees which make the legendary Greek Hymetus honey have been gathering their nectar from tiny thyme flowers for centuries.

Fresh or dried, thyme is dearly loved in the Middle East for its lively savory flavor. The fresh leaves are stripped from their stalks and scattered into salads and salad dressings. The dried leaves retain their intense flavor and are often combined with cheese dishes. *Shankleish* – golf balls of chalky-dry yogurt cheese – are often rolled in thyme with a little chili and then marinated in olive oil.

In many Middle Eastern countries, the most common use of thyme is in the aromatic mixture za'atar, which is eaten on a daily basis throughout Lebanon. *Za'atar* is the Arabic word for both thyme, the herb, and the seasoning mix made with dried thyme, sour red sumac berries, and sesame seeds. When we traveled through Lebanon a few years ago, our favorite breakfast was *mankoushi*, a flat, round bread rather like a pizza, thickly spread with za'atar and eaten hot from a wood-fired oven. The aroma of this bread fills the streets early in the morning and is quite irresistible. At home we make our own instant version by mixing za'atar with a little olive oil to make a paste which is delicious spread on toast.

SELECTING AND STORING THYME

There are many different varieties of thyme, but the only two you are likely to find in the shops are common thyme and lemon thyme. They are quite different and should, therefore, be used differently. Lemon thyme really does have distinct lemony overtones and works well with poultry, veal, or baked fish dishes. Common thyme is spicier, with a strong, savory flavor, and is better suited for seasoning heavier dishes like rich stews, soups, or even stuffings – either on its own or as part of a bouquet garni.

Thyme is a perennial and is readily available all year round, either picked from your own herb patch or in little twiggy bundles from greengrocers and most supermarkets. Fresh thyme is a hardy herb and will keep happily in the refrigerator for at least a week. Dried thyme lasts several months before losing its potency.

USING THYME

Carefully wash and dry the thyme before you start on the fun task of stripping the tiny little leaves from the woody stalks. Then scatter them liberally over grilled meats, toss them through salads, or mix them into stuffings. Some resourceful people keep a little bunch of thyme to use as a handy brush for dousing olive oil and flavor directly onto grilling meat.

Some recipes specify dried herbs. Thyme dries particularly well, retaining much of its flavor for several months. Ideally you should hang your bunch upside down in a dry, airy place for 2–3 weeks, until it is completely dry.

To make Lebanese-style za'atar spread, you need to buy a bag of sumac and a bag of dry za'atar from a Middle Eastern grocer. Keep them separately, stored in airtight containers, until you want to make up the mix. It is best to make za'atar spread in fairly small quantities to ensure that the flavors stay fresh and zingy. The proportions are three of za'atar to one of sumac (start with a tablespoon measure). Combine the two loosely together and then drizzle in enough oil to make a loose paste. No, it doesn't look very exciting – but just wait until you taste it!

LEBANESE BREAD WITH ZA'ATAR

Breadmaking often ends up being much less of a chore than you anticipate. If, like many of us, you are totally sick of focaccia, then try making these stubby little bread sticks for a change. This quantity makes 20 sticks, which might seem like a lot, but somehow they always seem to disappear quite swiftly.

~~~~~~

BREAD DOUGH
5 cups plain flour
1 tablespoon salt
1½ tablespoons fresh yeast
1 tablespoon sugar
1½ cups warm water

LEBANESE SPICED OIL
3 tablespoons za'atar
1 tablespoon sumac
7 tablespoons olive oil

PLACE THE FLOUR AND SALT in your electric mixer. In a separate bowl, whisk together the yeast, sugar, and water to a smooth, creamy liquid and add it to the flour. Mix with the dough hook for 5–10 minutes until the ingredients form a smooth, glossy dough. Cover the dough with a cloth and leave it in a warm place to rise for around an hour.

For the Lebanese spiced oil, mix the za'atar, sumac, and olive oil.

Punch down the dough and roll out on a floured work surface to a 30- x 10-inch rectangle, about ⅔ inch thick. Brush it with the Lebanese spiced oil and sprinkle it with a little salt. Then cut it into sticks about 1 inch wide. Place them on a baking sheet and leave them to rise in a warm place for a further 10 minutes.

Preheat the oven to 350°F and bake for about 10 minutes, until the sticks are golden brown.

MAKES 20 BREAD STICKS.

SLOW-COOKED SALMON WITH ARAB SPICES

These days it is very fashionable to grill or fry salmon quickly, so that the outer edges cook to a neat little border around a bright pink – often raw – center. This recipe is the complete antithesis, and is pleasurably simple to make. The slow cooking merely sets the salmon's firm, oily flesh to a gelatinous, almost buttery, soft wobble. The spices are a good way of livening up farmed salmon's predictable flavor. Serve with a tangy sauce, like Avgolemono (page 173), or with Soused Zucchini and Eggplant (page 328), or even with crunchy croutons spread with a little Black-Olive Cream (page 197).

1 tablespoon za'atar
1 teaspoon sumac
1 teaspoon fresh thyme leaves

4 salmon medallions, skinned
 (6-ounce portions)
¼ cup olive oil
salt and pepper

PREHEAT THE OVEN to the lowest possible heat. Mix the za'atar, sumac, and thyme together. Brush the salmon pieces generously with the oil. Lightly season with salt and pepper and then sprinkle the herb mixture all over the salmon, so pieces are completely covered. Line a heavy baking sheet with baking parchment (this helps slow the heat conduction from the metal sheet to the fish).

Place the salmon on the sheet in the center of the oven. Leave for 15 minutes and then check that it is not cooking too fast (if opaque milky liquid has started to ooze from the fish, then the oven is too hot). If necessary, leave the oven door ajar while cooking a further 20 minutes. When it is ready, the salmon should look opaque and almost gelatinous.

GARFISH GRILLED WITH THYME, LIME, AND SUMAC

The garfish is native to coastal and estuarine waters around Australia. Similar fish are found around the Mediterranean and the Gulf of Mexico. It is a thin, bony fish that can be difficult to clean but has a sweet, delicate flavor. If you can't obrain garfish, try the recipe with fillets of another small, flaky white fish.

~~~~~~

zest of 2 limes, finely grated
1 tablespoon fresh thyme leaves, chopped
1 teaspoon sumac

8 garfish, cleaned and filleted into butterflies, so that the two halves remain attached to each other
salt and pepper
¼ cup olive oil

DRY THE LIME ZEST OVERNIGHT, or for about ½ hour on very low heat.

Mix the lime zest with the thyme leaves and sumac.

Open out the garfish and fold them in half widthways, to form a fattish rectangle. Sprinkle with salt and pepper and a little of the lime-thyme-sumac mixture. Heat the olive oil and cook the garfish, head end down, until nicely colored. This will take about 1 minute on high heat. Turn the fish over and sprinkle with more of the spice mix. Cook for another minute and then remove from the pan.

Serve straightaway with Baba Ghanoush (page 120) and Parsley Salad (page 211).

SERVES FOUR (TWO GARFISH EACH).

turkish coffee

Café culture in the Middle East is largely men's business. Anyone who has ever visited this region, where alcohol is often prohibited, will be aware of how central cafes are to men's daily lives. They spend many long hours sitting at tables – alone or with friends – sipping small cups of fierce black coffee, puffing on water pipes, playing backgammon or cards, arguing, reading the papers, watching the TV, or listening to the radio. Any excuse to linger will do, at any time of day of night!

Hospitality in the home is also unthinkable without coffee. A visitor's arrival is the cue to prepare fresh coffee, which is then brought to the guest and poured with much ceremony from elegant long-handled pots into tiny china cups. Coffee is always drunk very strong, usually sweet, and often flavored with cardamom seeds or orange-blossom water. When coffee is served, the goodies come out also – no self-respecting Arab household would be without a tin of buttery little *raybeh* cookies or perfumed, nut-stuffed *ma'amoul*, and of course on special occasions there is always a huge range of sticky, sweet pastries to be sampled.

If you are lucky, when the coffee is finished someone will suggest a reading of the cups. The empty cups are turned over and the dregs allowed to trickle down the insides and dry. The resulting patterns usually predict imminent romance, vast wealth, or hordes of children, depending on one's circumstances!

Originating in Ethiopia, the wild *Coffea arabica* bush is believed to have been cultivated by African tribes from the sixth century AD and enjoyed for its stimulating properties – rather in the same way that we enjoy it today. It is likely that at first the berries were just chewed, and then later on they were crushed to a wet paste and infused in water. Later still, a more sophisticated coffee drink was made by fermenting the juice from the ripe berries. However, the modern drink was not invented until the thirteenth century, when beans were cleaned and roasted before infusing. Despite all the fancy coffee-making contraptions which litter our kitchens nowadays, in Middle Eastern households they still make coffee by finely pulverizing the roasted beans and combining the powder with boiling water to make the strong infusion we call Turkish (or Arab) coffee.

From Ethiopia, the use of coffee spread across the Red Sea to Aden in Yemen, and its popularity swept rapidly through Arabia. By the sixteenth century, its consumption had become fashionable in Mecca, Damascus, and Constantinople, where the first true coffeehouse was established in 1554. It is not hard to see why coffee was such an immediate hit in these intensely religious Muslim lands, where alcohol was forbidden. In fact, our word *coffee* comes from the Turkish word *kahveh*, which itself comes from the old Arabic word for wine, *kahwah*. Denied the real thing, Muslims had to invent a new drink. Coffee was so popular in Constantinople, according to the French food writer Alexandre Dumas in his *Dictionnaire de Cuisine*, "that the imams complained their mosques were empty while the coffeehouses were always full."

SELECTING AND STORING TURKISH COFFEE

Chez Malouf, one is just as likely to enjoy a cup of instant coffee or to jiggle a tea bag in a mug, but as a special treat Greg will make Turkish coffee. We tend to choose a popular Lebanese blend — from a Middle Eastern grocer — which is already flavored with cardamom seeds. However, there are many different types of Turkish and Arab coffees available, and it is a good idea to try different ones to find the brand you like. Otherwise, any dark-roasted coffee beans will be quite acceptable (perhaps Mocha beans from Yemen for the sake of authenticity), and additional flavorings (like cardamom or cinnamon) can be added later on.

If you prefer to let the store grind the coffee beans for you, then make sure you ask for the very finest grind possible: it should end up being closer to a fine powder than the coarser grind we use for European methods of coffee making. One thing to avoid above all, though, are the instant powdered versions of so-called Turkish coffee available from supermarkets. They just don't come anywhere near the real thing!

As with all good-quality coffee, the oil content means that it will deteriorate over time. Coffee beans and ground coffee should be stored in the refrigerator or in the freezer.

TURKISH COFFEE

Turkish or Arab coffee is best made in small quantities in the traditional long-handled pot called a *rakweh*, but a very small saucepan will just about do. The whole process is extremely simple but, like so many things, tends to be shrouded in mystique, everyone having their own particular method for making plenty of the desirable golden froth. Each family, too, tends to have its own little traditions and rituals: the Maloufs, for instance, favour tapping the side of the pot with a spoon at various points in the procedure. Nobody quite knows why; it's just something they do.

Various aromatics may be used to flavor the coffee. The Lebanese and Syrians like to add a few cracked cardamom pods or a pinch of ground cardamom to the pot. In the Persian Gulf states they add a splash of rose water, or occasionally even saffron. In North Africa they enjoy cinnamon and sometimes coriander seeds, while in Yemen they favour ginger and cloves.

6 small cups water

3 heaped teaspoons dark-roasted, plain
   Turkish coffee, finely ground

2 teaspoons sugar

3 cardamom pods, lightly crushed

BRING THE WATER TO THE BOIL and add the coffee, sugar, and cardamom pods. Bring the mixture back to the boil, and as soon as the froth begins to rise, remove the pot from the heat.

Once the froth has settled, return the pot to the heat and repeat the process twice. Serve the coffee straightaway, taking care to give everyone a share of the froth. Let it settle in the cup for a minute or two before sipping.

SERVES SIX.

TURKISH COFFEE ICE CREAM

Turkish coffee makes a simply superb ice cream. Rich, smoky, and very adult, it is delicious with a steamed chocolate pudding, a hot chocolate soufflé, roasted pears, or hazelnut Florentine cookies. Even a simple mix of summer berries works beautifully.

1 cup sugar

½ cup water

½ cup liquid glucose

3 cardamom pods, cracked

1 cup dark-roasted plain Turkish coffee,
    finely ground

2 ounces best-quality dark chocolate

12 egg yolks

¼ cup Tia Maria or other coffee liqueur

1 quart cream

PLACE THE SUGAR, water, glucose, cardamom, and coffee in a pan and slowly bring to the boil, making sure the sugar dissolves completely. Simmer for 5 minutes, then pour over the chocolate and stir until it melts.

Whip the egg yolks at high speed until they are light and fluffy. Strain the coffee-chocolate mixture though a coffee filter into the egg yolks and beat for 1 minute. Add the Tia Maria and cream and refrigerate for 1 hour. Pour into an ice-cream maker and churn according to the manufacturer's instructions.

SERVES EIGHT.

TURKISH COFFEE PETITS POTS

½ cup dark-roasted plain Turkish
   coffee, finely ground

1 cup cream

1 cinnamon stick

1½ ounces best-quality dark chocolate,
   grated

4 egg yolks

¼ cup sugar

MOISTEN THE GROUND COFFEE with warm water and tie it in a muslin square.

Bring the cream to the boil with the coffee bag and cinnamon stick. Simmer for 5 minutes to infuse the coffee and cinnamon. Turn off the heat and squeeze the muslin bag to extract as much coffee flavor as possible. Add the grated chocolate and stir until it is completely melted.

In a separate bowl, whisk the egg yolks with the sugar and then pour them over the hot cream mixture. Stir well and return to the saucepan. Stir over low heat until the mixture thickens to the consistency of custard. You should be able to draw a distinct line through the custard on the back of a spoon.

Pour the custard into a glass bowl and immediately place it in a sink of cold water or crushed ice. Stir gently while the mixture cools down.

Spoon into petits pots or little ramekin dishes and chill. Serve with a sprinkle of Pine-Nut Praline (page 231), or Sesame-Honey Wafers (page 280).

MAKES AROUND EIGHT PETITS POTS.

vine leaves

As winemaking has expanded dramatically in the New World over the last few decades, a sadly neglected by-product of all this excellent industry has been the vine leaf. Throughout the Mediterranean and the Middle East, however, people make good use of vine leaves as a kind of edible wrapping paper. Grape vines grow wild throughout these regions, and many people have a handy supply of the leaves right outside their back door.

There can't be many of us who haven't tried stuffed vine leaves as part of a Greek or Lebanese banquet. Dolmades, as they are best known to us, can be served hot or cold, with slightly different but equally delicious fillings. Cold, they usually have a rice stuffing, flavored with subtle combinations of cinnamon, allspice, and mint, and sometimes even enriched with the pungency of saffron. The flavors merge beautifully into the lemony backdrop provided by the vine leaf itself. Turkish and Iranian cooks also like to include pine nuts and currants, and yet another popular version uses dill.

Hot vine leaves are traditionally filled with ground meat – usually lamb – bulked out with rice and onion and flavored with plenty of spices. They may not sound quite as exotic, but braised slowly, they develop a lovely rich, lemony flavor. Greg's mother, May, cooks her vine leaves on top of lamb ribs or shanks, with handfuls of garlic cloves, lots of lemon, and fresh mint. In good one-pot-cooking style, the meat can then be enjoyed as a main meal after the vine leaves.

Vine leaves are not just used for making dolmades. Their chief attraction is the slightly tart, lemony flavor they impart, so they have a natural affinity with fish and poultry. A favorite Mediterranean cooking technique is to wrap vine leaves around small fish such as sardines and red mullet and char-grill or roast them. They not only look very pretty, but they also help protect the delicate flesh from the flames and keep the flesh moist, while adding a subtle hint of citrus. Meatier and oily fish, such as tuna and swordfish, and even poultry and game birds benefit from this technique. Brush the meat with a little oil and lemon juice first, sprinkle with oregano, wrap in a large vine leaf, and bake in the oven.

SELECTING AND STORING VINE LEAVES

Even if you don't live next to a vineyard, vine leaves are still widely available. The leaves preserved in brine are perfectly acceptable, even if the process of buying them is not quite as romantic as plucking them straight from the vine. If you can lay your hands on some fresh leaves, they can be frozen for future use. Small, younger leaves are more tender and have a more delicate flavor.

USING VINE LEAVES

Fresh vine leaves need to be blanched before using. Plunge them into boiling water and count to ten, then remove them and refresh them in cold water. Squeeze them dry before carefully unfurling and spreading them out on a countertop, ready to stuff.

Preserved vine leaves are stored in brine and need to be well rinsed in warm water before use.

GOAT CHEESE BAKED IN VINE LEAVES

This is one of the most delicious starters we can imagine. It is a great way of using any dried-out ends of goat-cheese logs you might have in the refrigerator, but very young fresh cheese works well, too. These fat little parcels should be served hot from the oven, all squelchy and lemony, with the hot, tangy cheese almost bursting through the skins. Serve lots of warm, crusty bread on which to smear the bubbling hot cheese.

3½ ounces vine leaves, rinsed and drained	extra-virgin olive oil
	a pinch of dried mint
1½ cups goat cheese	pepper

IF YOU USE FRESH VINE LEAVES, quickly blanch them before use. Brine-pickled leaves need to be well rinsed and dried first.

Lay the vine leaf, vein side up (or two together if small), on a kitchen counter. Mold a portion of cheese into a small sausage shape and place across the base of a leaf. Drizzle a little oil over the cheese and add a pinch of mint and a grinding of pepper.

Roll the leaf over once, then fold the sides in and continue to roll it into a neat sausage shape. Repeat with the remaining leaves. Brush them with a little oil and cook under a preheated broiler for 4–5 minutes or until they start to color and blister.

MAKES EIGHT LITTLE PARCELS.

CHICKEN AND PISTACHIO DOLMADES

Shop-bought dolmades often have a nasty, tinny flavor, suggesting that the vine leaves have been used straight from a commercial-sized tin, with barely adequate rinsing. The chicken and pistachios make these home-made dolmades more delicate than traditional lamb versions.

~~~~~~

8 ounces vine leaves

½ cup long-grain rice

8 ounces ground chicken

¼ teaspoon allspice

¼ teaspoon cinnamon

¼ teaspoon fresh black pepper

½ cup unsalted, shelled pistachio nuts

zest of 1 lemon, finely chopped

a pinch of salt

½ teaspoon pepper

4 tomatoes, sliced

4 cloves garlic, cut in half

1 bunch mint

1 quart chicken stock

juice of 1 lemon

IF YOU ARE USING PRESERVED VINE LEAVES, soak them well, then rinse them and pat them dry. Fresh vine leaves should first be blanched. Wash the rice and mix it with the chicken, allspice, cinnamon, black pepper, pistachio nuts, and lemon zest.

Lay a vine leaf on the work surface, vein side up, and place a spoonful of filling across the base of the leaf. Roll it over once, fold the sides in, and then continue to roll it into a neat sausage shape. The dolmades should be around the size of your little finger; don't roll them too tightly, or they will burst during the cooking. Continue stuffing and rolling until the filling is all used.

Line the bottom of a heavy-based casserole with vine leaves and a layer of sliced tomatoes.

Pack the dolmades in tightly on top of the tomatoes, stuffing the halved garlic cloves in among them. Lay the bunch of mint over the top, then pour in the chicken stock and lemon juice. Cover with a plate and slowly bring to the boil. Once boiling, lower the heat and simmer gently for 45 minutes.

Allow to cool, then turn out into a serving dish and serve hot, warm, or even cold, with plenty of yogurt.

MAKES AROUND TWENTY DOLMADES.

PORTOBELLO MUSHROOMS BAKED BETWEEN VINE LEAVES

Portobello mushrooms are readily available from supermarkets. Tangy and fragrant with thyme, these meaty baked mushrooms are a lovely accompaniment to grilled meats. Or, for a quick and easy light meal, they can be served with a small salad, with plenty of bread to mop up all the lovely lemony, garlicky juices.

3½ ounces vine leaves, rinsed well in cold water and dried well
⅓ cup olive oil
16 medium-size portobello mushrooms
⅓ cup shallots, sliced finely

1 clove garlic, sliced thinly
8 sprigs fresh thyme
juice of 1 lemon
salt and pepper

IF YOU ARE USING PRESERVED VINE LEAVES, soak them well, then rinse them and pat them dry. Fresh vine leaves should first be blanched and refreshed.

Brush the base and sides of an ovenproof dish (11 x 8 inches, and 2 inches deep) with a little oil. Lay the vine leaves on the bottom of the dish and around the sides, reserving enough to cover.

Wipe the mushrooms and trim the stalks so they are flush with the base of the mushroom.

In a large bowl, combine the mushrooms, shallots, and garlic with half the remaining olive oil. Place the mushroom mix in the ovenproof dish, with the mushrooms stalk side down, and scatter the sprigs of thyme over the top.

Sprinkle with lemon juice, season with salt and pepper, and cover with the remaining vine leaves, tucking them around the sides. Brush with oil and cook in a preheated 350°F oven for 30 minutes.

watermelon

There is something childishly appealing about watermelons, with their vivid mouthwash-pink flesh, slick black seeds, stripy, green skin, and simple sweet flavor, that satisfies our primitive desire for sugar. It is hard to retain a sense of dignity when you munch a big, smiley slice of watermelon and feel the juice run down your chin!

Watermelons are believed to have originated in Africa. Their first recorded harvesting was nearly 5,000 years ago in Egypt, where there are numerous paintings in pharaonic tombs depicting their beauty. Watermelons still grow wild in desert watering holes in some parts of Africa, and one can only admire Mother Nature for her foresight in arranging for such a welcome source of liquid refreshment in harsh desert lands.

From Egypt, watermelons were spread along ancient Mediterranean trade routes by traders who carried the seeds in the holds of their boats. By the tenth century, they had crossed the Middle East to reach China, and by the thirteenth century, the Arabs had enthusiastically spread them around the rest of Europe, although they were not known in England until the end of the sixteenth century. The southern states of America took to the watermelon – brought there by African slaves – with alacrity. The watermelon seems to have been a particular favorite of Mark Twain, who wrote in 1894: "When one has tasted it, he knows what the angels eat."

For the hot and dusty countries of the Middle East and southern Mediterranean, watermelons have long provided a welcome liquid relief to parched throats. Anyone who has visited Asia or southern Europe during the hot summer months will recall the relief of spying a street vendor with a barrow piled high with chilled watermelons. An icy-cold wedge sliced from one of these monsters does more to slake one's thirst than any fizzy soft drink!

In the Middle East, endless varieties of fruit are available during the summer, and an extravagant selection is always offered at the end of a meal. Melons and watermelons are great favorites and are always served chilled. Persians have known how to store winter snow and ice for use in the summer months for at least 2,000 years, and it doesn't require much of an imagination to see how easily watermelons, with their crunchy, granular, almost icy flesh, could have been transformed, perhaps with the addition of a few drops of rose water, into sweetly perfumed sherbet.

SELECTING AND STORING WATERMELON

Nowadays watermelons come in manageable sizes. The Minilee, for instance, is closer in size and shape to a honeydew or Galia melon. This makes them much less daunting to the shopper and far easier to cart home.

When purchasing, look for fruit which feels firm and heavy. Once cut, watermelons can be wrapped in plastic wrap and kept in the refrigerator for up to a week. Instead of reaching for ice cubes or cans of soft drinks on hot summer days, why not try a slice of delicious, thirst-quenching watermelon instead?

USING WATERMELON

In Middle Eastern and Mediterranean countries, watermelon is most often enjoyed as a thirst-quenching snack or as part of a dessert fruit plate, perhaps with a few slices of creamy halvah. Watermelons are ideal for making sorbets and, simpler still, only require a little mashing to make a granita.

With the large, thick-skinned varieties of watermelon it is also possible to pickle the white layer of rind under the outer green skin. Watermelon pickles are a very popular condiment on Greek and Eastern Mediterranean tables and are also much loved in the southern United States. In France and Spain the rind is also popular as part of a candied fruit selection. And then there are the seeds. In many Middle Eastern countries they are toasted, wrapped in little packages, and sold as a popular street snack.

WATERMELON WITH WHITE PORT AND PISTACHIOS

Served well chilled, this watermelon salad makes a lovely light ending to a meal and has an interesting alcoholic kick! Dried limes are a Persian speciality, available from Middle Eastern grocers. They need to be cracked with a heavy rolling pin and then infused to impart their musty, citrusy flavor.

½ cup sugar
½ cup water
1 stick cinnamon
peel of 1 lemon or 1 cracked
   dried lime (optional)

4 cracked cardamom pods
2 pounds watermelon flesh
¾ cup white port
⅔ cup unsalted, shelled pistachio nuts
1 pint blackberries

PUT THE SUGAR AND WATER IN A PAN and bring them slowly to the boil, making sure the sugar dissolves completely. Add the cinnamon stick, lime or lemon peel, and cardamom pods, lower the heat, and simmer for about 5 minutes to make a syrup. Remove from the heat and allow to cool.

Peel the watermelon into ¾-inch-thick wedges. Place them in a bowl, sprinkle them with port, and macerate them in the refrigerator for 1 hour. Roughly crush the pistachio nuts and mix them with 1 tablespoon of the sugar syrup. To serve, stack the watermelon slices in the center of the plate, sprinkle them with pistachio nuts and blackberries, and douse the lot with syrup.

SERVES SIX.

WATERMELON SALAD WITH CHERRY-VANILLA ICE CREAM

½ cup sugar

½ cup water

1 stick cinnamon

peel of 1 lemon or 1 cracked
  dried lime (optional)

4 cardamom pods, cracked

1 teaspoon rose water

2 pounds watermelon flesh

1 pint raspberries

1 pint blueberries

1 pint blackberries

½ cup shredded mint leaves

CHERRY-VANILLA ICE CREAM

8 egg yolks

1 cup sugar

¾ cup water

1 vanilla bean, split and scraped

2½ cups cream

1 pound cherries (stoned weight)

½ cup sugar

¼ cup water

juice of 1 lemon

TO MAKE THE ICE-CREAM BASE, first whisk the egg yolks in an electric mixer until they are light and fluffy. Bring the sugar, water, and aromatics to the boil. Pour the boiling syrup over the whisked egg yolks, mixing slowly. Then add the cream and turn off the mixer. Allow the mixture to cool for a few moments. Pour it into an ice-cream maker and churn according to manufacturer's instructions.

Place the cherries, sugar, water, and lemon juice in a heavy pot. Stir gently to ensure the sugar dissolves, and slowly bring to the boil. Lower the heat and simmer for about 5 minutes. Remove from the heat and purée in a blender. Strain through a sieve to remove the skins.

Put the sugar and water in a pan and bring slowly to the boil, ensuring that the sugar dissolves completely. Add the cinnamon stick, lime or lemon peel, and cardamom pods, lower the heat, and simmer for about 5 minutes to make a syrup. Remove from the heat and allow to cool. Strain and add half the rose water. Chill until needed.

Cut the watermelon into small bite-size pieces and place in a large mixing bowl with the berries. Add the shredded mint leaves and enough syrup to moisten, mix gently, and then sprinkle with the remaining drops of rose water.

Allow to cool. Swirl the cherry purée into the ice cream when you transfer it to the freezer.

Serve the watermelon salad with a scoop of Cherry-Vanilla Ice Cream.

SERVES SIX.

WATERMELON SORBET

Early Persian sherbets and iced fruit drinks must surely have made use of the icy-cold, sweet watermelon. This sorbet is extremely simple to make. Enlivened with a splash of lemon juice and the merest hint of rose water, it is quite delicious served with fresh berries and finely chopped mint leaves as a refreshing summer dessert.

~~~~~~

1¾ pounds watermelon
1½ cups sugar
¾ cup water

juice of 2 lemons
a splash of rose water

REMOVE THE PEEL from the watermelon, chop the flesh into largish chunks, and remove the seeds. Blend to a purée in a food processor and sieve.

To make a sugar syrup, bring the sugar and water to the boil over medium heat, then lower the heat and simmer for 5 minutes. Mix the fruit purée with the syrup and allow to cool. Then add the lemon juice and rose water. Pour into an ice-cream maker and churn according to the manufacturer's instructions.

SERVES FOUR TO SIX.

yogurt

Yogurt is one of those foods which firmly divide people: you either love it or loathe it! Greg, for instance, in true Lebanese style, will happily eat yogurt as an accompaniment to just about every meal, and when he gets home from work late at night will open the refrigerator and eat great spoonfuls of icy-cold yogurt straight from the tub. I share this enthusiasm, and well remember a holiday in the Greek islands when, as an impoverished student, I survived for almost an entire month on yogurt and honey, with the odd piece of fruit thrown in for dietary balance.

Yogurt has come a long way. It used to be that the only yogurt readily available was a gloppy, gelatinous substance, usually sweetened beyond belief and colored pink (raspberry), yellow (banana), or even brown (chocolate). The so-called fruit flavors had certainly never seen a real raspberry or strawberry. On the other hand, "natural" yogurt was something eaten only by earnest hippie types, and you had to either hunt it down in a health food shop or make it yourself.

Yogurt has now become very fashionable and is just one product in an ever-expanding range of dairy desserts. Supermarkets stock dozens of exotic flavors, ranging from mango, guava, and passion fruit to coconut. There are yogurts made from cow's milk, goat's milk, sheep's milk, and even buffalo milk. Fat contents range from nearly o to as much as 8 percent. The latest marketing idea for this ever-growing industry is that yogurt is the key to a longer life. The current buzz-word is *probiotic*, and we are all getting used to hearing about the health-giving properties of lactobacillus-this, acidophilus-that, and casei-Shirota-the other.

While laboratory research has shown that these new strains of bacterial cultures, such as the acidophilus, bifidus, and casei strains, do promote the growth of beneficial bacteria in a test tube, whether the benefits can be transferred to the human digestive system remains to be proved. If we are to believe the experts, though, humble yogurt can provide, if not exactly eternal life, help with digestive problems such as constipation and irritable bowel syndrome, as well as some allergies, and with counteracting the adverse side effects of antibiotics.

The good news is that regardless of all the pseudoscientific claims of the manufacturers, all yogurts are protein- and calcium-rich and extremely delicious, something which Middle Easterners have always known. The even better news is that yogurt (although fat content varies widely) is not nearly as high in fat as many ricottas and all types of cream and mascarpone. Needless to say, the higher the fat content of the yogurt, the more voluptuously rich and velvety smooth the result.

Yogurt is enjoyed throughout the Arab world, although almost never as the oversweetened dairy dessert we know in the West. Middle Easterners would hardly recognize yogurt in these forms, which bear so little resemblance to the refreshingly sour original. In hot, sunny countries yogurt is enjoyed as a cooling drink or to dampen the fire of chili dishes. It is used in soups, stews, marinades, pastries, and cakes. It is served as an accompaniment to all kinds of savory dishes. Hung in a bag until the whey drains away, it thickens into a delectably creamy version, which is delicious with a drizzle of honey, a sprinkle of cinnamon, or mixed with summer berries. Longer straining – for up to three days – results in a very soft, slightly sharp fresh cheese, which may be flavored with fresh herbs and served with crusty bread.

FAT CONTENT OF YOGURT, CREAM, AND CHEESE PRODUCTS

Product	Fat content (%)	Product	Fat content (%)
Low-fat yogurt	0.2–1	Low-fat cream	18
Full-fat yogurt	3.5–5.5	Light sour cream	18–25
Fromage frais	4	Sour cream	25
Goat's milk yogurt	7	Light cream cheese	32
Sheep's milk yogurt	7	Cream cheese	33
Buffalo milk yogurt	8–9	Heavy cream	35
Strained yogurt	10	Crème fraîche	min. 35
Ricotta	8–15	Mascarpone	40

SELECTING AND STORING YOGURT

For cooking, always buy plain natural yogurt. These days there are numerous brands and styles of yogurt available. In particular there are some excellent European-style and biodynamic yogurts which we use at home. It is worth experimenting to find out which style you prefer – a thinner, sourer type or the richer, creamier Greek style. The creamier and softer the flavor, though, the higher the fat content is likely to be. Yogurts range from full fat (4 percent) to low fat (around 1 percent).

It is sensible to buy the freshest possible yogurt, not just because it is perishable, but also because the flavor sharpens over time (even when properly stored in the refrigerator). Most natural yogurts contain live cultures, which continue to munch on the milk sugars (lactose) and cause acidity levels to slowly increase. However, most very fresh store-bought yogurts will keep perfectly well for up to two weeks after purchase.

USING YOGURT

Straining yogurt for a few hours in a muslin cloth gives a richer, more concentrated product. It is delicious eaten like a very soft fresh cheese, lightly salted and drizzled with olive oil, and maybe flavored with garlic and fresh herbs. Sweetened with one of the lovely floral honeys or sprinkled with rose water or orange-blossom water, chopped pistachios, or fresh berries, yogurt makes a luscious and creamy dessert.

SAFFRON YOGURT CHEESE

The basic method described here works without the saffron, too. It is equally delicious plain or swirled with a variety of different flavorings. Try adding a spoonful of spicy harissa, smoked paprika, or purées of fresh herbs such as basil, oregano, or dill. Swirl into the yogurt and strain as outlined below.

Rose water also adds an exotic dimension. Salt and drain the yogurt and, when ready to serve, form into smooth round balls or quenelle shapes using spoons. Make an indentation in the top and fill with rose water and a big drop of extra-virgin olive oil. Serve it with Seven Vegetable Couscous with Onion Jam and Green Harissa Broth (page 98).

For a sweet treat, beat 2 tablespoons of honey and 1 teaspoon of orange-blossom water into the yogurt, sprinkle in the lightly crushed seeds from 4 cardamom pods, and drain for up to 48 hours. Serve with fresh strawberries or as an accompaniment to syrupy cakes or puddings instead of cream.

2 pounds natural yogurt (use sheep's milk for a richer result)

1 clove garlic, crushed with 1 teaspoon salt

10 saffron strands, lightly roasted and crushed

SCOOP THE YOGURT INTO A CLEAN MUSLIN SQUARE, cheesecloth, or towel. Mix in the garlic paste, then sprinkle the saffron over the top and swirl it in roughly. Tie the four corners of the cloth together to form a hanging bag and suspend it from a wooden spoon over a deep bowl. Allow it to drain in the refrigerator for 48–72 hours (the longer the time, the firmer the result).

Use the 48-hour soft cheese as an accompaniment for spicy dishes such as tagines, Indian curries, or most rice dishes. Or drizzle with extra-virgin olive oil and eat with crusty bread and a dish of olives. At the end of 72 hours, you will have a very firm lump of fresh cheese.

Gently remove it from the bag and roll it into small balls with oiled hands. Place the balls in jars with olive oil and the herbs of your choice. They will keep for up to 2 weeks in the refrigerator.

BASIL TZATZIKI

Mint is traditional in tzatziki, but try adding shredded basil for a change. This creamy tzatziki is terrific served with grilled meat or as an accompaniment to couscous dishes.

2 cups natural yogurt, strained overnight
1 Lebanese cucumber, deseeded and grated (leave the skin on)
1 clove garlic, crushed with 1 teaspoon salt

1 teaspoon dried mint
½ cup fresh basil leaves, chopped
juice of 1 lemon
salt and pepper

MIX ALL THE INGREDIENTS TOGETHER in a large bowl and season. Line a sieve with muslin or a tea towel and strain for a further 4–6 hours.

Chill until required.

STICKY LEMON-YOGURT CAKE

This moist, tangy cake is delicious on its own with a cup of coffee, or served with a big blob of thick cream and some fresh berries.

8 ounces (2 sticks) butter
1 cup sugar
4 teaspoons lemon zest
4 eggs
½ cup plain flour
2 teaspoons baking powder
1½ cups fine semolina
2¼ cups ground almonds

6 tablespoons lemon juice
1 cup plain yogurt

SYRUP
1 cup lemon juice
1 cup sugar
½ tablespoon brandy

CREAM TOGETHER THE BUTTER, SUGAR, AND LEMON ZEST until the mixture is pale and smooth. Then beat in the eggs, one by one, ensuring each one is completely incorporated before adding the next. Sift the flour and baking powder over the top, and gently fold in with the semolina and ground almonds. Then mix in the lemon juice and yogurt. Pour the mixture into a well-greased 8-inch springform pan and bake in a preheated 325°F oven for 50–60 minutes, or until the cake is firm to the touch and golden brown.

Combine the lemon juice, sugar, and brandy in a small pan and bring them to the boil. Reduce the heat and simmer for 5 minutes to make the syrup.

Remove the cake from the oven and pierce it all over with a skewer. Pour the syrup over the hot cake and allow it to soak in. The cake will keep well in an airtight container for 3–4 days.

zucchini

One of Greg's favorite home-cooked meals – cooked by his mother, that is – is koussa mahshi. This is zucchini stuffed with a mixture of rice, ground lamb, and pine nuts, flavored with allspice, and gently braised in a tomato sauce. It is a hugely popular Lebanese dish, and just one way of cooking the infinitely versatile zucchini.

Like its cousins the marrow and squash, the zucchini is a type of edible gourd which grows close to the ground under a riot of lush leaf cover. The best zucchini are small to medium in size and firm to the touch. They can be a lovely, shiny dark green, or paler and speckled looking, or even a butter-bright yellow. Sadly, they are often allowed to grow too large, which makes their flesh spongy and bitter. Greg's father has a fantastically productive vegetable garden, and we are often the lucky recipients of his bounty. The best zucchini of all are picked fresh and tender from his vines, no bigger than a finger, with their gorgeous golden flower still attached.

SELECTING AND STORING ZUCCHINI

Ideally, zucchini should be firm, shiny, and unscarred, but all too often they are droopy, soft, wrinkled, and blemished. Avoid these! Zucchini do not keep terribly well, and even in the refrigerator they have a tendency to get wet and slimy quickly, so eat them within a day or so of purchase. Choose larger ones for stuffing, medium or small ones for slicing and frying.

USING ZUCCHINI

Wash larger zucchini well and carefully pat them dry. Slice off and discard the ends. The zucchini can then be sliced into rounds, on the angle, or lengthways into long strips, or they can be grated. It is best not to boil zucchini, as they quickly become waterlogged and collapse into a soggy, flavorless mass. They are far better steamed, or sautéed in a hot pan with a little olive oil or butter. Add a good squeeze of lemon juice at the end of cooking and throw in a handful of fresh herbs – dill, mint, and thyme are all good choices. The tiny babies can be sautéed whole, for the briefest of moments, in a little olive oil, with a hint of garlic and a good squeeze of lemon juice.

Zucchini are also excellent char-grilled on a griddle pan or on the barbecue. Slice them lengthways, brush with extra-virgin olive oil, season well, and sear on the grill until they are soft and golden. Grilled zucchini are equally delicious eaten hot or allowed to cool and dressed with lemon juice and garlic-infused olive oil.

In the eastern Mediterranean, zucchini are often prepared as a salad for a mezze selection, in a yogurt dressing with mint or dill; or sliced wafer-thin and tossed in a vinaigrette with thin slices of Spanish onion, currants, and pine nuts.

Cheese and eggs are natural allies of zucchini. Grate zucchini and combine with beaten eggs, onion, parsley, and a touch of garlic to make a sort of Arab frittata called an *eggah*. Zucchini and cheese is a classic Judeo-Spanish combination. Bake lightly steamed slices of zucchini in the oven with a mixture of creamy ricotta-style cheese, a couple of eggs, and a pinch of nutmeg. Another, equally good version uses salty feta and mint.

Zucchini flowers are considered very chichi. Some upmarket greengrocers sell baby zucchinis with the flowers attached, and they are very pretty cooked whole. The flowers from larger plants can be removed and stuffed. The preparation method is described on page 327, but always make sure you cook them as quickly as possible after purchase. The petals will start to close up once they have been picked, which can make the whole exercise very fiddly and frustrating.

KOUSSA MAHSHI

This is probably one of the most popular home-cooked Lebanese family meals. Ideally, choose pattypan squash, which are squat and bulbous – they are easy to hollow out. Zucchini work well too, but require a little patience and a long, thin knife (like a fish-filleting knife) to scrape out the insides while preserving the whole long shape of the vegetable. Koussa makes a simple supper dish, served with a big blob of thick, creamy yogurt.

8 pattypan squash (at least 5 ounces each)

STUFFING

½ pound ground lamb
⅔ cup long-grain rice
¾ teaspoon allspice
¾ teaspoon cinnamon
¾ teaspoon fresh black pepper
½ teaspoon salt
1 teaspoon extra-virgin olive oil
⅓ cup cold water

SAUCE

1 tablespoon butter
1 tablespoon olive oil
1 medium onion, finely chopped
2 cloves garlic, finely chopped
½ teaspoon dried mint
1 can crushed tomatoes (14 ounces)
2 tablespoons tomato paste
1⅔ cups water
salt and pepper
¼ teaspoon cinnamon

TRIM OFF THE SQUASH at the stem end. With a melon baller or a long, thin knife, carefully hollow out the inside of each marrow. The idea is to have as thin a shell as possible, but without piercing the skin. Reserve the pulp for the sauce.

To make the stuffing, use wet hands to mix the lamb, rice, black pepper, salt, extra-virgin olive oil, and cold water. Divide the mixture into 8 portions and loosely stuff each squash about three-quarters full, which leaves space for expansion during cooking.

Melt the butter with the oil and gently sauté the onion for about 5 minutes, until it is soft and translucent. Then add the garlic and mint. Cook for a few more minutes, then add the roughly chopped squash pulp, followed by the tomatoes, tomato paste, and water. Season with salt, pepper, and additional spices. Stir well.

Place the squash in the sauce and bring to the boil. Then cover and simmer over low heat for 40–45 minutes. About 10 minutes before the end of the cooking time, remove the lid and raise the heat to reduce the sauce by a quarter.

BATTERED ZUCCHINI FLOWERS STUFFED WITH GOAT CHEESE

One of the most pleasing aspects of zucchini is their summery-looking yellow flowers, which are delicious dipped in a light batter and fried, or carefully stuffed with a light cheese and bread crumb filling.

4 ounces goat cheese
1 teaspoon dried mint
1 teaspoon parsley leaves, chopped
1 tablespoon extra-virgin olive oil
12 baby zucchini, with flowers attached

2 cups olive oil and vegetable-oil blend
  for deep-frying
½ cup plain flour for dusting
Chickpea Batter (page 62)
salt
2 cups mixed baby salad leaves

MASH THE CHEESE WITH THE MINT, parsley, and extra-virgin olive oil.

Carefully open each zucchini flower and pinch out the stamen. Roll a lump of the cheese stuffing into a thumb-size sausage shape between the palms of your hands, and gently stuff it into the flower. Twist the top of the flower to seal.

Heat the oil olive and vegetable oils to 400°F (when a blob of batter will sizzle to the surface and color within 30 seconds). Hold the zucchini and carefully dust each flower in the flour and then dip in the Chickpea Batter. Gently place in the oil – cook no more than four at a time – until the batter turns crisp and golden. Remove and drain on kitchen paper. Season with salt and serve immediately with a small handful of lightly dressed mixed salad leaves.

SERVES FOUR AS A STARTER.

SOUSED ZUCCHINI AND EGGPLANT

This is one of our favorite ways of preparing zucchini. Serve them with all meat, poultry, and fish.

2 medium eggplants
4 medium zucchini
½ cup olive oil
2 cloves garlic, finely sliced
1 tablespoon parsley, chopped
1 tablespoon oregano leaves
½ teaspoon sumac

MARINADE
8 teaspoons sherry vinegar
4 teaspoons honey
8 teaspoons water

TRIM THE ENDS FROM THE EGGPLANTS and cut them lengthways into ½-inch-thick slices. Place them in a colander, lightly salt, and let them sit for half an hour. Rinse well and pat dry.

Trim the ends from the zucchini, slice in half lengthways, and season with salt.

Heat the oil in a large, heavy pan and fry the zucchini and eggplant slices until they are lightly colored. Tip them into a large dish.

Boil the marinade ingredients for 1 minute and pour over the pan-fried vegetables. Sprinkle with the garlic, chopped parsley, oregano leaves, and sumac. Leave in the marinade overnight.

When you are ready to serve, remove the vegetables from the marinade and warm them through gently in a pan or in the oven. Serve with a drizzle of extra-virgin olive oil.

bibliography

Alexander, Stephanie, *Stephanie's Australia*, Allen and Unwin, Sydney, 1991.

—— *The Cook's Companion*, Viking, Melbourne, 1997.

Al Hashimi, Miriam, *Traditional Arabic Cooking*, Garnet, Reading, UK, 1993.

Bareham, Lindsay, *Onions without Tears*, Michael Joseph, London, 1995.

Beer, Maggie, *Maggie's Orchard*, Viking, Melbourne, 1997.

Boxer, Arabella, *Mediterranean Cookbook*, Penguin, London, 1981.

David, Elizabeth, *Mediterranean Food*, Penguin, London, 1950.

—— *Harvest of the Cold Months*, Penguin, London, 1994.

Davidson, Alan, and Davidson, Jane, *Dumas on Food*, Oxford University Press, Oxford, 1978.

Danon, Simy, and Denarnaud, Jacques, *La Nouvelle Cuisine Judeo-Marocaine*, ACR, Paris, 1994.

Der Haroutunian, Arto, *The Yogurt Book*, Penguin, London, 1983.

Dosti, Rose, *Mideast and Mediterranean Cuisines*, Fisher Books, Tucson, AZ, 1993.

Greenberg, Sheldon, and Lambert Ortiz, Elisabeth, *The Spice of Life*, Michael Joseph, London, 1983.

Grigson, Jane, *Vegetable Book*, Michael Joseph, London, 1978.

—— *Fruit Book*, Michael Joseph, London, 1982.

Grigson, Sophie, *Ingredients Book*, Pyramid Books, London, 1991.

Guinaudeau, Madame, *Traditional Moroccan Cooking*, Serif, London, 1994.

Humphries, John, *The Essential Saffron Companion*, Grub St, London, 1996.

Jaffrey, Madhur, *Eastern Vegetarian Cooking*, Arrow Books, London, 1990.

Lassalles, George, *Middle Eastern Food*, Kyle Cathie, London 1991.

McGee, Harold, *On Food and Cooking*, Collier Books, New York, 1988.

Owen, Sri, *The Rice Book*, Doubleday, London, 1993.

Roden, Claudia, *A New Book of Middle Eastern Food*, Penguin, London, 1986.

—— *The Book of Jewish Food*, Viking, London, 1997.

Root, Waverley, *Food*, Simon and Schuster, New York, 1980.

Saleh, Nada, *Fragrance of the Earth*, Saqi Books, London, 1996.

Shaida, Margaret, *The Legendary Cuisine of Persia*, Penguin, London, 1994.

Simmons, Shirin, *Entertaining the Persian Way*, Lennard Publishing, London, 1988.

Tannahill, Rheay, *Food in History*, Penguin, London, 1973.

Time-Life, *Food of the World* series, Time-Life, New York, 1968–78.

—— *The Good Cook* series, Time-Life, New York, 1978–81.

Toussaint-Samat, Maguelonne, *The History of Food*, Blackwell, Cambridge, MA, 1992.

Visser, Margaret, *Much Depends on Dinner*, Penguin, Canada, 1986.

Whittaker, Noel, *Sweet Talk*, Macmillan, London, 1998.

Wolfert, Paula, *Good Food from Morocco*, John Murray, London, 1973.

—— *Mediterranean Cooking*, Harper Collins, New York, 1994.

index

NOTES

NOTES